Berossos and Manetho, Introduced and Translated

Berossos and Manetho, Introduced and Translated

Native Traditions in Ancient Mesopotamia and Egypt

Gerald P. Verbrugghe
John M. Wickersham

Ann Arbor
THE UNIVERSITY OF MICHIGAN PRESS

First paperback edition 2000
Copyright © by the University of Michigan 1996
All rights reserved
Published in the United States of America by
The University of Michigan Press
Manufactured in the United States of America
⊗ Printed on acid-free paper

2003   2002   2001   2000   4   3   2   1

A CIP catalog record for this book is available from the British Library.

Library of Congress Cataloging-in-Publication Data

Verbrugghe, Gerald
    Berossos and Manetho, introduced and translated : native
traditions in ancient Mesopotamia and Egypt / Gerald P. Verbrugghe
and John M. Wickersham.
        p.   cm.
    Includes bibliographical references and index.
    ISBN 0-472-10722-4 (hardcover : alk. paper)
    1. Berosus, the Chaldean Babylōniaka. 2. Babylonia—History.
3. Manetho.   4. Egypt—History—To 332. B.C. I. Wickersham, John
M. (John Moore), 1943-. II. Title.
DS73.2.V47 1996
932—dc20   96-1860
                                                               CIP
ISBN 0-472-08687-1 (pbk. : alk. paper)

Contents

Berossos

Manetho

Conventions

T + # refers to an ancient source in our edition that contains information or testimony about Berossos, Manetho, Berossos's *History*, or Manetho's *History* and other writings.

F + # refers to an ancient source in our edition that contains information which originally appeared in Berossos's *History* or Manetho's *History* and other writings.

... indicates that text of an ancient author has not been translated, as it did not concern Berossos or Manetho or it did not form part of Berossos's or Manetho's writings.

lac. indicates that text of an ancient author is missing or illegible in the manuscript tradition or that a document is defective.

( ) Words, phrases, and sentences enclosed in parentheses are additions we have made in our translations of the ancient texts, usually to make them more readily understandable.

$ANET^3$ = James B. Pritchard, *Ancient Near Eastern Texts Relating to the Old Testament*, third edition (Princeton 1969).

BM = British Museum (with index number for the tablet).

CAH^2 = *Cambridge Ancient History*, vols. 3–5, 2d ed. 1982–92.

CAH^3 = *Cambridge Ancient History*, vols. 1–2, 3d ed. 1970–75.

FGrHist = Felix Jacoby, *Die Fragmente der griechischen Historiker*, vols. I–III (Leiden and Berlin, 1923–1958)—a collection of the fragments of those historical works written in Greek, which survive mainly by being quoted or cited by more fortunate authors whose works have been preserved. Some of the volumes of fragments are accompanied by companion volumes of commentary. Some of these volumes of commentary are in German, some in English. Unfortunately, Jacoby did not live long enough to write a commentary for the fragments of either Berossos or Manetho.

Testimony and fragments of Berossos are in *FGrHist* vol. III C 1 (1958), pp. 364–97. Berossos = *FGrHist* #680. Testimony and fragments of Manetho are in *FGrHist* vol. III C 1 (1958), pp. 5–112. Manetho = *FGrHist* #609.

FHG = Carolus Müller, *Fragmenta Historicorum Graecorum*, 5 vols. (Paris, 1841–1870). The testimony and fragments of Manetho are in *FHG* 2:511–616.

Karst = Josef Karst, *Die Chronik aus dem Armenischen übersetzt*, vol. 5 of *Eusebius, Werke* (Leipzig 1911), five volumes which offer a translation of Eusebius's surviving writing. Volume 5 contains a German translation of the Armenian translation of Eusebius's *Chronicon* (*The Chronicle*).

With one exception, only passages that ancient authors specifically attributed to Berossos or to Manetho are given, not passages for which Berossos or Manetho is the presumed source. The one exception is Manetho F29b.

Testimony or information about Berossos and Manetho is arranged in chronological order of the authors of that information.

Fragments of Berossos's *History* and Manetho's *History* and other writings are in the order they would have appeared in those works, that is, for the most part in chronological order.

We used what might be called reformist spelling for transliterating proper names from ancient Greek to English, as we try to preserve the Greek spelling and sound rather than give a spelling derived from the original or supposed original Mesopotamian or Egyptian script. We have tried to be consistent, but it is difficult. Some Mesopotamian and Egyptian names have become standardized in English, and it seemed at times too strange to change those already so familiar names by using a straight transliteration from Greek to English letters. We therefore apologize for any inconsistencies the reader may notice. In addition, we have standardized our transliteration of the Greek spelling of our two authors' Greek names. Berossos is always spelled *Berossos*, even though his name appears in various different Greek forms in the manuscripts, and Manetho is always spelled *Manetho*, even though in Greek it more properly is *Manethon*. In chapters 4 and 9, where the individual rulers named by Berossos and Manetho are listed, for names derived from Mesopotamian or Egyptian lists we give modern equivalents, which are more closely based on the supposed Mesopotamian and Egyptian pronunciation of proper names.

We give the numbers assigned by Jacoby in *FGrHist* to the historians mentioned in the texts we translate. Where possible, we also give the testimony number or fragment number.

We give both Latin titles and English titles of the ancient authors' works that preserve the histories of Berossos and Manetho. We give the standard English names for the Latin authors and the standard latinized forms for the surviving Greek authors, for example, Pliny for the Latin *Plinius*, Josephus for the Greek transliteration *Josephos*. For fragmentary Greek authors, however, we use a reformist transliteration, since these names have not become standardized in English—for example, Hestiaios rather than Hestiaeus. In rare cases, when we translate the names of Greek authors from a Latin original, we give the Latin spelling of the Greek name.

For the names of the kings of Judah, we use the standard English transliterations of the Hebrew.

For Eusebius's text, when both treat the same material, we have preferred the Greek text of Syncellus's *Ecloga Chronographica* (*Chronological Excerpts*), which preserves parts of Eusebius's *Chronicon* (*The Chronicle*), to Karst's German translation of the Armenian translation of Eusebius's *Chronicon*.

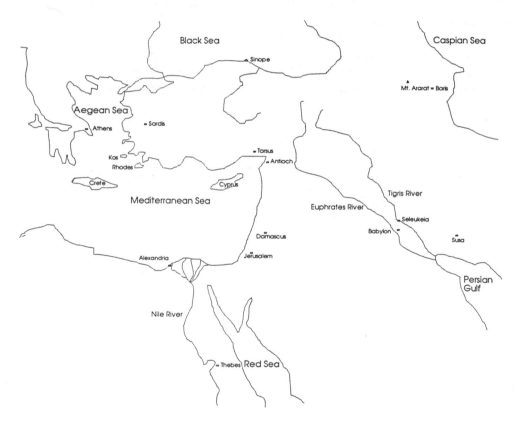

Map 1. Berossos's and Manetho's Hellenistic World

General Introduction

Before Alexander the Great and the Greeks, both ancient Mesopotamia and Egypt had known foreign conquerors. These rulers, however, had usually lasted only a short time, or, if they were able to establish themselves for an extended period, the native traditions of Egypt and Mesopotamia overwhelmed them. Even the Persians, who had conquered and then ruled both Mesopotamia and Egypt for the two hundred years before Alexander, had had little effect on the traditional society of either. The Hellenistic kingdoms, established after Alexander's conquest of Egypt in 332 B.C. and of Mesopotamia from 331 to 330 B.C., had a much different and much greater effect. It is not that they changed the traditional civilizations of ancient Mesopotamia and Egypt. These would continue for many more centuries as they were before Alexander. Rather, the establishment of Hellenistic kingdoms in Mesopotamia (the Seleucids in 311 B.C.) and Egypt (the Ptolemies in 305 B.C.) began a new civilization that became equal and parallel to the native civilizations.

This new civilization did not seriously threaten the existence of native Mesopotamian and Egyptian civilizations, but it did become the vehicle by which new ideas about religion, government, literature, and art were brought to Mesopotamia and Egypt. The languages and scripts, which had served so well the older, traditional native civilizations for millennia, were not used to express these new ideas. More important, fundamental changes caused by the introduction of new languages, new scripts, and new religions in Mesopotamia and Egypt meant loss of knowledge about the old languages and the old scripts that had preserved ancient Mesopotamia's and ancient Egypt's past. The native histories of Egypt and Mesopotamia before Alexander the Great, created and preserved by the older civilizations and continued during the Hellenistic kingdoms, were ultimately forgotten and lost. The new languages and scripts would not preserve the past of the older civilizations.

Languages and Scripts of Ancient Mesopotamia

Shortly after 3500 B.C., the Sumerians in extreme southern Mesopotamia began to develop a system of writing. All those who ruled after the Sumerians in Mesopotamia (the area drained by the Tigris and Euphrates Rivers)—Akkadians, Amorites, Mittani, Kassites, and Assyrians—as well as ancient peoples who did not even inhabit Mesopotamia, such as the Hittites, from the third millennium through the first millennium B.C. used the Sumerian script to write their own languages. Cuneiform is the modern name of this script. Cuneiform means "wedge–shaped," derived from the Latin word for wedge. In the seventeenth and eighteenth centuries A.D., travelers from western Europe in the Turkish Empire began to notice, collect, and bring back to western Europe clay tablets incised with wedge-shaped written symbols that they could not read. Clay tablets were the preferred writing medium for the cuneiform script.

Of all the languages written with cuneiform, the two most important for the civilization that developed in Mesopotamia were Sumerian and Akkadian. No other language is related to the Sumerian language, and it is, therefore, not possible to place Sumerian in any family of languages. Akkadian, however, belongs to the Semitic family of languages, the eastern branch, with two main dialects: Assyrian and Babylonian. The Babylonian dialect belonged properly to Babylonia, the lower valleys of the Tigris and Euphrates Rivers, that is, south of a line drawn between Hit on the Euphrates River and Samarra on the Tigris River to the Persian Gulf, but centered on ancient Babylon. The Assyrian dialect of Akkadian was the language of Assyria, the upper Tigris River valley, most especially the area around and between the Greater Zab River and the Little Zab River, near where various capitals of the Assyrian Empire were located: Ashur, Kalhu (biblical Calah), and Nineveh. Although Sumerian was no longer a spoken language after 1800 B.C., it remained a religious and literary language for the eastern Semites of Mesopotamia. They continued the use of the Sumerian cuneiform system of writing and developed it further to represent their own Akkadian language. Indeed, the cuneiform system of writing for the eastern Semites remained stable and constant even as their language changed or evolved over 1,500 years. Thus, the well-trained scholars and scribes of Mesopotamia, both of Babylonia and Assyria, could read and maintain the entire literary output of Mesopotamia, preserved in cuneiform, whether the text was in the Sumerian language or in one of the dialects of Akkadian. A tradition of learning that had begun in the fourth millennium B.C. survived intact to the beginning of the first millennium A.D.

In the eighth century B.C., Chaldeans, who had settled in the extreme southwest of Babylonia, the marshlands north and west of the mouths of the Tigris and Euphrates Rivers, began to vie with Assyrians and native Babylonians for control of all of Mesopotamia. Scholars debate today whether or not the Chaldeans were native speakers of Aramaic, a western Semitic language. Whether they were or not, in Babylonia under the Chaldeans or Neo-Babylonians, with the fall of the Assyrian Empire in 609 B.C., Aramaic began to replace Akkadian, which had predominated in Mesopotamia since the fall of the Third Kingdom of Ur at the end of the third millennium B.C. Indeed, even earlier, in the eighth and seventh centuries B.C., the Assyrians had used Aramaic as a sort of official bureaucratic language to run their empire, which had included native Aramaic speakers in what is today Syria, Lebanon, Israel, and Jordan. It is most likely then that even before the Neo-Babylonian Empire, when the Assyrians ruled all of Mesopotamia, Aramaic had became the lingua franca of the entire Ancient Near East, and it would remain the predominant language under the Chaldeans, the Persians, and the Greeks. Aramaic was, however, written in its own alphabet, not with the cuneiform script or on clay tablets. The usual writing material for Aramaic, papyrus or animal skins, was, however, much more perishable than clay, and this accounts for the relatively few surviving official documents in Aramaic from the first millennium B.C. compared to the many thousands of clay tablets written in cuneiform in either the Sumerian or Akkadian language.

The arrival of Greek rulers with their Greek armies, Greek colonists, and Greek traders in the fourth century B.C. meant the introduction of yet another language and script, Greek. The eastern Semitic languages and their script, cuneiform, thus were suffering, so to speak, a double blow after Alexander's conquest. Mesopotamian scholars continued their literary tradition by incorporating the new Chaldean, Persian, and Greek kings into their lists and chronicles of kings written with cuneiform for the next two hundred years.[1] Indeed, examples of cuneiform writing on clay tablets survive even from the first century A.D. and indicate the strength of that tradition. Nevertheless, that tradition would come to an end, as the changes introduced by the new Greek rulers did not help preserve the old traditional civilization.

---

1. For example, the Uruk King-List, *ANET*[3] 566, given in chapter 4, table B.5; and Chronicles 10–13 from the Seleucid Period in A. K. Grayson, *Assyrian and Babylonian Chronicles* (Locust Valley, N.Y., 1975), 113–124.

To be sure, many things continued as before: the new Greek rulers maintained the satrap system of government introduced by the Persians and gave generous monetary and other practical support to millennia-old religious practices. It was reasonable that they not interfere with long-established traditions. Nevertheless, there were changes. Babylon on the Euphrates, the center of old Semitic empires and of the Persian Empire, lost its governmental position of preeminence, as Seleukos founded on the Tigris a new capital for Mesopotamia, Seleukeia, named for himself. Papyrus from Egypt was becoming the standard writing material, and as Aramaic had become the standard spoken language of the people, it assumed more and more importance. In addition, Greek was now another language of the bureaucracy, which ran the empire. True, cuneiform texts were still being copied. Traditional old Babylonian texts from the school curriculum for scribes were even being transliterated into Greek letters.[2] Perhaps, and of this there is no proof, cuneiform texts were even being translated into Aramaic or Greek. The traditions, however, of Assyria and Babylonia ended. After the first century A.D., there are no more cuneiform texts, and there are no more attempts to use the Greek alphabet to write Akkadian; no translations of Sumerian or Akkadian literature, religious or secular, survive; no mention in Greek or Aramaic literature of there ever having been such translations exists.

Instead, the Greek and Aramaic languages, so to speak, prospered and thrived. They were used to carry the new literature and the new religions. Due to the Greek language's spread from Syria to the Indus River valley during Hellenistic times and its continued acceptance both by the Parthians after they assumed control of Mesopotamia around 150 B.C. and by the Romans as they came to rule the eastern Mediterranean, Greek became a world language. With the spread of Christianity and its adoption as the religion of the Roman Empire, Greek then became the preeminent religious language of the Ancient Near East, as the sacred texts of Christianity are written in Greek and major Christian writers throughout the East from Egypt, Asia Minor, Syria, and northern Mesopotamia used Greek. Greek, of course, remained the second language of the Roman Empire for its first three centuries, but with the establishment of Constantinople in A.D. 330 as a capital city equal to Rome and with the emergence of a thoroughly Greek empire in the east after the end of a Roman empire in the west in the fifth century A.D.,

---

2. See Susan Sherwin-White and Amélie Kuhrt, *From Samarkhand to Sardis* (Berkeley, 1993), 160, for mention of these texts with attendant bibliography.

the Greek language and its literature, both religious and secular, survived, with some great losses, as a living and still vital tradition to the modern age.

Aramaic, of course, even with the new Hellenistic kings after Alexander, remained the spoken language of the vast majority of people, whether rich or poor, in Mesopotamia and along the eastern Mediterranean. It along with Greek also served the educated elite as a major written language. For example, Josephus originally wrote his account of the Jewish revolt of A.D. 66–73 in Aramaic, but he translated his work into Greek (*Bellum Judaicum* [*The Jewish War*] 1.3) to find an even wider audience. The Greek version has survived from antiquity; the Aramaic original has not. The Parthians adapted the Aramaic alphabet, not the Greek alphabet, to write their own Parthian language. Mani, the third-century A.D. religious leader, the founder of Manichaeism, wrote his seven main canonical religious treatises in Aramaic. Unfortunately, none of those works survive, and modern scholars wishing to reconstruct his teachings are forced to use secondary sources that describe or translate in part what he wrote.[3] The Jews of Palestine and Mesopotamia used Aramaic as the language of both the Babylonian and Jerusalem Talmuds, written between 400 and 600 A.D.; and the eastern Christians of Syria and northern Mesopotamia from the fourth to the fourteenth century used Syriac, a local dialect of Aramaic centered in ancient Edessa (modern Urfa in Turkey), to compose a rich and varied Christian religious literature.[4] The spread of Islam, however, with the introduction of Arabic, another western Semitic language, but one with its own alphabet, meant the end of both Syriac and Aramaic as mainstream literary languages, although they remained sacred languages for a very small minority of Christians and Jews. After the Islamic conquest, neither Syriac nor Aramaic remained a living language, as Arabic became the spoken language of the vast majority of people in Mesopotamia as well as along the eastern Mediterranean coast in what today is modern Syria, Lebanon, Israel, and Jordan.

The religious, civil, legal, and historical texts written with cuneiform and representing Sumerian and eastern Semitic dialects with a tradition over 3,000 years old were therefore totally alien to the Greek, Parthian, Roman (Byzantine), Sassanid, and Islamic empires and were completely forgotten.

---

3. See Samuel N. C. Lieu, *Manichaeism in the Later Roman Empire and Medieval China*, 2d ed. (Tübingen, 1992), 8.

4. For a survey of Syriac religious literature see William Wright, *A Short History of Syriac Literature*, in *Encyclopaedia Britannica*, 9th ed., 1887, vol. 22 (reprinted and enlarged, Philo Press, 1894 and 1966) and W. Stewart McCullough, *A Short History of Syriac Christianity to the Rise of Islam* (Chico, Calif., 1982).

With the vast changes introduced by new peoples with new languages, new scripts, and new religions, there was no concern to preserve the old. No provision was made to safeguard the past contained on clay tablets written with cuneiform; there were no translations into either Aramaic or Greek; there was no preserving of the old languages, the old script, the old religious texts, the old ways. The past of Mesopotamia disappeared, as Mesopotamia became in succession Greek, Parthian, Sassanid, and Islamic, part of different empires with different religions, languages, and scripts over the course of a thousand years. The skills necessary to read Mesopotamia's past were lost. Only in the nineteenth century were they relearned.

Languages and Scripts of Ancient Egypt

Many of the same forces that worked to remove Mesopotamia's ancient past also removed ancient Egypt's. Egypt, soon after 3,000 B.C., began to develop its own writing system, and two different scripts emerged: (1) the hieroglyphic script, usually reserved for texts or inscriptions on monuments, that is, carved or painted on stone; and (2) the hieratic script, more cursive and much less pictorial than the hieroglyphic script, for more literary or religious texts to be written on papyrus. These scripts were used to preserve in written form the languages or dialects spoken in ancient Egypt from the predynastic period through the New Kingdom and into the Third Intermediate Period. Modern scholars have given these names to these scripts, but both names are derived from the ancient Greek name for all native Egyptian writing. Educated ancient Greeks usually did not bother to learn foreign languages. Indeed, only one Greek ruler of Egypt, Cleopatra VII (69–30 B.C.), is said to have learned to speak Egyptian (Plutarch *Antony* 27.4–5). Educated Greeks, because they could not read the native Egyptian writing, but since so much of it was written on temple walls, referred in Greek to all native Egyptian writing as "holy writing," that is, "hieroglyphics."

After 700 B.C. a new script, the demotic, began to emerge in Egypt. It became the script of choice for bureaucratic use. Although there were foreign invasions of Egypt before the Greeks (e.g., the Hyksos, the Libyans, and the Nubians, as well as the Persians), Egypt did not have to endure, so to speak, the introduction of a new language as Mesopotamia had with Aramaic. Nevertheless, the spoken language of the Egyptians naturally changed over the course of three thousand years. The maintenance, though, of the hieroglyphic and hieratic scripts, even with the introduction of demotic script, enabled scribes to read texts written over two thousand years earlier. It was, however, with the introduction of the Greek language and its alphabet that the demise of the hieroglyphic, hieratic, and demotic scripts began.

As in Mesopotamia, so in Egypt Greek was the language of the court and the highest-level bureaucrats under the new Greek pharaohs with their new capital at the newly founded Alexandria. The Romans, after they came to rule in Egypt in 30 B.C., kept Greek as the "national" language. To be sure, native Egyptian was maintained at all levels in society; many Greeks, most likely those with native wives or husbands and especially those living on the land far from cities, certainly spoke Egyptian; and Hellenization was thorough only at the king's court or governor's palace at Alexandria, not really located in the Egypt of the Egyptian pharaohs. Pharaonic Egypt consisted of two Egypts: Upper Egypt, the long, narrow Nile River valley from the first cataract at Elephantine in the south to the delta, and Lower Egypt, the Nile Delta, where the Nile divides into many streams to empty into the Mediterranean. Alexandria actually is situated to the west of the delta. Nevertheless, Greek language and script, even if seemingly isolated, began to edge out the native languages and scripts. By A.D. 200 the native Egyptian language, now called by scholars Coptic, had changed into its final form and was being written with the Greek alphabet. Coptic with its Greek script became the language of the native Egyptian Christian church.

During the Greek, Roman, and Byzantine rule of Egypt, the religious, philosophical, and historical material of Egypt from the Old Kingdom through to the Third Intermediate Period, written in hieroglyphics or hieratic, was no longer being copied and was not even, so to speak, brought up to date. Old texts were not rewritten in the demotic script, nor, later, were they written or transformed into Coptic. New works were being written in traditional Egyptian genres in demotic,[5] and, indeed, after 100 B.C., pagan religious texts of Egypt were even being written in Greek in the Greek language. But the texts written under Egyptian pharaohs were neither translated nor written in demotic, Coptic, or Greek. Thus, the literary output of over two thousand years was not preserved as part of continuing Egyptian-Greek culture and life under the Greeks, Romans, and Byzantines, pagan or Christian. Knowledge of how to read and write the old scripts would take a long time to die out, and there is an inscription in hieroglyphics that dates from the fourth century A.D., the last we know of. Most telling, however, of the

---

5. Thus, for example, Miriam Lichtheim, *Ancient Egyptian Literature, Volume III: The Late Period* (Berkeley, 1980), 125–217, which includes typical classic genres of Egyptian literature in demotic: narratives and instructional literature.

real situation in Egypt about the old scripts and the languages of Egypt used during the third and second millennium is a scene Tacitus describes (*Annals* 2.60). When Germanicus, heir apparent to the Roman Empire, traveled in Egypt in A.D. 19 and was naturally curious about the hieroglyphics he saw on the walls of ancient monuments, an old priest was found who could interpret the writing. He told of a vast and strong empire that could field large armies, as he translated a list of contingents of a New Kingdom army. But no attempt was made to preserve for the new masters of Egypt, the Romans, Egypt's written past by translating into Greek what was there on the walls of Egypt's great temples. It was a tradition closed to Greeks, maintained by the native Egyptian priestly caste. When that caste died out, replaced by Christian priests and monks, its history was lost. Only in the nineteenth century A.D. did it become possible to write ancient Egypt's past by using again what the ancient Egyptian scripts told.

Two Native Attempts to Preserve the History of Ancient Mesopotamia and Egypt

Only two men partially succeeded in preserving the old Mesopotamia and Egypt for the new Greek Mesopotamia and Egypt. Berossos wrote a history of Babylonia in Greek, and Manetho wrote a history of Egypt in Greek. Unfortunately, their works have not survived from antiquity. Especially unfortunate is that neither Berossos nor Manetho inspired successors who would build on the history each had written and so ensure the continuation and flowering of histories of Babylonia and Egypt before the Greeks arrived. With such writers as Berossos and Manetho, who produced what one might legitimately consider authoritative histories, one would think that the survival of Mesopotamian and Egyptian history was assured.

Both Berossos and Manetho were men of two cultures.[6] Both were native priests of their lands and both knew Greek, yet the only remains of their histories survive in the works of others who happened to cite or quote them.

---

6. Wolfram von Soden, "Zweisprachigkeit in der geistigen Kultur Babyloniens," *Österreichische Akademie der Wissenschaften, Philosophische-Historische Klasse* 235 (1960): 1–33 describes the ability of the ancient Mesopotamians to have a two-cultured society, which was both Sumerian and Semitic, as the carriers of this culture were fluent in two different languages and cultures, Sumerian and Akkadian. Both Berossos and Manetho, because of their ability in both their native languages (for Berossos the ability to read cuneiform and for Manetho the ability to read hieroglyphic and the hieratic script) and Greek, were thus able to participate fully in each of the cultures now dominant in their native lands.

Other men after them also wrote histories of Mesopotamia and Egypt, but none was as uniquely qualified to write history as Berossos and Manetho, and little or nothing remains of those histories. Although Jacoby in *FGrHist* gives the names of over twenty men who wrote histories of Mesopotamia (included in his section on the histories of Babylonia, Assyria, Media, or Persia, #680–96), not one was also a priest in Mesopotamia. Indeed, almost all have Greek names and almost all came from Greek cities. And again, although Jacoby in *FGrHist* (#608–65) gives the names of over fifty men who wrote histories of Egypt, almost all have Greek names and are Greek scholars. It is true that some of these men, even though they have Greek names, were priests—for example, Khairemon of Alexandria (*FGrHist* #618) and Ptolemaios of Mendes (*FGrHist* #611)—and perhaps they built on what Manetho had started. Almost nothing, however, of their work survives, and it is impossible to know if they added anything to what Manetho had already written by doing their own research and investigation of Egypt's pre-Greek past. Certainly in what does survive, nothing indicates new research into pharaonic records written in the hieroglyphic or hieratic script. Indeed, we do not know of what cult these later Egyptian historians were priests, whether of old native Egyptian cults or of the Greco-Egyptian cults that emerged during the Greek rule of Egypt. We are, therefore, almost totally dependent on Berossos and Manetho for what knowledge the Greek world managed to preserve of Mesopotamian and Egyptian history, and we are totally dependent on what survives from Berossos and Manetho for an organized attempt to present the entire history of ancient Babylonia and ancient Egypt from a native standpoint.

Because of the great importance of Berossos and Manetho, in this book we want to present what remains of them. We have three basic aims. The first is to give in a concise and relevant form what information we have about these two native historians of Babylonia and Egypt. The second is to present an interpretation of their accomplishments based on what survives of their works. We want to make intelligent judgments about the accuracy of their works, their purpose in writing, and the reasons why their works did not survive and were not successful in integrating the early history of Babylonia and Egypt into Greco-Roman civilization. The third is to present what remains of their works in translation into English with, where needed, short explanatory notes. At times it is necessary to present more information on a topic than Berossos or Manetho gives, to make clearer for the modern reader what Berossos and Manetho meant. Also, at times, the text that preserves what Manetho or Berossos wrote is not clear, and we must give some explanation or justification of our translation. In addition, we present various tables, lists, maps, and so on that will serve most conveniently to help readers understand better the histories of Babylonia and Egypt that Berossos and Manetho tried to present. We want to add that it is not our goal to present a complete and scholarly commentary on Berossos's and Manetho's histories. There are many difficulties in their texts, and a lengthy scholarly bibliography has grown around these difficulties at which we can at times but hint. Rather, we want to present in one volume an accurate translation of what remains of Berossos's and Manetho's histories in a form that will appeal to the student interested in ancient Mesopotamia and Egypt as well as to one interested in Hellenistic Mesopotamia and Egypt.

Berossos

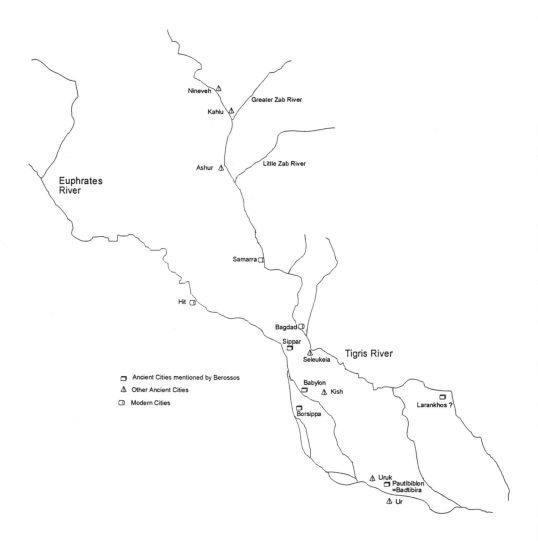

Nineveh

Kahlu

Greater Zab River

Ashur

Little Zab River

Euphrates
River

Samarra

Hit

Bagdad

Sippar

Seleukeia

Tigris River

Ancient Cities mentioned by Berossos
Other Ancient Cities
Modern Cities

Babylon

Kish

Larankhos ?

Borsippa

Uruk
Pautibiblon
=Badtibira

Ur

Map 2. Berossos's Mesopotamia

CHAPTER 1

Introduction to Berossos

Berossos's Life and Work

Berossos was born during Alexander's reign over Babylon (T6), between 330 and 323 B.C., and became a priest of Marduk or Bel at Babylon (T2). *Belu* means lord or master in Akkadian, and Bel became another name for Marduk, the head god of Babylonia, who was the lord or master of all the gods, of all of creation. Scholars postulate that Berossos's native Akkadian name was *Bel-re-ušu*, a name that would mean "Bel is his shepherd."[1] The name, when Hellenized, had a variety of spellings, as there was no agreement in antiquity on how the sound of the Akkadian vowels should be rendered into Greek, and both the Akkadian *š*, a sh sound, and the consonant combination *lr* had no equivalent in ancient Greek. *Berossos* is a transliteration of one of the main Greek spellings of his name, as other Greek spellings of his name have survived in the Greek manuscripts. He probably served at the Great Temple of Esagila, where he would have had access to its records (T7a). He published his *History of Babylonia* in Greek (T4), most likely around 290 B.C. for the Macedonian king Antiochos I (T6), co-ruler of the Seleucid Empire, which stretched from the Indus River in the east to the Mediterranean Sea in the west. Antiochos I was first associated with the rule of his father, Seleukos I, as king of the eastern satrapies in 292 B.C. (Plutarch *Demosthenes* 38.10; Appian *Syriaca* 59).[2] Later, Berossos moved to the island of Kos off the coast of modern Turkey in the Mediterranean,

---

1. See G. Komoroczy, "Berosos and the Mesopotamian Literature," *Acta Antiqua Academica Scientiarum Hungarica* 21 (1973): 125, with attendant references.

2. See Susan Sherwin-White and Amélie Kuhrt, *From Samarkhand to Sardis* (Berkeley, 1993), 23 24, with attendant references.

where he founded a school of astrology or astronomy (T1a–b). Here he was no longer a subject of King Antiochos but a subject of the king of Egypt, who controlled most of the Aegean Islands at this time. We do not know when Berossos died.

Not all modern scholars accept the brief outline given above of Berossos's life. Some argue that Berossos was born sometime before 340 B.C.—because Berossos is called a contemporary of Alexander the Great (T7), when he conquered Babylonia—and that our ancient sources have in fact information about two different men named Berossos and have combined their lives: there was a Berossos who was an astrologer and another who was the historian. It is difficult, some scholars maintain, to imagine the same Berossos writing a historical work for a Seleucid and then, so late in his life, moving to start a school in astronomy or astrology in an area controlled by a Ptolemy. The Seleucids and Ptolemies in the 280s B.C. were usually at war over eastern Mediterranean lands. Our most ancient sources (T1a–T3b) mention a Berossos interested exclusively in astronomy, while it is only later historical writers who mention a Berossos who wrote history. It is difficult, some scholars maintain, to place in the history of Babylonia, which a Berossos wrote, the astronomical and astrological fragments (F16–F22), which are also attributed to a Berossos, and there is no indication that the Berossos who wrote a historical work also wrote an astrological work (F19).[3]

These objections to treating everything that survives about a Berossos as a reference to one man are not convincing. Our ancient sources know only one Berossos, and there is nothing inherently contradictory in the pieces of information they preserve about him. Even if Berossos were born before 340 B.C. and published his *History of Babylonia* in 278 B.C., the third year after Seleukos I's death and the beginning of Antiochos I's sole rule, Berossos's departure for a more central area of Greek culture is readily understandable. His skill in astronomy or astrology made him, so to speak, much in demand. His fame in antiquity must have been considerable, since Athens even erected a statue to honor him (T3b). Although there is no information to account for Berossos's leaving the patronage of Antiochos I to take up residence in an area controlled by Egypt, it is easy to imagine reasons why Berossos might find it practical to move. Babylon under the Seleucids, whatever religious favors Seleukos I or Antiochos I showed to the Great Temple at Babylon, was no longer the intellectual center of the now Greek empire of

---

3. See Robert Drews, "The Babylonian Chronicles and Berossus," *Iraq* 37 (1975): 51–52, for a summary of the arguments that there were two different men named Berossos, one a historian and the other an astrologer.

the Seleucids. The foundation in 312 B.C. of Seleukeia on the Tigris created a great economic and political rival to Babylon. Seleukeia became the major city of Mesopotamia. Babylon was becoming an intellectual backwater.[4] The Seleucids depended on Greeks, not native Babylonians, to run their government. But whatever the reason for Berossos's desire to emigrate, it is not difficult to believe that the same Berossos who wrote a history of his native land for the Macedonian king of that land would leave Babylon for the Greek Aegean of the Ptolemies. Berossos's age when he left Babylon, whether he was in his 30s or 40s (born after 330 and publishing his *History* in 290) or in his 60s (born before 340 and publishing his *History* in 278), does not have to be considered an important factor in deciding whether there were one or two men named Berossos. Most important, Josephus (T4) mentions that Berossos the historian also wrote about ancient Babylonian astronomy.

There is no proof that Berossos the historian wrote a separate astronomical work. There is a reference in Latin that indicates such a work by a Berossos (F21), called *Procreatio* (*The Creation*), which would be the translation of the Greek title *Genesis*. The citation of a particular work by a title, however, is very rare in antiquity. Rather, the subject matter of a work or of a particular part of a work is most often used to refer to a work or part of a work, and the phrasing of that citation can vary. Thus, what is referred to in F21 is most likely a part of Berossos's *History*, book 1, which dealt with primordial creation and the establishment of order in the world by Marduk (Bel). Astronomical or astrological references and information (F16–F22) as part of a work of Babylonian history by someone with a professional interest in those matters are easily understandable. Such information could play an especially important role in a description of creation based on ancient wisdom given by the gods (F1).

Berossos's *History of Babylonia*—Sources, Methods, and Reliability

In what remains of Berossos's *History* there is no indication of what specific or particular sources he used. The ancient authors who cite what Berossos

---

4. It is a matter of debate how well or how badly Babylon was treated under its new Greek rulers. For a description of how favored Babylon was under the Seleucids, see R. J. van der Spek, "The Babylonian City," in *Hellenism in the East*, ed. Amélie Kuhrt and Susan Sherwin-White (London, 1987), 60–70. Even if he is correct and "Babylon continued as a traditional Mesopotamian city with its own institutions" (69), it was still an intellectual backwater compared to what was going on in Greek circles.

had to say about the sources he used report that he did use ancient, but un-
named records (T4 and F1). Perhaps Berossos cataloged his sources in his
History to impress on his readers the antiquity and, therefore, the reliability
of his own *History*. Ancient cuneiform sources with what might be called
primary historical information have survived from the Mesopotamian past,
and it is possible to compare what Berossos wrote with them. Because, however, so much of the literary output of Mesopotamia has not survived, it is
not possible to form a judgment on how accurately Berossos has transmitted
the Babylonian past from the written records he would have had at his disposal. That Berossos gives information different from what survives in exist-
ing cuneiform texts may be due to Berossos's use of cuneiform texts that did
not have the good fortune to survive to the present.

What Berossos intended in his statement that he had used ancient records
is not that the information he had at his disposal was more trustworthy than
the information others had published but that he had access to information,
temple records, sacred priestly lore, and so on that had not been used before
by anyone attempting to write Babylonia's history and that was surely not
available to any ordinary citizen of Babylon. Rather, Berossos's *History* is
the result of the effort and care he took in assembling what information he
had available to construct a connected narrative of the history of Babylonia
to his present. He had no native narrative history to follow and was writing a
history in a form foreign to the literary traditions of Babylon.

In Berossos's first book he described the creation of the world and how
humans learned about creation. Berossos has retold the *Creation Epic*, the
Enuma Elish, as Marduk saved creation from Tiamat, the goddess of the
primeval salt waters, and brought order to it (F1). Berossos used as the basis
of his description of creation in his work of history the main religious text of
ancient Mesopotamia, which was recited at the beginning of every new year.
Numerous copies of it exist. Although no extant text is older than the first
millennium B.C., all scholars think that it was composed centuries earlier.
The view that it dates to the early second millennium, the Old Babylonian
period, is no longer held, as scholars now date it to the second half of the
second millennium.[5] No matter when it was composed, Babylonians of the
first millennium B.C. held it sacred. They were devoted to their god, Mar-

---

5. See *ANET*[3] 60 for the view that the *Creation Myth* is early second millennium B.C., but
most recent scholarship divides between a date in the fifteenth century B.C. and a date in the late
second millennium. Thus, see Benjamin R. Foster, *Before the Muses: An Anthology of Akkadian
Literature* (Bethesda, 1993), 1:351, for the view that the poem belongs to the late second millennium B.C.

duk, and Berossos was one of his priests. There are a few instances in Berossos's account where his narrative differs from that of the *Creation Myth*, but
they are relatively minor.

Berossos also in his first book tells how humans learned about what Marduk had done in creating order in the world from Oannes and other similar
monsters from the sea. These monsters not only taught humans about creation but gave them the gift of civilization. Oannes and the others who are
named in Berossos's text do not appear in ancient Semitic literary texts and
are not mentioned with the antediluvian kings in king-lists. They are not,
however, Berossos's creations. A late Babylonian tablet found at Uruk mentions these teachers of humans with antediluvian kings:[6] the tablet is based
on Sumerian mythology or speculation on it by Kassites (in the late second
millennium B.C.) and Neo-Babylonians (in the early first millennium B.C.).
Based undoubtedly on Berossos's account are the names of the kings and
monsters preserved in the *History* Abydenos wrote in the second or third
century A.D.[7] The similarities of the names on the list preserved on the tablet
and those found in Berossos and Abydenos are striking. In addition, images
of these teacher-creatures were most likely set up in the Great Temple of
Marduk in Babylon, and Berossos's description of them was undoubtedly
based on their likenesses. Berossos is not merely preserving ancient Mesopotamian traditions by copying or translating them into Greek. He is integrating what information he has found from disparate sources and presenting to
his readers his understanding and interpretation of what happened.

It is in the first book of Berossos's *History* that the astronomical and astrological fragments (F16–F19), which ancient authors attributed to him,
should be placed. No reference to book numbers survive in these fragments,
but there is no more logical place for them. There is no evidence of a separate book on Babylonian astronomy or astrology by Berossos. According to
Berossos, all knowledge was revealed to humans by Oannes in the very first
year after creation (F1). Therefore, the narrative of how Marduk created order in the world after subduing Tiamat would have been the proper place to
reveal all the knowledge about the universe that ancient Babylonian science
possessed.

In his second book, Berossos narrated the history of the world after creation down to the reign of Nabonassaros (747–734 B.C.). He undoubtedly has
made use of ancient king-lists originally compiled in the third, second, and

---

6. See chap. 4, table B.2b, Tablet W 20030,7.
7. See chap. 4, table B.2b, Abydenos's List.

first millennia B.C. In addition, his story of the Great Flood is very similar in general outline to that found in the *Epic of Gilgamesh*, the *Sha nagba imuru*.

The ancient Mesopotamians did not have what modern scholars call narrative history, such as the ancient Greeks wrote. Nor does it seem that the ancient Mesopotamians, even in the last stages of their civilization under the Neo-Babylonians or the Persians, developed a narrative in any way similar to that which the ancient Israelites had in the biblical books of Samuel or Kings. Rather, the ancient Mesopotamians had only what modern scholars call king-lists, annals, and chronicles.[8] Of these three, only the Assyrians had annals, which celebrated an individual king's reign and achievements. Berossos most likely had no familiarity with or knowledge of such documents, since all the archival centers of the Assyrian Empire were completely destroyed two hundred years before he wrote. Of the remaining two, not all modern scholars agree that a distinction is to be made between king-lists and chronicles,[9] and there can be scholarly disagreements into which class an ancient document should fall. Certainly the ancient Mesopotamians never recognized a difference between these two categories of what modern scholars call historical documents. Nevertheless, this distinction can serve to illustrate well how Berossos used his ancient sources.

A king-list is a document that basically lists kings, usually with a set phrase preceding or following each king's name, such as "The king ruled for (*x* number) years." The king's filiation may be mentioned. In addition, there may be bits of information about individual kings, but the information given in a king-list is in no way comparable to the amount of information a chronicle had. Thus, in a chronicle, events that occurred during a king's reign are mentioned in a sober, dispassionate, and seemingly objective narrative. Royal defeats, internal problems, even rebellions are cataloged, some of them with what might be considered lengthy descriptions. An ancient chronicle, though, is not a historical narrative of a king's reign. Although many of the events described in a chronicle may be intimately connected with the king, such as a military campaign, some of the events may have nothing at all to do with the king. No attempt is made in the narrative part

---

8. There are other documents that modern historians would also class as ancient Mesopotamian attempts at history. For example, besides chronographic texts, A. K. Grayson, *Assyrian and Babylonian Chronicles* (Locust Valley, N.Y., 1975), 4 mentions "pseudo-autobiographies, prophecies, historical epics, royal inscriptions, and miscellaneous texts." These all undoubtedly had an influence on Berossos, although it is impossible to attribute specific pieces of information that survive in Berossos to a specific prophecy, epic, inscription, and so on.

9. For a discussion of this, see A. K. Grayson, "Assyria and Babylonia," *Orientalia* 49 (1980): 171–72.

of the chronicle to draw logical or specific connections between the events mentioned during a king's reign or, if a number of kings' reigns are treated, between kings. Some scholars have argued that there are implicit connections between events mentioned or described and the kings who are listed, and that these connections would be known to the ancient reader and can, with some imagination, be found by the modern reader. It is, however, very difficult to prove this convincingly, since the connection that is presumed is usually either so trivial or so general as to be useless in an analysis of chronicles. For example, a chronicle that included a king's victories in various battles obviously contributes to the glory of that king. But such a chronicle on a clay tablet in an archive can not be meant for a general reading public. There was no general reading public in ancient Mesopotamia, with a literacy rate probably at less than 1 percent. Even if there were a relatively large number of people who knew how to read, an inscription commemorating a specific victory or victories would be much more appropriate to a king's glory than a chronicle of his victories with a great deal of other information stored in an inaccessible archive. We have no evidence that these tablets would have been read aloud at specific events or on certain days during the year. Indeed, why they were even compiled is as puzzling a question as why they were preserved.

There are many differences between what Berossos records in his second book and information the ancient king-lists and chronicles record. As an example, in chapter 4, tables B.1a–b there is the list of Berossos's antediluvian kings of Babylon (F3) and the list of antediluvian kings mentioned by what might be called the main canonical copy of the *Sumerian King-List*, compiled at the time of the Third Dynasty of Ur (ca. 2200–2000 B.C.).[10] Numerous exemplars of it have been found in Mesopotamia, as it became what one might call a mainstay of Mesopotamian historiography, although its major purpose was religious and mythic, not historical. The *Sumerian King-List* cataloged a time long before its present and established the divine and long tradition of kingship in Mesopotamia. The differences between it and Berossos's list are striking. Berossos has two more kings than the *Sumerian King-List*, although most of the names mentioned there have counterparts in Berossos's list (e.g., Euedorankhos and En-men-dur-Anna of Sippar). The lengths of the reigns of the kings are different as is the total of the years all the kings reigned before the Great Flood. Most interesting is Berossos's last king of Babylon before the flood, Xisouthros, who is rewarded by the gods

---

10. Thorkild Jacobsen, *The Sumerian King List* (Chicago, 1939), 140–141.

with immortality after surviving the Great Flood. He does not appear in the main canonical copy of the *Sumerian King-List*, nor is that the name of the man to whom the gods gave immortality in the *Epic of Gilgamesh*. Although there are a number of short Sumerian epic poems that mention the Great Flood and a number of short poems about individual exploits of Gilgamesh, it is the Semitic *Epic of Gilgamesh* that has the longest and most popular account of the Great Flood. It might be called the national poem of Mesopotamia. It was written in Akkadian sometime between 1900 and 1600 B.C. and reached its final form on twelve tablets around 1250.[11] In the *Epic of Gilgamesh* the name of the man to whom the gods give immortality is Utanapishtim, and he is not a former king of Mesopotamia.

Berossos has not simply reproduced the *Sumerian King-List* in its standard form or recounted the Great Flood by translating the *Epic of Gilgamesh*. Xisouthros is most likely the Greek equivalent of the Sumerian name Ziusudra, who in Sumerian mythology is connected with the Great Flood. There is a Sumerian poem on the Great Flood that mentions Ziusudra as king,[12] and Ziusudra appears in the Diyala and Sippar king-lists as the last king before the flood. Berossos has used his research to present an older and perhaps to him, therefore, more historically accurate account of the Great Flood based on Sumerian records and myths, which are anterior to Semitic records and myths.

For the kings after the Great Flood, Berossos gave only the names and number of years that kings reigned, with scarcely any mention of anything that an individual king did down to the reign of Nabonassaros (F3). While the *Sumerian King-List* and other king-lists give the names of kings from after the Great Flood to the reign of Nabonassaros and the length of their reigns as well as the length of their dynasties, it is difficult to compare them with what survives from Berossos, since hardly any names of kings survive from Berossos's account. In addition, there are possible problems with the text of Berossos, as scribes copying ancient manuscripts could easily make mistakes when transcribing numbers. Thus, scholars are not sure to whose reigns or to what dynasties Berossos is referring in his mention of eighty-six kings who ruled for 33,091 years, eight kings of the Medes, or nine kings of the Arabians; nor are they sure what sources or what lists he had at his disposal. Thus, for example, it seems Berossos did not use the *Sumerian King-List* as he does not mention the first two kings of the First Kingdom of Kish

---

11. *ANET*[3] 72–73, 97.

12. *ANET*[3] 42–44.

who, according to the *Sumerian King-List*, ruled immediately after the Great Flood (see chap. 4, tables B.2a–b).

Most interesting in the second book of Berossos's *History* is his refusal to include information that was most likely available to him. Berossos simply, it seems, compiled a listing of the kings of Babylon. For example, there were narratives or information available on the reign of Sargon of Akkade (ca. 2300 B.C.), as there survive three distinct sources about Sargon that would probably have been available to Berossos. There is a document that contains a birth-legend about Sargon from the first millennium B.C.[13] There is also an epic poem on Sargon written during the second millennium B.C., which has been preserved at El-Amarna in Egypt, but also exists in a later Assyrian version found at Nineveh.[14] Last, there is a Neo-Babylonian chronicle on Sargon which survives on two clay tablets in the British Museum.[15] Berossos chose to ignore whatever information had survived about Sargon. Surely the great king Hammurabi (ca. 1750 B.C.) would have been worthy of more than just mention, and the history of Babylonia under the Kassites (ca. 1500–1150 B.C.), a rather brilliant historical period with its international relations with Egypt, would have provided abundant material for his history.

It is, therefore, surprising, given Berossos's lack of specific information in his second book, that he specifically contradicts Greek historians about what they had written on Semiramis, fabled queen of Babylon. If there is any truth behind the stories Greeks told of her, she was in reality Sammuramat, a wife of Samshi-Adad V of Assyria (824–811) and the mother of Adad-Nirari III (810–782), and she was perhaps a queen of Assyria, although there is no evidence she bore a title equivalent to the modern conception of what a queen is. A newly discovered and published inscription, a boundary stone, does give her, however, a prominence that is uncommon for Assyrian women. It mentions her threefold relation to kings of Assyria, "palace woman of Samshi-Adad, mother of Adad-Nirari, and daughter-in-law of Shalmaneser."[16] Greek historians, however, had made her not only the queen of Assyria but Babylon's founder and builder. Herodotus mentions her in passing (1.184), but Ktesias of Knidos in his *Persica* had a lengthy description of her reign (*FGrHist* #688). He wrote twenty-three books, of

---

13. *ANET³* 119 = Benjamin R. Foster, *Before the Muses: An Anthology of Akkadian Literature* (Bethesda, 1993), 2:813.

14. Foster, *Before the Muses*, 1:250–59.

15. *ANET³* 266–267 = BM 26,472 and BM 96,152.

16. Veysel Donbaz, "Two Neo-Assyrian Stelae in the Antakya and Kahramanmaraš Museums," *Annual Review of the Royal Inscriptions of Mesopotamia Project* 8 (1990): 9.

which books 1–6 dealt with history before Cyrus established the Persian Kingdom. In these books he narrated Assyrian and Babylonian history. Although Ktesias's *Persica* has not survived to modern times, his narrative on Semiramis has, as part of Diodorus Siculus's *World History* (2.4–20 = *FGrHist* #688 F1). Although Diodorus correctly says she was not responsible for constructing the Hanging Gardens of Babylon, his account is, nevertheless, full of astounding misinformation. He described her as the daughter of Derketo, a Syrian goddess, and as married to Ninos, the legendary founder, for the Greeks, of Nineveh and the Assyrian Empire. How much information Berossos gave about her is, of course, unknown. Since she would have been a queen, so to speak, of Assyria and not of Babylon, and since Berossos is said to have given hardly any information about individual rulers in his second book anyway (F3), perhaps all he did was to say that she was not a queen of Babylon, as Greek historians had written.

Berossos's third book, which covered the history of Babylon from the reign of Nabonassaros (747–734 B.C.) to, presumably, King Antiochos I (joint rule with his father 292–281 B.C.; sole ruler 281–261 B.C.), included extensive historical narrative. It is not possible to state which particular ancient sources, king-lists, and chronicles he followed. Among the sources that survive to the present, which modern historians use as a source for Mesopotamian history and which might have served Berossos, are *King-List A* and *Chronicle 1*. Berossos, however, if he used them, felt free to construct his own chronology and narrative, as what remains of his history at times does not agree with what they have preserved. In chapter 4, tables B.3a–b, we list the kings Berossos mentions and the length of their reigns for comparison with those of *King-List A* and *Chronicle 1*. In addition, we include the names and length of reigns preserved by the *Synchronistic King-list* and the *Ptolemaic Canon*.

King-List A was originally a date-list. A scribe usually dated an important or legal document in Mesopotamia by noting the name and the year of the reigning king when the document was drawn up. How old a document was or in what year a document was drawn up could be found by finding a match in *King-List A*. It survives in only one copy, made most likely sometime in the sixth or fifth century B.C.[17] *Chronicle 1* survives in three copies—one of which was written in the twenty-second year of Darius,[18] around 500 B.C.— and recounts events from the third year of Nabu-nasir's reign to the first

---

17. J. A. Brinkman, *A Political History of Post-Kassite Babylonia 1158–722 B.C.*, vol. 43 of *Analecta Orientalia* (Roma, 1968), 16.

18. Grayson, *Assyrian and Babylonian Chronicles*, 69.

year of Shamash-shuma-ukin's reign (741–667). The *Synchronistic King-list* gave the names of the Babylonian and Assyrian kings in parallel columns. While it is possible that Berossos consulted either *King-List A* or *Chronicle 1*, the *Synchronistic King-list*[19] undoubtedly was not available to Berossos. Only four such texts are known, all four found at Assur. This royal city of Assyria was sacked and completely destroyed at the end of the seventh century B.C., and therefore its records lost or covered over until archaeologists of the nineteenth and twentieth centuries A.D. discovered them. Furthermore, Berossos was not interested in writing or compiling lists of contemporaneous kings in Mesopotamia. He was interested only in the one king of Babylonia. Unfortunately, hardly anything of Berossos's narrative survives about the various kings of Babylon during the last century of the Assyrian Empire. Some information that originally appeared in Berossos's account does survive about Senakheirimos (Sennacherib), Assyrian king from 704 to 681 B.C. and king of Babylon twice, from 704 to 703 and from 688 to 681 B.C.

It is impossible, however, from the pieces of information that survive, to derive what interpretation, if any, Berossos made about the struggles that were occurring within the Assyrian Empire or between the Assyrian Empire and other peoples. Not only were there terrible dynastic struggles in Assyria, but there were wars between Assyria and Elam for control of Babylonia, as well as an ever-present struggle between the dying Assyrian Empire and the coming Neo-Babylonian or Chaldean Empire. What Berossos chose to describe and how he determined what kings deserved mention as legitimate kings of Babylon are questions just as intriguing as the question of what sources Berossos used. As there are differences between the list of kings that can be made from Berossos's account and the list that survives in *King-List A* or *Chronicle 1*, so are there differences between them and the list of kings that survives in Claudius Ptolemy's *Canon of Babylonian Kings* from the second century A.D.,[20] which is itself based on a source different from Berossos, *King-List A*, and *Chronicle 1*.

Much more survives, however, of Berossos's account about the foundation of the Neo-Babylonian or Chaldean Empire, the height of its power under Naboukhodonosoros (Nebuchadnezzar II, 604–562 B.C.), and its demise under Nabonnedos (Nabonidus) in 539 B.C. For the first time there survive in Berossos's account moral judgments that most likely indicate his interpretation of historical events. Thus, for example, Berossos describes Euilmara-

---

19. *ANET*[3] 272–74 which calls it *Synchronistic Chronicle*.
20. See chap. 4, table B.4.

dokhos (Evil-Merodach) as ruling capriciously and Laborosoardokhos (Labashi-Marduk) as evil. He seems to approve of their removal from the kingship, even of the murder of Laborosoardokhos, when the king was still a child. There are a number of chronicles that survive about the kings of the Neo-Babylonian Empire, such as the *Chronicle of Nabonidus*.[21] These chronicles appear to modern scholars to take a moral stand also. Thus, in the *Chronicle of Nabonidus* various facts of Nabonidus's reign are mentioned: the occurrence or nonoccurrence of the celebration of the *Akitu*, which was the great New Year Festival held in March or April; Cyrus's defeat of the Babylonian army by the Tigris; the fall of Sippar and then of Babylon without another battle or a siege; and the capture of Nabonidus in Babylon. Some modern scholars maintain that the *Chronicle of Nabonidus* offered an explanation of why Cyrus was able to take Babylon, that is, the gods were displeased with Nabonidus and his neglect of them, and, therefore, they made Cyrus victorious. If such an interpretation is true and if Berossos offered a similar interpretation of events of the sixth century B.C. (i.e., moral conduct determined the success or failure of a king), then it would seem that Berossos has mirrored the value system of the Babylonian chronicle writers. Although there does dominate in some Greek historical writing a rationalistic interpretation of human activity, there is also a heavy strain of moralizing in many Greek historical writers, both classical and Hellenistic. For example, Xenophon in his *Hellenica* (*Greek History*) 5.4.1 interprets a Spartan defeat as punishment for the Spartans' failure to live up to an agreement they had made. Thus, it is very difficult to determine from what survives of Berossos's *History* not only which Babylonian chronicles he used as sources for his *History* but also whether he adopted a typical Babylonian outlook on life or used the moralizing tone that appears in a large number of Greek historians. It is clear, however, that Berossos did not give a rationalistic Greek interpretation of events, such as the Greek historian Thucydides tried to offer in his history of the Peloponnesian War.

Although a number of chronicles do survive about the last Babylonian kings of all of Mesopotamia, it is difficult to compare their narrative of events with Berossos's to judge how accurately Berossos has transmitted Babylonian history. Both the native chronicles and Berossos's account, as it survives, are meager in their narrative and in details. Nevertheless, there are some differences between them, as there are also differences between Berossos's account and what some Greek historians have recorded. We note these where they occur in the fragments of his work.

---

21. Grayson, *Assyrian and Babylonian Chronicles*, 104–11.

Whatever the difficulties in assessing how well Berossos used his sources, his achievement was unique. He combined Mesopotamian and Hellenistic historiography, as he took lists, legendary and mythic accounts, and bare chronicles—all that Mesopotamian literature had produced—and turned them into a connected Greek narrative of the past, chronologically ordered. What marks Berossos's *History* as a Greek history, besides the language in which it was written, is his direct imitation of Greek historical form.

First, Berossos identified himself to his readers at the beginning of his *History*. This is the source of what knowledge we do have of him. Similar, for example, would be the beginnings of the histories written by Herodotus or Thucydides, where each identified himself to his reader and stated what particular resources he brought to writing his history. We have practically no knowledge about any author of any piece of Mesopotamian literature. We do know the names of a number of Mesopotamian scribes and of some supposed authors of Mesopotamian literature, but there is no comparison possible between the personal and pertinent information Berossos gave about himself and what meager scraps of information can be gleaned from a cuneiform tablet about a scribe who copied lists or poems or about the reputed author of a poem or hymn.

Second, Berossos offered in his *History* a narrative account of the sacred myths of the Mesopotamians. Stories about the gods were an integral part of the early histories produced by the Greeks in the fifth century B.C. For example, both Hellanikos (*FGrHist* #5) and Pherekydes (*FGrHist* #3) wrote, either as separate works or as parts of other historical works, cosmologies or theogonies. These contained the stories or the myths of the gods. While these early Greek historians may have had some misgivings about the veracity or accuracy of these stories about the gods, Berossos most likely would not have doubted that what he described about the gods had taken place. The philosophical or naturalistic interpretation, then, of Mesopotamian myths, mentioned in F1, is most likely due not to Berossos but to later Greek writers who could not imagine that Berossos had not seen the myths of Mesopotamia as allegories.

Third, Berossos included in his *History* a geographical description of Babylonia. This is typical of Greek history writing. Indeed, the Greeks even developed a specific genre of writing that might be called geographical writing, which could be combined with history. For example, Herodotus, the father of history, gave a physical description of Egypt (2.5–34) as part of his history of Egypt. Such descriptions of foreign lands found a natural audience among Greeks. Besides, it would hardly be necessary to describe Babylonia for native Babylonians. In addition, in the geographical section of his *His-*

tory of Babylonia Berossos uses terms and descriptions typical of Greek classifications, such as his list of grains that grew in Babylonia (F1).

Fourth, Berossos seems to have taken very seriously his task of investigation. He has presented only that information for which there was evidence. He does not add information. Hence, in book 2 he presents a long, almost recipe-like list of kings who have ruled Babylonia. Only as his narrative neared his present, after Nabonassaros's (Nabu-nashir's) rule, when there were evidently records he trusted to be accurate, does his *History* resume a true narrative form.

Unfortunately, no direct evidence survives from Berossos's *History* to explain why he wrote his *History*. In keeping with the usual form of a Greek historical work, he most probably explained in an introduction to his work not only who he was and what his credentials for writing a history were but also why he was writing. Modern scholars have given various reasons to account for Berossos's *History*. Perhaps there was a commission either from King Antiochos I or from the priests of the Great Temple. It may be that King Antiochos wanted a history of the land that was part of the Seleucid Empire, just as it may be that the priests found in their number someone who could explain or justify to the new king or his court the important role that the Great Temple and the worship of Marduk had always played in world history.[22]

It is, however, possible to come to some conclusions about the purpose of Berossos's *History* from what survives. First, his history was obviously meant for Greeks. It was written in Greek and presented in Greek form, that is, Greek narrative history. The ordinary means by which a literary work was published in classical antiquity was by a public reading. Then the author or patron of the author would give copies of the work to those to whom he wanted to give copies. Others who wanted to have a copy of the work would have to procure one for themselves by finding someone who had the work and by arranging to have it copied. There was no copyright in antiquity, and authors did not earn money by selling copies of their work. Although we have no information about what patronage Berossos may have enjoyed, it is impossible to imagine that such a work as Berossos's *History* was produced without the monetary support of the Seleucid King or the Great Temple.[23]

---

22. For speculation on why Berossos wrote, see Amélie Kuhrt, "Berossus' *Babyloniaka* and Seleucid rule in Babylonia," 53–56 in *Hellenism in the East*, Amélie Kuhrt and Susan Sherwin-White (London, 1987).

23. There is little reason to believe Moses of Chorene's statement (see T10) that the Egyptian ruler, Ptolemy II, urged Berossos to write his history.

Second, since Berossos was a Babylonian and since he was, so to speak, writing national history with the support of either the king or the priests of the Great Temple or perhaps of both, it is not difficult to believe that the purpose of Berossos's *History* was to treat Mesopotamia's history favorably. There survives nothing in Berossos's *History* that could be considered detrimental to Mesopotamia, although there is nothing to survive that could be considered favorable to Mesopotamia. Nevertheless, it does not seem improbable that one of the purposes Berossos had in writing his *History* was to glorify Babylonia by describing its great age, the importance of the city of Babylon, and the importance of the worship of Marduk.

Berossos's *History of Babylonia*—Reception and Transmission

Classical antiquity did not value highly Berossos's *History*. It was not thought worth the effort to preserve, as no copy of it has survived to the present. It was also little read and consulted in antiquity; Ktesias of Knidos's *Persica*, ca. 400 B.C. (*FGrHist* #688, F1–F33) remained the standard narrative account of the history of ancient Mesopotamia. Berossos's account served only as a mine for information on astronomical opinions and miscellaneous information or as a sourcebook for scholarly abbreviated accounts of Mesopotamian history.

Ancient authors whose works have survived to the present and have preserved parts of Berossos's *History* most likely did not do so directly. All those ancient writers on astronomy or astrology who cite Berossos as a source of information about Babylonian science probably never read Berossos's *History* themselves. They are most likely dependent on what Poseidonios of Apamea (135–50 B.C.), a Greek philosopher and historian, recorded about Berossos in his various works.[24]

Only three ancient authors who mention Berossos as their source for astronomical or astrological information consulted Poseidonios directly for their knowledge of what Berossos wrote:

1. Vitruvius Pollio (T1a–c and F16), a contemporary of the emperor Augustus and the author of a book on architecture;
2. Pliny the Elder (T3a–b, F15a, and F20), who died in A.D. 79 and was the author of a compendium of all knowledge; and

---

24. What follows on the transmission of Berossos's text is dependent on Paul Schnabel, *Berossos und die Babylonisch-Hellenistische Literatur* (Leipzig, 1923), 33–171; see especially the charts on Schnabel's pp. 169 and 171.

3. Seneca the Younger (T2 and F19), who died in A.D. 65 and was an author
   of numerous philosophical works.

The seven later pagan writers who mention Berossos as their source for
astronomical or astrological information are most likely dependent on at
least one intermediary source, who would then have reported what Poseidonios had preserved from Berossos. These seven writers are:

1. Cleomedes (F18) of the last half of the second century A.D., who was a
   writer on astronomy;
2. Aetius (F17a–c) of the first or second century A.D., who summarized the
   opinions of various Greek thinkers on natural phenomena;
3. Pausanias (T5), a writer of a travel description of Greece ca. A.D. 150;
4. Athenaeus (F2), author of *The Philosopher's Learned Banquet*, ca. A.D.
   200, which contained witty conversations, allusions, and so on of diners
   well educated in classical learning;
5. Censorinus (F15b), a third-century A.D. Roman grammarian, who wrote a
   work brimming with classical erudition as a birthday gift for Q. Caerel-
   lius for his forty-ninth birthday in A.D. 238;
6. Palchus (F22) of the sixth century A.D., who was a writer on astronomy;
   and
7. the anonymous author (F21) of a Latin commentary on the Greek poem
   Phaenomena by Aratus of Sikyon (ca. 315–240/239 B.C.).

While Poseidonios is the most likely main source for all surviving citations of Berossos by pagan writers of antiquity, the most likely main sources
for Christian or Jewish writers who cite Berossos were two epitomators who
incorporated portions of Berossos's *History* in their compendia of world
history: Alexander Polyhistor (*FGrHist* #273), ca. 65 B.C., and Juba of
Mauretania (*FGrHist* #275), ca. 50 B.C.–ca. A.D. 20. Alexander wrote numerous works, one of which was on Assyrian and Babylonian history. One
of his main sources for this work was Berossos. We do not know how long
Alexander's history was, but undoubtedly it was shorter than Berossos's
three books. Juba of Mauretania wrote a work titled *On the Assyrians* in two
books, which also used Berossos's *History* as a principal source. Josephus
(T4, F4b, F6, F8a, F8c, F9a, F10a, and F15c), who lived during the last half
of the first century A.D. and who wrote a number of historical works[25]—all

---

concerned with the history of the Jews—most likely did not use Berossos's *History* directly, although he cites Berossos as if he had that work in front of him. Rather, he is dependent on Alexander Polyhistor's epitome of Berossos's *History*. The three Christian apologists of the second and third century A.D. are also most likely dependent on Alexander's historical work, as well as on Juba's for their citations of Berossos. These three apologists are:

1. Tatianus of Syria (T7) of the second century A.D., born in Assyria, but educated in Syria;
2. Theophilus (F9c), a bishop of Antioch ca. A.D. 180; and
3. Titus Flavius Clemens (T7, F12) from Alexandria, in exile in A.D. 200 in Cappadocia.

Unfortunately, both Alexander's and Juba's works have not survived to the present, but even by the second century A.D. their historical works were considered too long and too detailed. Thus, Abydenos (*FGrHist* #685) of the second or third century A.D., who wrote about the ancient Assyrians and Babylonians, and Sextus Julius Africanus of the early third century A.D., who wrote a *Chronographiae* (*Chronologies*), a five-book history of the world from creation to A.D. 221, excerpted passages from the works of Alexander Polyhistor and Juba of Mauretania that contained parts of Berossos's history. But just as the works of Alexander and Juba, their works have not survived to the present and were considered too long. Therefore, Bishop Eusebius of Caesarea (ca. A.D. 260–340) in his work *Chronicon* (*The Chronicle*), an epitome of world history that sought to synchronize pagan (Greek, Roman, Egyptian, Mesopotamian, etc.) history with Hebrew and Christian history, excerpted passages from the works of Abydenos and Sextus Julius Africanus. *Chronicon* contained lists of kings, magistrates of cities, bishops, and so on. *Chronicon* itself has not survived to the present and exists only in what survives from Jerome's Latin translation of Eusebius's chronological tables, in an Armenian translation of the entire work (F1, F3, F5, F8b, F10b, F11) made between A.D. 500 and 800, and in excerpts from it in Georgius Syncellus's *Ecloga Chronographica* (*Chronological Excerpts*—T11a–c, F1, F3, F4a, F7). What remains of Jerome's Latin translation of the chronological tables in Eusebius's *Chronicon* preserves nothing of Berossos's history. We know practically nothing about the circumstances of the Armenian translation. Syncellus was a Byzantine monk who in the first decade of the

---

against Rome (A.D. 66–73) but came over to the side of the Romans early in the war and won great favor. His historical works are apologetic in nature, for his religion, his people, and himself.

ninth century wrote his epitome of world history that sought to bring together pre-Christian and Christian times up to his present. His work, however, reached only to Diocletian's time (A.D. 285–305). Besides citing
Berossos in his *Chronicon*, Eusebius also cites him a number of times in his
Praeparatio Evangelica (*Preparation for the Gospels*). Unfortunately these
citations do not increase our knowledge of Berossos's text, as almost all of
them are excerpts from the surviving works of Josephus (F4b, F6, F9a, F10a,
F15c) and another is from a work of Tatianus (T7). The only citation not
taken from another surviving author is inconsequential (F9b).

Thus, for the majority of the historical excerpts that survive from Berossos's *History*, there is a rather long line of authors through whom a passage
had to travel to survive—from Berossos's *History* to either Alexander Polyhistor or Juba of Mauretania, then from them to either Abydenus or Sextus
Julius Africanus, then from them to Eusebius, and from Eusebius to either
the Armenian translation of the *Chronicon* or Syncellus. Only the fragments
of Berossos's *History* from Josephus have come down to us in a somewhat
direct line—from Berossos to Alexander Polyhistor to Josephus. Unfortunately, because of the constant excerpting ancient authors did from what
were already excerpts of Berossos's *History*, most of the names of the kings,
which Berossos's original text had given, are now lost. Only the names of
the ten antediluvian kings and some of the names of the kings of Babylon
after Tiglath-pileser III (728–727) to Berossos's own time have survived.
Excerptors have preserved the numbers of kings Berossos mentioned with
some attempt to localize groups of them in time (see F5), but it is impossible
to compare what has survived from Berossos with the *Sumerian King-List* to
determine either how accurately Berossos has reproduced it or where he
disagreed with it. It seems, however, that whether Berossos used it as a
source or not, he adopted the same convention the *Sumerian King-List* used.
Both assume that there was only one king of Babylonia (Mesopotamia) at a
time. Modern historians, however, when they try to use the *Sumerian King-
List* as an historical source that mentions the names of actual kings who
ruled, disregard the long life spans recorded and make several of the king-
lists of different cities contemporaneous (see chap. 4, tables B.3a–b). What
survives from Berossos helps not at all in clarifying what has survived from
the *Sumerian King-List*.

For later Christian writers or sources after A.D. 400 who incidentally cite
Berossos, Eusebius's *Chronicon* was their most likely source. These writers
and sources are:

1. Agathias (F13), A.D. 536–82, who wrote a history of the reign of Justinian

(A.D. 552–58), although he might have had still available to him Alexander Polyhistor's work;

2. Moses of Chorene (T10), who lived most likely in the eighth century A.D., an Armenian historian of Armenia whose first book dealt with the origin of the Armenian people;
3. Hesychius of Alexandria (F14), a compiler of a Greek glossary in the fifth century A.D.;
4. Pseudo-Justinus (T8), who wrote, sometime between the third and fifth centuries A.D., apologetic works that were attributed to Justin Martyr of the second century A.D.;
5. an anonymous geographer (T9) of unknown date who mentions Berossos in passing; and
6. the *Suda* (T12), a Byzantine dictionary or encyclopedia compiled in the tenth century A.D.

Berossos's *History of Babylonia*—Goals and Accomplishments

Whatever the original purpose Berossos had for his *History*, it had very little effect on classical antiquity. His *History* failed to become the standard work on Mesopotamia before Alexander the Great's conquest, and his chronology of ancient Babylonian rulers failed to be adopted by later Christian writers. Ktesias of Knidos's *Persica*, written in the fourth century B.C., remained for the Greco-Roman world the standard account of Mesopotamian history, with an emphasis on Assyria and Media. Berossos's *History* was little read and copied. We owe what does remain to chance quotations on obscure matters from pagan writers and to the need felt by one Jewish writer of the first century A.D., Josephus, and by one Christian writer of the fourth century A.D., Eusebius, to give some corroborating evidence for what Hebrew Scripture said.

Why did Berossos's *History* neither survive nor have influence? It is not that his *History*, especially his first book, contained too many unbelievable stories about Mesopotamian gods, wise monsters, or Babylonian kings. Diodorus has preserved in his first book basic Egyptian mythology, which was as strange to the Greco-Roman world as anything Berossos wrote. The fault lies in the failure of Berossos to produce stories that would interest his readers and in the loss of Babylonia to the Greco-Roman world.

Although the Seleucid Empire was the largest of the successor states in Alexander's Empire and although Babylonia was an important and rich area, after 150 B.C. Mesopotamia was no longer part of the Greco-Roman world. The Parthian Empire, an enemy of Rome, controlled the ancient river valleys. Only under the emperor Trajan did Babylonia become once again for three years (A.D. 114–117) part of a Mediterranean empire. Under the Parthians, Babylon did not regain the political importance (as capital of a large empire) it had lost when Seleukeia on the Tigris was founded. For the Parthians, Ktesiphon, on the Tigris across from Seleukeia, became the most important city of Mesopotamia, and by 50 B.C. Babylon was practically deserted. The cults of its ancient temples no longer functioned. In addition, since the Mesopotamians used sun-dried bricks, not stone, as their main building material, there did not survive to arouse interest great monuments to a great imperial past, as had survived from ancient Egypt. Babylonia was not an area of importance or interest to the Greco-Roman world.

More important, Berossos seems not to have written a history that contained interesting stories about people, about great rulers. His second book for Mesopotamian history after the Great Flood was little more than a list of rulers, and his third book, at least as far as can be judged from what remains, did not have narratives that stirred readers. It is not the fault of the material that Mesopotamian history provided. The death of Sennacherib by his own son, the fall of the Assyrian Empire, the fall of the Chaldean Empire, the revolts of the city of Babylon, and many other events would have provided ample raw material for the type of stories that could have fascinated the reading public of the Greco-Roman world.

Perhaps Berossos was a prisoner of his own methodology and purpose. He used ancient records that he refused to flesh out, and his account of more recent history, to judge by what remains, contained nothing more than a bare narrative. If Berossos believed in the continuity of history with patterns that repeated themselves (i.e., cycles of events as there were cycles of the stars and planets),[26] a bare narrative would suffice. Indeed, this was more than one would suspect a Babylonian would or could do. Those already steeped in Babylonian historical lore would recognize the pattern and understand the interpretation of history Berossos was making. If this, indeed, is what Berossos presumed, he made a mistake that would cost him interested Greek readers who were accustomed to a much more varied and lively historical narrative where there could be no doubt who was an evil ruler and who was not. In addition, if Greek readers were accustomed to think of a succession of empires—Assyrian, Median, Persian, Macedonian, and Roman[27]—

---

26. For a fuller development of this line of reasoning, see Drews, "The Babylonian Chronicles and Berossus."

27. See Aelius Aristeides *Panathenaic Speech* (Jebb) 183 as an example of this commonplace on the successive five empires. See also Robert Drews, "Assyria in Classical Universal Histories,"

without mention of Babylon, Berossos could not overcome the preconceived notion of the succession of empires with his own devotion and love for the eternal kingship that remained centered at Babylon.

Later ancient pagan historians, impressed by the lists that Berossos had compiled, did continue to give either his lists of rulers or the total number of regnal years for the dynasties he had compiled, but neither the later historians nor Berossos himself found favor with an audience who needed what they had written. When the Roman Empire became Christian, only Berossos's antediluvian Babylonian kings with their long reigns and his narrative of now false gods were maintained, since they were obviously incorrect as they contradicted the Bible and needed to be refuted. Berossos's lists of kings after the Great Flood, however, were of no interest. Not only did their names disappear from Christian literature, but the names and lengths of their various dynasties became garbled (see F5). The names and some of the events of the last independent Babylonian dynasty, the Chaldeans, did survive due to interest in the biblical account of the Chaldean capture of Jerusalem, the exile of the Jews, and their return. Only two men preserved Berossos's narrative: a Jewish apologist, Josephus, who wrote in Greek and found favor with later Christian writers; and a Christian bishop of the fourth century A.D., Eusebius. Josephus needed to refute the charges that other peoples were older than the Jews; Eusebius needed to construct a consistent chronology of the pagan and Jewish-Christian world; hence, they needed to quote Berossos and prove the chronology of the Bible correct.

Therefore, what remains of Berossos is not of major importance in reconstructing the history of ancient Mesopotamia. To understand what Berossos is describing it is necessary to integrate what he writes with the information that survives from other ancient sources. In our notes, we try to give enough historical data to make his text comprehensible. Unfortunately, Berossos's *History* does not close the large gaps in our knowledge of ancient Mesopotamia. Only a small number of names of kings survives in Berossos, unlike the long list of pharaohs' names that survives from Manetho's *History*. It is equally unfortunate that the numbers of years that excerptors say Berossos covered in his list of kings do not help solve the major difficulty facing ancient historians in setting dates for the dynasties of Mesopotamia in the second and third millennia B.C.

Historia 14 (1963): 129–42 and D. Mendels, "The Five Empires: A Note on a Propagandistic *Topos*," *American Journal of Philology* 102 (1981): 330–37, with addendum by H. Tadmor, 338–39. See also F8b.

Because the king-lists of the Neo-Babylonians are connected to the king-lists of the Persians and the Seleucids and thus grounded in the history of the classical world, and because they are in turn connected to the king-lists of the Assyrians and Kassites, a firm chronology exists for the first millennium B.C. and for the first half of the second millennium B.C. The king-lists that mention the First Dynasty of Babylon, however, which included Hammu-rabi, are anchored to neither Assyrian king-lists nor Babylonian king-lists. Therefore, it is impossible to know for sure when to date an astronomical event mentioned as occurring in the reign of one of the kings of the First Dynasty of Babylon. Three dating systems, labeled high, middle, and low, have been proposed for the end of this dynasty caused by the raid of the Hittites on Babylon: high—1651, middle—1595, low—1531. The preceding dynasties of Larsa, Isin, and Ur III and the First Dynasty of Babylon thus float at the end of the third millennium and the beginning of the second millennium B.C. The middle chronology, given in chapter 4, tables B.3a–b, has found the most favor with modern scholars. In addition, nothing has been found to close the gap in the king-lists between the Third Kingdom of Ur and the Akkadian dynasties, that is, the Gutian period.[28] While Berossos's numbers, even if they had survived, would not have solidly grounded the dynasties of the Early Dynastic Period, his list of the length of reigns and names for the kings of the late third and early second millennium B.C. would have been invaluable.

It seems, therefore, that the remains of Berossos's *History* have not provided much of value. This is too harsh a verdict. What does survive shows an attempt to put forth in Greek format the history of an ancient land and people from its beginnings to the then present. It is an attempt to establish historical narrative for the Babylonians.

---

28. Jean-Jacques Glassner, *La Chute d'Akkadé: L'événement et sa mémoire* (Berlin, 1986), 53–54, especially the table of events on pp. 96–98, postulates no gap at all between the Third King-dom of Ur and the Akkadian dynasties; that is, the dismemberment of the Akkadian Empire hap-pened contemporaneously with the raids of the Gutians.

CHAPTER 2

Berossos—Ancient Testimony

T1a

Vitruvius *de Architectura* (*On Architecture*) 9.6.2: Concerning astrology: in determining what effects the twelve signs, the five planets, the sun, and the moon have on the course of human life, the calculations of the Chaldeans must hold first place, because they have the ability to cast horoscopes[1] so that they can explain the past and the future from their calculations of the heavens. They have, moreover, left their findings, and those who are descended from the Chaldean nation have the greatest skill and wisdom in these matters. The first of these was Berossos who settled in the city of Cos on the island and opened a school. Afterward, Antipater was a student there, as was Athenodorus,[2] who had a method to cast not only horoscopes based on birth dates but also horoscopes based on conception dates.

---

1. The casting of horoscopes based on the situation of the heavens to explain either what happened or what would happen was for the Greeks and Romans a specialty of Babylonian or Chaldean lore. The ancients divided the heavens into the twelve signs of the zodiac and knew of only five planets: Mercury, Venus, Mars, Jupiter, and Saturn. Although a number of records—called astronomical diaries, which preserved on a daily basis observed celestial phenomena—survive from the seventh century to the second century B.C. and are, so to speak, the raw material from which horoscopes could be cast, horoscopes, whether in Mesopotamia or among Greeks and Romans, are rare. Our earliest Greek horoscope comes from after 100 B.C., and our earliest Mesopotamian horoscope comes from the Persian period, late fifth century B.C.; see O. Neugebauer and H. B. van Hoesen, *Greek Horoscopes* (Philadelphia, 1959), 161. Nevertheless, Cicero in his *de Divinatione* (*On Divination*) devotes a long section (2.87–99) to debunking such belief, which must indicate how popular such practices really were.

2. The manuscripts' reading for this name is in doubt. Neither Antipater nor Athenodorus, if Athenodorus is an accurate restoration of the manuscripts' reading, can be identified with certainty.

T1b

Vitruvius *de Architectura* (*On Architecture*) 9.2.1: Berossos, who emigrated from the city in the land of the Chaldeans (Babylonia) to Asia, opened up a school in the Chaldean discipline. He taught as follows about the moon. (Continued in F16.)

T1c

Vitruvius *de Architectura* (*On Architecture*) 9.8.1: Berossos the Chaldean is said to have invented the half-circle sundial cut out of a square block.

T2

Seneca *Naturales Questiones* (*Questions About Science*) 3.29.1: Berossos, who interpreted the prophecies of Bel, (Continued in F19.)

T3a

Pliny *Naturalis Historia* (*Natural History*) 1.7: My research (for the contents of book 7)[3] comes from the following authors ... Berossos ...

T3b

Pliny *Naturalis Historia* (*Natural History*) 7.123: In knowledge of various sciences, innumerable men stand out. It is, nevertheless, proper for me to pick out the best. In astrology it was Berossos, in whose honor, because of his divine predictions, the Athenians set up in the gymnasium a statue of him with a gold tongue. In grammar it was Apollodorus[4] (*FGrHist* #244 T19)...

---

3. Unfortunately, Pliny the Elder does not specifically cite Berossos as a source in book 7, although he lists him here as one of his sources for book 7 and does mention him later (see T3b) as an especially famous astrologer. Book 7 has a number of themes, but one that would be very relevant to Berossos is "gentium mirabiles figurae, prodigiosi partus de homine generando" [wondrous shapes of people, marvelous births from human beings]. For examples of these shapes, see F1.

4. Apollodorus was a second-century B.C. Athenian, who also resided in Pergamon and Alexandria. He was the author of a number of works, none of which has survived.

T4

Josephus *contra Apionem* (*Against Apion*) 1.128–31: I will now mention what the Chaldeans have to say about us in their writings and history. They are in basic agreement with what our writings say on various matters. (129) Berossos is proof of this. He was a Chaldean by birth, but known in educated Greek circles, because he translated into Greek works on the astronomy and the philosophy of the Chaldeans. (130) This Berossos followed carefully the most ancient writings and wrote both about the Great Flood that occurred and about the destruction of mankind that followed, just as Moses himself had done.[5] Berossos also mentions the ark in which Noah, the father of our race, was saved and how it came to rest on the peaks of the Armenian mountains.[6] (131) Then Berossos catalogs the descendants of Noah down to the time of Nabopalassaros, a king of the Babylonians and the Chaldeans, and tells how long they reigned. (Continued in F9a.)

T5

Pausanias *Graeciae Descriptio* (*Description of Greece*) 10.12.9: There was a woman prophet, later than Demo, who lived among the Hebrews beyond Palestine. Her name was Sabbe. Her father was, they say, Berossos, and her mother Erymanthe. Some say she was the Babylonian Sibyl; others called her the Egyptian Sibyl.[7]

T6

Tertullian *Apologeticum* (*The Defense*) 19.4–6: Even if the other prophets are not as great as Moses, even the most recent of them are not inferior to your leading philosophers, lawgivers, and historians. (5) It is not so much a difficult task as it is an enormous one, not so much a laborious task as it is a time-consuming one to prove this … one must even open up the archives of the gentiles—Egyptians, Babylonians, Phoenicians. (6) One must call up

---

5. According to later Jewish belief, Moses was the author of the Torah or Pentateuch, the first five books of the Hebrew sacred scripture: Genesis, Exodus, Leviticus, Numbers, and Deuteronomy.

6. See F4a. Josephus identifies Berossos's Xisouthos as the Bible's Noah (Genesis 6.5–9.17).

7. There were a number of Sibyls (ancient sources disagree on the exact number, but range from two to ten) who the Greeks and Romans believed could foretell the future, as they became divinely inspired or possessed. As Berossos was closely identified with horoscopes (see T1), it would be natural for him in popular opinion to have some connection with the Sibyls. See also T8.

those of their citizens who made records: a certain Manetho, an Egyptian; Berossos, a Babylonian; and Hieronymus (*FGrHist* #794 F5c), a Phoenician, king of Tyre; as well as their followers: Ptolemy of Mendes (*FGrHist* #611 T2), Menander of Ephesus (*FGrHist* #783 T2), Demetrius of Phaleron (*FGrHist* #643 T2), King Juba (*FGrHist* #275), Apion (*FGrHist* #616 T12), and Thallus (*FGrHist* #256 T3),[8] and, for critical commentary on the others, Josephus of Judea, a native defender of Jewish antiquities.

T7

Tatianus *Oratio ad Graecos* (*Speech to the Greeks*) 36 (= Clemens of Alexandria *Stromata* [*The Carpets*] 1.122.1; Eusebius *Praeparatio Evangelica* [*Preparation for the Gospel*] 10.11.8–9): Berossos, a priest of the god Bel, was born and raised in Babylonia during Alexander's reign. In the third year of King Antiochus, he published his work in which he described the course of Chaldean history in three books and told of the deeds of their kings. He singled out one of them, Naboukhodonosoros by name, who led an army against the Phoenicians and the Jews. We were already informed by our prophets of these events that happened long after Moses's time, seventy

---

8. Tertullian has merely assembled a list of writers who dealt with non-Roman, non-Greek peoples. It is doubtful he had direct knowledge of them, but, as he himself indicates, he knew of them because Josephus had mentioned them. Most of them had connections to the great libraries of antiquity, either at Alexandria or Pergamon, are most likely dependent for whatever knowledge they had of Babylonia or Egypt on Berossos and Manetho, and, seemingly, drew up chronological tables of events, kings' reigns, and so on.

Hieronymus was not a king of Tyre but was rather an Egyptian who wrote a history of Tyre and its kings. Josephus identifies him correctly (see F15c).

Ptolemy of Mendes was an Egyptian priest who wrote about the deeds of the Egyptian kings in three books. His work was filled with accounts of natural wonders. When he lived and wrote is not known, but since Josephus mentions him, he was active sometime before A.D. 90.

Menander of Ephesus wrote on Phoenician history. When he lived and wrote is not known, but most likely he was active sometime before 133 B.C.

Demetrius of Phaleron was more a philosopher and statesman than a historian. He found refuge in Egypt around 307 B.C.

On Juba, king of Mauretania, a contemporary of Augustus, who wrote a number of historical works, see "Berossos's History of Babylonia—Reception and Transmission" in chap. 1.

Apion, who lived ca. A.D. 30, wrote *Aigyptiaka* (*Egyptian History*) in five books. Josephus wrote his *contra Apionem* (*Against Apion*) to dispute what Apion had written that depicted the Jews in an unfavorable light.

Thallus, who lived sometime during the Roman Empire, wrote a universal history or history of the world.

years before the Persian rule.[9] Berossos is a most able man. An indication of this is that Juba (*FGrHist* #275 F4), writing about the Assyrians, says he learned their history from Berossos.

T8

Pseudo-Justinus *ad Gentes* (*To the Gentiles*) 37: Of the ancient Sibyl, ... they say she was sired by the Babylonian Berossos, a daughter of the man who wrote the Chaldean history. I do not know how she got to Campania to deliver her oracles.[10]

T9

Expositio Totius Mundi et Gentium (*Description Of the Whole World and Its Peoples*) 2 (Riese *Geographi Latini Minores* p. 104): After Moses, the order of regions and seasons was described by Berossos, a learned Chaldean, whose writings were followed by the Egyptian prophet Manetho, and also by the learned Egyptian Apollonius[11] ...

T10

Moses of Chorene *Historia Armeniae* (*History of Armenia*) 1.1: Many famous and illustrious men of letters from Greece have not only actively sought to have works that were housed in the royal archives and temples of other peoples translated into Greek, as we understand Ptolemy (II) Philadel-

---

9. Jeremiah 25.11 and 29.10 prophesied that the land of Judah would endure an exile of seventy years. For the author of 2 Kings 24.12–17, the exile began in 597 B.C. when the Babylonian king exiled the king of Judah and a large number of important people to Babylon and installed a new king on the throne. To calculate the seventy years of Jeremiah, however, most believers in Jeremiah's prophecy would follow the author of 2 Chronicles 36.20–21, who saw the exile begin with the destruction of the temple in 587/6, and the author of Ezra 6.15, who saw the exile end with the return of temple vessels and the completion of the second temple in 516 under King Darius. Cyrus, the first Persian king, had initially allowed the Jews to return home in 538 B.C. (Ezra 1–6).

10. One of the most famous locations of a Sibyl was in Campania. According to legend, she had originally been the Sibyl of Erythrai before moving, so to speak, to Cumae, and her name was Herophile. Here Pseudo-Justinus has confused the Babylonian Sibyl (see T5) with the much more famous Sibyl of Campania. Virgil *Aeneid* 6.9–13 has the most famous description of the Campanian Sibyl.

11. This Egyptian writer, Apollonius, is unknown.

phos[12] urged on a Berossos, a Chaldean, skilled in every discipline, but they have ...

T11a

Syncellus, *Ecloga Chronographica* (*Chronological Excerpts*) 25–27: Berossos, who recorded the foundation stories of the Chaldeans, was a contemporary of Alexander of Macedon, as he himself says. He found the public records of many of those who had settled in Babylonia carefully preserved. These records covered a little more than 150,000 years,[13] and he recorded in a somewhat boastful tone their stories about the sky, the earth, and the sea, about the ancient history of the kings and their deeds, about the settlement of Babylonia and its fertility, about beings who appeared out of the Persian Gulf and who had forms unlike all others in nature, and about other mythic creatures as well. All of these are, to make some logical sense out of what he wrote, representations of natural forces. Nevertheless, I think it necessary to record the times of all the events in Berossos's history and list them beginning in the actual 1,059th year of the creation of the world,[14] just as if I were convinced of the truth of what Berossos and those who followed him, Alexander Polyhistor (*FGrHist* #273 F79) and Abydenos (*FGrHist* #685), recorded in their desire to prove and demonstrate that the Chaldean people are the oldest people of all. It is, though, much more logical to conclude from the Holy Scripture, from the writings of our own ancestors, and from the natural order of things as well, that all the land we now live in, including the land of the Babylonians and Egypt, was uninhabited before the Great Flood. (26) Scripture itself (Genesis 3.24) says: "And God expelled Adam, and they dwelt on the other side of the garden of Paradise." Babylonia and all the land we now live in lie far from Eden in the east where we say paradise was located... . (27) ... I think that for those of the faith this is sufficient proof that those who lived before the Great Flood inhabited the land

---

12. Although Ptolemy II is closely identified with the library at Alexandria, this very late notice by Moses of Chorene is difficult to believe. Most likely, Moses simply associated Berossos's *History* and Ptolemy II's concern to acquire texts.

13. The manuscript reading of this number is in doubt. Pliny the Elder (see F20) says Berossos had records going back 490,000 years; Khairemon of Alexandria (*FGrHist* #618 F7), who was the emperor Nero's tutor and was most likely referring to Berossos, says that Babylonian records go back over 400,000 years; and Cicero *de Divinatione* (*On Divination*) 1.36 gives the number of years for which Babylonian records supposedly existed as 470,000.

14. This is, according to Syncellus's calculations, the year in which the flood Berossos described (F4a) really occurred. Syncellus identifies that flood with the one described in *Genesis* (see T4).

between the ocean and Paradise and that Babylonia had not yet come into existence, nor was there yet kingship in Babylonia, as it seems to be for Berossos and those who follow him in direct contradiction of the Holy Scripture, nor was there yet an Egyptian dynasty, as there seems to be for Manetho, that fabricator and boaster, in his writings about Egyptian affairs.

T11b

Syncellus *Ecloga Chronographica* (*Chronological Excerpts*) 29–30: It is very clear that the Chaldean Empire began with Nebrod,[15] and it is just as clear, if not more so, that what Manetho of Sebennytos wrote to Ptolemy (II) Philadelphos about the Egyptian dynasties is full of lies, written both in imitation of Berossos and at about the same time as Berossos or a little later. Moreover, what these men wrote is still useless even though many historians were to draw up chronological lists based on what Berossos and Manetho wrote. ... (30) If one carefully examines the underlying chronological lists of events, one will have full confidence that the design of both is false, as both Berossos and Manetho, as I have said before, want to glorify each his own nation, Berossos the Chaldean, Manetho the Egyptian. One can only stand in amazement that they were not ashamed to place the beginning of their incredible writing each in the one and the same year.[16]

T11c

Syncellus, *Ecloga Chronographica* (*Chronological Excerpts*) 32: Manetho of Sebennytos ... born later than Berossos, in the time of Ptolemy (II) Philadelphos, wrote to this same Ptolemy, telling lies just as Berossos did, ...

T12

Suda (*Fortress of Knowledge*), s.v. "The Delphic Sibyl": Berossos is called the father of the Chaldean Sibyl, her mother Erymanthe.[17]

---

15. Nebrod = Nimrud, founder of the Assyrian Empire according to the ancient Hebrews in Genesis 10.8–12.

16. On the calculations needed to place in the same year both Berossos's and Manetho's story of creation, see footnote 15 on Manetho T10b.

17. See T5 and T8.

CHAPTER 3

Berossos—Fragments

History of Babylonia, **Book 1**

F1

Eusebius *Chronicon* (*The Chronicle*), p. 6, line 8–p. 9, line 2 Karst, in an Armenian translation: Whatever Berossos wrote in his first book, I will report and add it to what I have already narrated from his first book. This is exactly what Polyhistor (*FGrHist #273 F79*) did when he cited Berossos's work. Polyhistor recorded one event in Berossos's history right after another, corresponding in the following manner in his form of presentation. (From here the Armenian version basically agrees with Syncellus's Greek.)	Syncellus *Ecloga Chronographica* (*Chronological Excerpts*) 50–53: From Alexander Polyhistor (*FGrHist #273 F79*), on the ten Chaldean rulers before the Great Flood, the Great Flood, and Noah and his ark. In his account, he mentions some incredible events, as recorded in Berossos's writings. (Syncellus continues as follows.)

Berossos reports in the first book of his Babylonian history that he was a contemporary of Alexander, the son of Philip, and that many public records, which covered a period of over 150,000 years ago[1] about the history of the sky and the sea, of creation, and of the kings and of their deeds, had been preserved with great care.

---

1. The manuscript reading of this number is in doubt. See T11a.

First he says that the land of the Babylonians lies between the Tigris and the Euphrates rivers. It produces wild wheat, barley, chickpea, and sesame, and even, in its marshlands, edible roots, called *gongai*.[2] These roots are the equal of barley in nutrition. The land also produces dates, apples, and all sorts of other fruit, as well as fish and birds, field birds as well as waterfowl.

There are also in the land of the Babylonians waterless and infertile regions near Arabia, while lying opposite Arabia there are hilly and fertile areas. In Babylonia there was a large number of people of different ethnic origins who had settled Chaldea. (51) They lived without discipline and order, just like animals.

In the very first year there appeared from the Red Sea (the Persian Gulf) in an area bordering on Babylonia a frightening monster, named Oannes, just as Apollodoros[3] (*FGrHist* #244 F84) says in his history. It had the whole body of a fish, but underneath and attached to the head of the fish there was another head, human, and joined to the tail of the fish, feet, like those of a man, and it had a human voice. Its form has been preserved in sculpture to this day. Berossos says that this monster spent its days with men, never eating anything, but teaching men the skills necessary for writing and for doing mathematics and for all sorts of knowledge: how to build cities, found temples, and make laws. It taught men how to determine borders and divide land, also how to plant seeds and then to harvest their fruits and vegetables. In short, it taught men all those things conducive to a settled and civilized life. Since that time nothing further has been discovered.[4] At the end of the day, this monster Oannes went back to the sea and spent the night. It was amphibious, able to live both on land and in the sea.

Later other monsters similar to Oannes appeared, about whom Berossos gave more information in his writings on the kings. Berossos says about Oannes that it had written as follows about the creation and government of the world and had given these explanations to man.

---

2. *Gongai* would appear to be a native name for these edible roots and has no Greek or English equivalent.

3. On Apollodoros the grammarian, see T3b. Jacoby (*FGrHist* #244 F83–F87, see Kommentar), however, considers mistaken late authors, such as Eusebius, who say that Apollodoros used Berossos as a source.

4. One of the concerns of the ancients was to account for how humans learned to do things. For those who saw the gods as responsible for all things, as here for Berossos, a solution to this question was to attribute all learning, all skills, all science, all art to the instruction of the gods, their gift. The idea of humans themselves learning how to do things, of making progress, was not taken into account. Also, on a purely logical basis, since the battle among the gods, which Oannes goes on to describe, took place before Marduk created human beings, it would be necessary for them to be informed of what had happened before Marduk created them.

(52) There was, he says, a time when the universe was only darkness[5] and water, and in it there were wondrous beings with peculiar forms who were able to engender other living beings. For men with two wings were born, as were other men with four wings and two faces. Some of these had one body but two heads, male and female, and two sets of sexual organs, male and female. Further, there were other men with the legs of goats and the horns of goats on their heads. Yet others had horses' feet, and others had the body of a horse for their lower extremities and human bodies for their upper body, which are the forms of hippo-centaurs. Bulls were engendered with human heads, as were dogs with four bodies, who had fish tails on their hindquarters. There were also horses with dogs' heads, men and other creatures with the heads and bodies of horses, men with tails of fish, and all sorts of creatures who had the forms of all sorts of animals. In addition, there were fish, snakes, crawling things, and many other amazing creatures that had the appearance of two different animals combined. Their images are preserved one next to the other in the temple of Bel. Over all these a woman had control, named Omorka, who in Chaldean is named Thalatth (Tiamat), but in Greek her name is translated as Thalassa (i.e., Sea) or, with the same value of the letters in the name, Selene (i.e., Moon).[6]

While the world was in this state, Bel rose up against the woman and cut her in half. (53) Out of the first half he made the earth and out of the second the heavens. The animals who were in her he destroyed. All this, he says, is an allegorical explanation. For when all was water and only monsters were in it, the god cut off his own head, and the other gods mixed the flood of blood with earth and created men. Because of this men have reason and share in the gods' wisdom.

But then Bel, whose name is translated into Greek as Zeus, cut through the darkness and separated the sky and the earth from one another and established order in the universe. The monsters could not endure the strength of the light and were destroyed. Bel, however, as he saw an empty and barren region, gave an order to one of the gods to cut off his own head and mix

---

5. Darkness most likely was not what Berossos wrote but was added later to make a reading more like the description of creation given in Genesis 1.2.

6. Greek letters also served as numbers. By adding the numerical value of each letter in a word, the word's numerical value could be determined. The Greek letters to spell *Omorka* have the same value when added together as those of the Greek letters that spell *Selene*. This use of numerology, ascertaining the numerical value of a word and then freely substituting like values, provides an interesting and entertaining, if not always logical, way to offer new interpretations or explanations of things.

earth with the flowing blood and to create men and the animals that could breathe the air.[7]

Bel created the stars and the sun and the moon and the five planets.[8] All this, according to Polyhistor (*FGrHist* #273 F79), Berossos reported in his first book.

F2

Athenaeus *Deipnosophistae* (*The Philosophers' Banquet*) 14.44: Berossos in the first book of his Babylonian history says that the feast of Sakaia begins on the sixteenth day of the month Loos,[9] and lasts for five days. During the celebration the custom is that the masters are given orders by their slaves and that one slave, wearing the royal robes of the king, rules the house. This slave is called Zoganes. Ktesias (*FGrHist* #688 F4) also relates this festival in the second book of his *Persica* (*Persian History*).[10]

History of Babylonia, Book 2

F3

Eusebius *Chronicon* (*The Chronicle)* p. 4, line 11–p. 6, line 4 Karst, in an Armenian translation:	Syncellus, *Ecloga Chronographica* (*Chronological Excerpts*) 53, 30, 71–72:
And in Berossos's second book he chronicled the kings, one after the other, as he says, "At the time	(53) In his second book, Berossos described the ten kings of the Chaldeans and the length of their reigns,

---

7. Syncellus in section 53 has preserved two different versions of how Bel (Marduk) created the human race. In the first, Marduk cuts off his own head and makes humans from his own blood. In the second, it seems that another god willingly at Marduk's order serves as the raw material not only for humans but for all life. The second is closest to the description found in the *Creation Epic*, the *Enuma Elish*, the central religious text of first-millennium B.C. Babylon. In it, Marduk defeated the forces of chaos led by Tiamat. He cut her in half and used one part of her for the sky and the other for the earth Then Marduk, after other gods incriminated Kingu, a god who had sided with Tiamat in her fight against him, has them make humankind from his blood. See *ANET*[3] 60–72.

8. See T1a–b.

9. The twelve months of the Babylonian year were Nisanu, Aiaru, Simanu, Duzu, Abu, Ululu, Tashritu, Arasamnu, Kislimu, Tebetu, Shabatu, and Addaru; see E. J. Bickerman, *Chronology of the Ancient World* (Ithaca, 1968), 20. Loos would most likely be Duzu, corresponding to June/July.

10. Zoganes does not appear elsewhere in Greek literature. In Strabo *Geographica* 11.8.4 Sakaia is an annual sacred festival in Zela in Armenia among the Sakai to celebrate a Persian defeat, but in 11.8.5 Strabo gives an alternate explanation that it was a Persian festival to celebrate a victory over the Sakai.

Nabonassaros was king." Either he merely lists the kings in chronological order and only as an aside does he even mention any of their deeds and then in no detail, or he only gives the number of kings that ruled, as he does not think their names even worthy of mention. He began to write in the following manner.

Apollodoros[11] (*FGrHist* #244 F83) reports that Berossos said the first king at Babylon was Aloros. He was a Chaldean, who reigned ten *saroi*. A *saros*[12] consists of 3,600 years, a *neros* of 600, and a *sossos* of 60. Such counting is due to some very old original method of the ancients.

Berossos reports, according to Apollodoros, that there were ten kings from Aloros, the first king, to Xisouthros, under whom, he says, the First and Great Flood took place, which Moses also described. The times of this rule of these kings he reckoned as 120 *saroi*, which approximately consists of 430,000 years. Individually he writes of each of these as follows. (From here the Armenian version agrees with Syncellus's Greek.)

altogether 120 *saroi* or about 432,000 years until the Great Flood.

... (30) Berossos used in his accounts *saroi*, *neroi*, and *sossoi*. A *saros* is a unit of time that consists of 3,600 years, a *neros* of 600 years, and a *sossos* of 60 years. ...

(71) Berossos records that Aloros, a Chaldean from Babylonia, was first king at Babylon. He reigned ten *saroi*. (Syncellus continues as follows.)

---

11. On the likelihood that Apollodoros used Berossos as a source, see F1.

12. Although modern astronomers use *saros* as the name of the cycle of eighteen years and ten and two-thirds days in which solar and lunar eclipses repeat themselves, there is no connection between it and the Babylonian *saros*. It is not known why the Babylonians used a base of sixty for recording years, although some scholars have tried to see a connection between the 360 degrees of a circle with the twelve signs of the zodiac (each sign roughly occupying 30 degrees of the heavens) and the numbering of time.

Alaparos next reigned, and after Alaparos, Amelon from the city of Pautibiblon. And after Amelon, Ammenon the Chaldean[13] reigned. During his reign, the monster Oannes, the Annedotos,[14] appeared from the Red Seas (the Persian Gulf). Alexander Polyhistor[15] (*FGrHist* #273) claims he appeared in the first year, Berossos after forty *saroi*, and Abydenos (*FGrHist* #685 F2) says he was the second monster, the second Annedotos who appeared after twenty-six *saroi*. After Ammenon Amegalaros from the city of Pautibiblon reigned for eighteen *saroi*. After him came the reign of Daonos, the shepherd from the city of Pautibiblon, for ten *saroi*. During his reign Berossos says monsters appeared again, four of them, from the Red Seas (the Persian Gulf) with the same form as those mentioned above, a mixture of man and fish. Then Euedorankhos from the city of Pautibiblon reigned for eighteen *saroi*. During his reign there also appeared from the Red Seas (the Persian Gulf) another man-fish being whose name was Odakon.[16]

(72) Berossos says that this monster explained in detail what Oannes had originally said in summary fashion. Abydenos (*FGrHist* #685) says nothing about him. Then came the rule of Amempsinos, the Chaldean from Larankhos. He was king for eighteen *saroi*. Then came the rule of Otiartes, a Chaldean from Larankhos. He reigned eight *saroi*. Then after the death of Otiartes, his son Xisouthros reigned eighteen *saroi*. During his rule the Great Flood occurred. All together there were ten kings, 120 *saroi*.

These then are the accounts taken from the grandiloquent historians Alexander Polyhistor (*FGrHist* #273) and Abydenos (*FGrHist* #685 F2) and Apollodoros (*FGrHist* #244 F83) on the Chaldeans. I have related all this to show their basic illogicality and unbelievability and to serve as an aid to those who read them. For those of our historians who record these stories and because of that are deceived should not believe them as if they contained anything of the truth.

(The Armenian text adds the table given below, which also appears in Syncellus, *Ecloga Chronographica* (*Chronological Excerpts*) 31–32, but without the implied attribution to Berossos that the Armenian text makes.)

---

13. Here Berossos obviously has written anachronistically by calling these early kings Chaldeans. For Berossos, Chaldean must have been synonymous with Babylonian.

14. Only Berossos and Abydenos (see chap. 4, table B.2b), a historian whose main source is Berossos, use the word *Annedotos*; its meaning is not clear.

15. Here Syncellus (or Eusebius) refers to what he had written earlier in 51 (in F1), but he did not specifically cite Alexander Polyhistor in that section.

16. See chap. 4, tables B.2a–b for a list of the monsters Berossos records and the corresponding kings with Abydenos's list and a Hellenistic list, roughly contemporaneous with Berossos.

1. Aloros   10 *saroi*
2. Alaparos   3 *saroi*
3. Amelon   13 *saroi*
4. Ammenon   12 *saroi*
5. Amegalaros   18 *saroi*
6. Daonos   10 *saroi*
7. Euedorankhos   18 *saroi*
8. Amempsinos   10 *saroi*
9. Otiartes   8 *saroi*
10. Xisouthros   18 *saroi*

In all ten kings, 120 *saroi*. 120 *saroi* ought to equal 430,000 years, if a *saros* is equal to 3,600 years. So Alexander Polyhistor (*FGrHist* #273) records.

F4a

Syncellus *Ecloga Chronographica* (*Chronological Excerpts*) 53–56: In the second book Berossos records the ten kings and the length of their reigns, 120 *saroi* or 432,000 years until the Great Flood. For Alexander (*FGrHist* #273) himself, from the writings of the Chaldeans, again proceeding from the ninth king, Ardates (Otiartes), to the tenth king, called by them Xisouthros, says the following. (54) After Ardates (Otiartes) had died, his son Xisouthros reigned for eighteen *saroi*, and in his reign occurred the Great Flood. He records the following.

Kronos[17] appeared to Xisouthros in a dream and revealed that on the fifteenth of the month Daisios[18] mankind would be destroyed by a great flood. He then ordered him to bury together all the tablets, the first, the middle, and the last, and hide them in Sippar, the city of the sun.[19] Then he was to build a boat and board it with his family and best friends. He was to provision it with food and drink and also to take on board wild animals and birds and all four-footed animals. Then when all was prepared, he was to make

---

17. Kronos was the father of Zeus, as Enki was the father of Marduk. Berossos or Syncellus here has used the Greek equivalent for the Babylonian god.

18. For the months of the Babylonian year, see F2 n. 9. Daisios would most likely be Aiaru, April/May.

19. These tablets would contain all the knowledge humans had that had been given by the gods through the wise sea-monsters (see F3). After the Great Flood, the tablets would be necessary for humans to relearn all that the gods had previously taught them.

ready to sail. If asked where he was going, he was to reply, "to the gods, to pray that all good things will come to man." He did not stop working until the ship was built. Its length was five stades (1000 yards) and its breadth two (400 yards). He boarded the finished ship, equipped for everything as he had been commanded, with his wife, children, and closest friends.

After the waters of the Great Flood had come and quickly left, Xisouthros freed several birds. They found neither food nor a place to rest, and they returned to the ship. After a few days he again set free some other birds, and they too came back to the ship, but they returned with claws covered with mud. Then later for a third time he set free some other birds, but they did not return to the ship. (55) Then Xisouthros knew that the earth had once again appeared. He broke open a seam on a side of the ship and saw that the ship had come to rest on a mountain. He disembarked, accompanied by his wife and his daughter together with the steersman. He prostrated himself in worship to the earth and set up an altar and sacrificed to the gods. After this, he disappeared together with those who had left the ship with him. Those who remained on the ship and had not gone out with Xisouthros, when he and those with him had disembarked, searched for him and called out for him by name all about. But Xisouthros from then on was seen no more, and then the sound of a voice that came from the air gave the instruction that it was their duty to honor the gods and that Xisouthros, because of the great honor he had shown the gods, had gone to the dwelling place of the gods and that his wife and daughter and the steersman had enjoyed the same honor. The voice then instructed them to return to Babylonia to go to the city of Sippar, as it was fated for them to do, to dig up the tablets that were buried there and to turn them over to mankind. The place where they had come to rest was the land of Armenia. After they understood all this, they sacrificed to the gods there and went on foot to Babylonia.

To this day a small part of the ship that came to rest in Armenia remains in the Korduaian Mountains in Armenia,[20] and some people go there and scrape off pieces of bitumen to keep them as good luck charms.

(56) And those who had arrived in Babylonia dug up the tablets in the city of Sippar and brought them out. They built many cities and erected temples to the gods and again renewed Babylonia.

---

20. Genesis 8.4 says Noah's ark came to rest on Ararat, which tradition identified with a mountain in ancient eastern Armenia, called today Mt. Ararat. It is in modern eastern Turkey, near the modern Armenian and Iranian borders. No other ancient author besides Josephus and Eusebius, who is in reality quoting Josephus, mentions the Korduaian Mountains.

All of the above is from Alexander Polyhistor (*FGrHist* #273), who in turn took it from Berossos, the false prophet of the Chaldeans. It is possible for those wishing to understand correctly what really happened to refer to the holy writings of Genesis (6.5–9.17) to see how much they differed from the above account of the Chaldeans, full of unbelievable stories.

F4b

Josephus *Antiquitates Judaicae* (*Jewish Antiquities*) 1.93: All those who wrote histories of non-Greek peoples record the Great Flood and the ark. Among these is Berossos the Chaldean. Writing about the Great Flood, he tells the following.

It is said that a part of the boat is still in Armenia on the Korduaian Mountains, and that men still take a piece of the bitumen used to cover it and they hold it sacred as they think it wards off evil. Hieronymos the Egyptian (*FGrHist* #787 F2), who wrote the foundation stories of the Phoenicians, also records these events, as does Mnaseas and many others. Even Nikolaos of Damascus in his ninety-sixth book (*FGrHist* #90 F72) recorded the story as follows.[21] There is lying opposite Minyas a large mountain in Armenia called Baris,[22] on which legend has it that many who fled the Great Flood were saved and that one man, carried by the ark, came to rest. There are still remnants of its wood in great part preserved there. This man might be the same man whom Moses, the lawgiver of the Jews, mentioned.[23]

F5

Eusebius *Chronicon* (*The Chronicle*) p. 12, line 17–p. 13, line 9 Karst, in an Armenian translation: Alexander Polyhistor (*FGrHist* #273) adds the following to the narrative. After the Flood, Euekhoios ruled over the Chaldean

---

21. On Hieronymos the Egyptian, see T6.

Mnaseas of the third century B.C. wrote numerous works on myth and natural wonders. He did not receive a specific number in *FGrHist*.

Nikolaos of Damascus, a contemporary of Augustus, wrote a universal history in 144 books, as well as a work concentrating on the different customs of various peoples.

22. Josephus is the only author who identifies the resting place of the ark on a Mt. Baris. See also F4a n. 20, on Mt. Ararat as the resting place of the ark.

23. Josephus identifies Berossos's story of the Flood with that in Genesis 6.5–9.17. On Moses, see T4 n. 5.

land four *neroi*. After him, his son Khomasbelos took over and ruled four *neroi* and five *sossoi*.[24]

From Xisouthros and the Great Flood until the Medes[25] took Babylonia, Polyhistor counts in all eighty-six kings. He mentions by name each of them from Berossos's books. Their reign he calculates altogether as lasting 33,091 years.[26]

And after this, after these great dynasties, the Medes, having assembled a large army, took Babylonia and established themselves as its lords. Here he adds the names of the kings of the Medes, eight in number who reigned 244 years and again eleven kings and 28 years, then the Chaldeans, forty-nine kings for 458 years, and then the Arabians, nine kings for 245 years. After these years, he records the reign of Semiramis over Assyria. Then he once again lists only the names of the individual kings, forty-five of them, and their total regnal years, 526.[27] After these, he says, the king of the Chaldeans was Phulos (Tiglath-pileser III), whom the history of the Hebrews mentions and also calls Phulos (2 Kings 15.19). About him they say that he campaigned against the land of Judea. And after him, so reports Polyhistor (*FGrHist* #273), Senakheirimos was king whom also the Hebrew books mention as king. He was king when Hezekiah was king of Judea and when Esau was prophesying. So says the Holy Scripture (2 *Kings* 18.13), which ...

---

24. The names and the length of their reigns Berossos gives for the first two post-flood kings in no way correspond to those in the *Sumerian King-List*. See chap. 4, tables B.3a–b.

25. *Medes* here most likely equals the Gutians, who came from the same general area the Medes later controlled, the Zagros Mountains to the east and north of Mesopotamia; see Paul Schnabel, *Berossos und die Babylonisch-Hellenistische Literatur* (Leipzig, 1923), 192–94. The Gutians invaded Mesopotamia during the twenty-second century B.C. and ended the dynasty that had been established by Sargon of Akkade.

26. Compare these figures, eighty-six kings and 33,091 years, with those given by the *Sumerian King-List*, chap.4, table B.3b.

27. Although there may be almost universal agreement that the Medes of Berossos's text can be identified as the Gutians (see n. 25 in this chapter), further attempts to make sense out of the names of succeeding dynasties and the lengths of their reigns founder. There are no easy correspondences in the surviving king-lists, and reconstructions need to do serious violence to the names and figures that survive from Berossos to bring them into line with other information surviving from cuneiform tablets. For an attempt, see Stanley Burstein, *The Babyloniaca of Berossus*, Sources and Monographs: Sources from the Ancient Near East, vol. 1, no. 5 (Malibu, 1978), 175–177, Appendix 2. The only relatively sure identification possible is that Semiramis is really Sammuramat, a wife of Samshi-Adad V of Assyria (824–811) and mother of Adad-Nirari III (810–782). See chap. 4, tables B.3a–b. for the dynasties and their lengths (which the *Sumerian King-List* and *King-List A* give) compared to the information that survives from Berossos's account.

F6

Josephus *Antiquitates Judaicae* (*Jewish Antiquities*) 1.158: Berossos records our father Abraham. He does not mention him by name but reports the following. After the Great Flood, in the tenth generation, among the Chaldeans there was a man, great, just, and all-knowing about the heavens.[28]

History of Babylonia, Book 3

F7

Syncellus *Ecloga Chronographica* (*Chronological Excerpts*) 390: The Chaldeans kept accurate records of the times of the movements of the stars from Nabonassaros's reign on. The Greek astronomers preserved the Chaldean records. As Alexander (*FGrHist* #273) and Berossos record, both of whom have recounted the foundation stories of the Chaldeans, Nabonassaros, having collected the deeds of the kings who ruled before him, destroyed them,[29] so that only from his reign on is there an accurate record of the Chaldean kings.

F8a

Josephus, *Antiquitates Judaicae* (*Jewish Antiquities*) 10.20: Herodotus (2.141) thus recorded the above about Senakheirimos, but Berossos, the writer of the Chaldean history, records the kingship of Senakheirimos and says that he ruled the Assyrians and that he campaigned throughout Asia and Egypt.[30] He wrote the following. (Our manuscripts do not preserve what Josephus wrote.)

---

28. It is not known whom from the text of Berossos Josephus identifies with Abraham. It is doubtful that it could be, after the Flood, another wise monster who would have come to teach humankind more about the world.

29. Based on the Armenian translation, the passage "having collected the deeds of the kings who ruled before him, destroyed them" could be translated as "kept only lists of kings but suppressed what they did as not worthy of mention."

30. On the campaigns of Senakheirimos (Sennacherib) in Judah, Phoenicia, and Philistia, see 2 Kings 18.1–19.36 and *ANET*[3] 287–88. Sennacherib had no campaigns in Egypt.

F8b

Eusebius *Chronicon* (*The Chronicle*) p. 13, line 18–p. 15, line 4 Karst, in an Armenian translation: The Chaldean historian (Berossos) records Senakheirimos and his son Asordanios and then Baladas. After these he mentions Naboukhodonosoros, as the excursus given here is written in reference to them in the following words: Alexander (*FGrHist* #273) on Senakheirimos and on Naboukhodonosoros and their deeds and accomplishments.

After the reign of the brother of Senakheirimos and after the reign of Akise over the Babylonians: before Akise had ruled thirty days, he was killed by Baladas. Baladas maintained himself as king for six months, and then a man whose name was Belibos killed him and became king. In the third year of his reign Senakheirimos, king of the Assyrians, led an army against Babylonia, showed a bold front, and conquered. He took captive Belibos and his friends and brought them to Assyria. He then ruled over Babylonia and made his son Asordanios king over them. Then he went back to Assyria.

When he was informed that Greeks were marching against Cilicia, he hurried against them, confronted them, and, after many of his troops had been struck down, he won the battle. As a memorial of his victory, he had a statue of himself erected on the battlefield and inscribed it in Chaldean script as a remembrance of his bravery and heroic deeds as a memorial for the future. He founded the city of Tarsus, as he records, on the plan of Babylon, and he called the city Tharsis.[31]

And after describing all the remaining deeds of Senakheirimos, he remarks by adding that he lived eighteen years, and then a conspiracy was readied against him by his son Ardumuzan, and he died.[32] This is what Polyhistor (*FGrHist* #273) records.

---

31. The modern city of Tarsus sits directly on ancient Tarsus. Therefore, archaeological work has not been able to establish a secure foundation date. The city seems to have been an ancient Semitic settlement but was not founded by Senakheirimos (Sennacherib). Indeed, in Senakheirimos's (Sennacherib's) own records, he records the taking of the city; see Daniel Luckenbill, *Ancient Records of Assyria and Babylonia* (Chicago, 1927), 2:137. And in 833 Shalmaneser in his twenty-sixth regnal year received tribute from Tarsus; see again Luckenbill, 1:207–08.

32. According to 2 Kings 19.37, two sons, Adrammelech and Sharezer, assassinated him, but Assyrian records say only one son conspired against him but do not name him; see A. K. Grayson, *Assyrian and Babylonian Chronicles* (Locust Valley, N.Y., 1975), 81 in Chronicle 1 = BM 75977. Abydenos, a second- or third-century A.D. historian who mainly followed Berossos's account of Babylonian history, gives the name of the murderer as Adramelos (*FGrHist* III C #685 F5), a name more similar to what the Bible gives than what has survived in Berossos's text. Simo Parpola, "The Murderer of Sennacherib," in *Death in Mesopotamia*, ed. Bendt Alster (Copenhagen, 1980), 171–

But here also the dates agree with those given in the Holy Scripture (see 2 Kings 18–25). When Hezekiah was king in Judah, Senakheirimos reigned, as Polyhistor records, eighteen years, and after him his son eight years.[33] Then Samoges reigned for twenty-one years, and then his brother for twenty-one years, and then Nabopalassaros for twenty years, and after him Naboukhodonosoros for forty-three years. Altogether from Senakheirimos to Naboukhodonosoros there are eighty-eight years. Also according to the Hebrew Scripture one finds corresponding numbers if one calculates carefully. For after Hezekiah, Manasses, the son of Hezekiah, reigned over those remaining Jews for fifty-five years. Then Amon was ruler for twelve years,[34] and after him Josiah for thirty-one years. Then Jehoiakim reigned. At the beginning of his reign Naboukhodonosoros invaded, besieged Jerusalem, and led the Jews away into exile to Babylonia. There were then eighty-eight years from Hezekiah to Naboukhodonosoros, eighty-eight just as Polyhistor (*FGrHist* #273) has calculated from the Chaldean written reports.[35]

---

82 has identified the murderer as Arad-Ninlil, or, more properly, Arda-Mulišši, if one reads the logographically spelled name with the neo-Assyrian form of the name *Mulišši* instead of the Babylonian form *Ninlil* in a Neo-Assyrian letter discovered in the nineteenth century, which concerned the murder of Sennacherib. This name, Arda-Mulišši, closely matches then the Hebrew (Adrammelech) and Armenian (Ardumuzan) names that the Bible, Berossos, and Abydenos give. Asordanios (Esarhaddon) did not participate in the conspiracy that removed his father, Senakheirimos (Sennacherib), from the throne, but in the civil war that erupted after Senakheirimos's (Sennacherib's) assasination, Asordanios (Esarhaddon) emerged triumphant.

33. There must be two mistakes here: (1) Senakheirimos (Sennacherib) ruled Babylon twice, the first time for two years and the last time for eight years, not eighteen years whether in one reign or in two separate reigns; and (2) his son, Esarhaddon, reigned for thirteen years (see chap. 4, table B.4). Perhaps, as Stanley Burstein suggests (*The Babyloniaca of Berossus* 178–79), there is confusion over how long Senakheirimos (Sennacherib) lived (eighteen years, as mentioned earlier in this text) after he installed his son Ashur-nadin-shumi as king of Babylon. Berossos or, more likely, Alexander Polyhistor has confused Senakheirimos's (Sennacherib's) two sons, Ashur-nadin-shumi and Esarhaddon (Asordanios), as there is no mention in what survives from Berossos of Ashur-nadin-shumi.

34. The manuscripts have twelve years as the length of Amon's reign, but twelve is a mistake for what should be two. Amon reigned for two years, and two are needed to make eighty-eight. See also n. 35 in this chapter.

35. The synchronism does not work. There are not eighty-eight years in the cuneiform records from the beginning of the last reign of Senakheirimos (Sennacherib) over Babylon to the eighth regnal year of Naboukhodonosoros (Nebuchadnezzar II). There are eight years for Sennacherib, thirteen (twelve for Esarhaddon and one for Assurbanipal before he placed his son Shamash-shum-ukin on the throne) for Esarhaddon, twenty for Shamash-shum-ukin, twenty-one for Kandalanu (= Sardanapallos), an interregnum of one year, twenty-one years for Nabu-apal-user, and then eight years into the reign of Nebuchadnezzar II to 597 B.C. when the first capture of Jerusalem took place (see T7, n.9); see chap. 4, tables B.4–5. These numbers (8+13+20+21+1+21+8) equal ninety-two, or counting inclusively from 688, the first year of Sennacherib's second reign over Babylonia, to 597 B.C., the eighth year of Nebuchadnezzar II's reign. The figures that survive in Eusebius's text can yield eighty-eight years: eighteen years for Senakheirimos (Sennacherib), eight years for his son,

And after all this Polyhistor lists numerous accomplishments and deeds of Senakheirimos. He also mentions his son and is even in agreement with the Hebrew scriptures (2 Kings 19.36) about this. He even totals everything up separately. It is mentioned that Pythagoras, the sage,[36] was a contemporary of these men. After Samoges, Sardanapallos[37] gained the throne (lac.) and (Sardanapallos) reigned over the Chaldeans twenty-one years. Nabopalassaros sent to Astyages, leader and satrap of the Medes, part of the royal army as aid in order to receive for his son Naboukhodonosoros a daughter of Astyages, Amytis, as his wife.[38] And Naboukhodonosoros reigned forty-

---

twenty-one (presumed) for Samoges (Shamash-shum-ukin), twenty-one for Sardanapallos (Kandalanu), and twenty years for Nabopalassaros (Nabu-apal-usur) equal eighty-eight years, with the eight years of Naboukhodonosoros's (Nebuchadnezzar II's) reign not counted. But as mentioned, Naboukhodonosoros (Nebuchadnezzar II) captured Jerusalem in the eighth year of his reign, not in the first year.

There are about eighty-eight years between Hezekiah's death (686 B.C.) and Nebuchadnezzar II's capture of Jerusalem (597 B.C.) The figures given in F8b, however, (55 for Manasseh, 2 for Amon, and 31 for Josiah), have nothing to do with the capture of Jerusalem by Nebuchadnezzar II. Pharaoh Necho, who killed Josiah, removed Jehoahaz from the throne, and installed Jehoiakim, never captured Jerusalem. It is at the beginning of Jehoiachin's reign, not at the beginning of Jehoiakim's reign, that Nebuchadnezzar II first captured Jerusalem. Below is a list of the last rulers of the southern kingdom of Judah from Hezekiah to the final destruction of Jerusalem by Nebuchadnezzar II in 586 B.C.

Hezekiah	716–686	29 years	2 Kings 18.2
Manasseh	696–641	55 years	2 Kings 21.1
Amon	641–639	2 years	2 Kings 21.19
Josiah	639–608	31 years	2 Kings 22.1
Jehoahaz	608	3 months	2 Kings 23.31
Jehoiakim	608–598	11 years	2 Kings 23.36
Jehoiachin	598–597	3 months	2 Kings 24.8
Zedekiah	597–586	11 years	2 Kings 24.18

The attempted synchronism involving eighty-eight years must be due to Eusebius, not to Alexander Polyhistor, and certainly not to Berossos.

36. Pythagoras, one of the seven wise men of Greece, born on the island of Samos, but achieving his fame in exile in southern Italy, most likely lived in the last quarter of the sixth century B.C. This synchronism is more likely due to Polyhistor than to Berossos.

37. Sardanapallos, or Sardanapalos, is first mentioned in Greek literature by Herodotus (2.150) and seems to have been described with great detail by Ktesias (*FGrHist* #688 F1 = Diodorus Siculus 2.23–8). He appears, however, in surviving Greek literature as the legendary last king of Assyria, who committed suicide while being besieged in Nineveh by the Medes, not as an Assyrian king in Babylon. He is pictured as a figure of great excesses (see Hellanikos, *FGrHist* #687a F2) but most likely corresponds in no way to Assurbanipal, the last great king of Assyria, who restored for a while the fortunes of the collapsing Assyrian Empire. Assurbanipal's end is not known, although there is some indication that two of his sons exiled him as they fought for the tottering throne of Assyria.

38. It is difficult to believe the report of Berossos, if Polyhistor has accurately transmitted Berossos's account. Berossos (through Polyhistor) implies that Astyages was the Median king when the

three years. After assembling an army, he captured Judea, Phoenicia, and Syria. Polyhistor (*FGrHist* #273) is in agreement with the Hebrew Scriptures on all of this, so there is no need of many words here.

F8c

Josephus, *Antiquitates Judaicae* (*Jewish Antiquities*) 10.34: Berossos also records the king of the Babylonians, Baladas.

F9a

Josephus *contra Apionem* (*Against Apion*) 1.131–44 (134–41 = Syncellus *Ecloga Chronographica* [*Chronological Excerpts*] 416–18 = Josephus *Antiquitates Judaicae* [*Jewish Antiquities*] 10.220–28): Berossos reports on Nabopalassaros, the king of Babylon and the Chaldeans. (132) He records the following about his accomplishments. He sent his son Naboukhodonoso-ros with a great army against Egypt and our land, when he learned they had rebelled against him. He conquered them and destroyed the temple in Jerusa-lem and caused all our people to settle in Babylonia. It happened then that our city was deserted for seventy years[39] until Cyrus the Persian king. (133) Berossos says that the Babylonians ruled Egypt, Syria, Phoenicia, and Ara-

---

Medes ended the Assyrian Empire with the help of the Babylonians under their king Nabopalassa-ros. In fact, Kyaxares was king of the Medes then, not Astyages, and Nabopalassaros (Nabu-apa-lusur) arrived too late for the decisive battle in 614 B.C. that resulted in the sack of Ashur: see Gray-son, *Assyrian and Babylonian Chronicles*, 93, Chronicle 3 = BM 21901; and Luckenbill, *Ancient Records of Assyria and Babylonia*, 2:419. Herodotus (1.103) also describes the Medes alone as having conquered the Assyrians. But Nabopalassaros (Nabu-apal-usur) was with Kyaxares two years later when the Medes and Babylonians sacked Nineveh in 612 B.C.: see again both Grayson, 94 and Luckenbill, 2:419.

Cyrus ended the rule of the Medes in 550 B.C. when he dethroned Astyages: see again Grayson, 106, Chronicle 7, Nabonidus Chronicle = BM 35382, and Herodotus 1.130. Berossos is the only author who says that Amytis was the daughter of Astyages and married to Naboukhodonosoros (Nebuchadnezzar II). According to Ktesias (*FGrHist* #688 F9), she also was the daughter of Asty-ages but the wife first of Spitamas and then of Cyrus the Persian. It is difficult to believe the report of Berossos not only on whose wife Amytis was, but, if Berossos is here reporting on the fall of the Assyrian Empire, that Astyages was king of the Medes when the Medes ended the Assyrian Empire. Berossos must not have had a correct synchronism of Median and Babylonian history. According to Herodotus the Median kings were:

Deiokes	53 years	(1.102)	
Phraortes	22 years	(1.102)	
Kyaxares	40 years	(1.106)	624–585
Astyages	35 years	(1.130)	584–550

39. On the length of the Babylonian captivity, see, T7 n. 9.

bia and that their king by his exploits surpassed all those who had ruled before him over the Chaldeans and the Babylonians.

(Since *Against Apion* 134 is irrelevant, it is not translated. For continuity,
we insert *Jewish Antiquities* 10.219. *Against Apion* resumes at 135.) The
king Naboukhodonosoros ruled forty-three years, a man vigorous and more
fortunate than all those who had ruled before him in Babylon, as Berossos
says in the third book of his Chaldean history. I will quote exactly what Berossos says. (135) His father, Nabopalassaros, heard that the satrap appointed for Egypt, Coele Syria, and Phoenicia[40] had rebelled. Since he was
not able to lead an army, as he was ill, he appointed his son Naboukhodonosoros, then in the prime of his life, as commander over part of his army and
sent him against the rebel. (136) Naboukhodonosoros drew up his forces and
joined battle with the rebel. He conquered the rebel and brought the country
under the rule of the Babylonians. It happened at this time that his father
Nabopalassaros fell ill and died in Babylon, having ruled twenty-one years.

(137) Naboukhodonosoros learned soon after of his father's death and
settled the affairs of Egypt and the rest of the country. He gave control of the
prisoners taken from Judea, Phoenicia and Syria, and Egypt to some of his
friends and ordered them with most of his army and the rest of the spoils of
war to march to Babylon. Then he with a few of his followers set out directly
for Babylon across the desert.

(138) He took over the government of the Chaldeans, which during his
absence had been ably administered and ruled by the noblest of them. He assumed command of the whole of his father's realm. He ordered that the most
suitable parts of Babylonia be found for the prisoners when they arrived.

(139) From the spoils of war he most zealously decorated the temple of
Bel and the rest of the holy places. He rebuilt the old city and added a new
one outside the walls and fixed it so that those who intended to besiege the
city could no longer divert the river's course. He built a triple wall around
the inner city and a triple wall around the outer city. The triple wall a-
round the inner city was made of baked brick and bitumen; the triple wall
around the outer city was made of rough brick.

---

40. Pharaoh Necho II (609–594 B.C.) of the Saite Dynasty ruled Egypt in his own right in the
last decade of the sixth century B.C. He was not a satrap (which was the Persian word for governor
of a province) of the Chaldean Empire, but he was its only rival for control of the eastern Mediterranean. The Chaldeans came to control the eastern Mediterranean, but they did not conquer Egypt.
Coele Syria is an imprecise geographical term, but in the third century B.C. it came to mean the land
between the coast of the eastern Mediterranean and the Euphrates river, not including Phoenicia. It
included what is today modern Syria, Jordan, and Israel, but it did not include Lebanon.

(140) After he had fortified the city and decorated its gates as if they were holy, he had a new palace built near the old royal palace of his forefathers. It would take a long time to describe this palace, its height and the rest of its dimensions. It took, however, only fifteen days to build it, even though it was exceedingly large and splendidly decorated.

(141) In this palace he had high stone terraces built that gave the appearance of being mountains planted with all kinds of trees. He had constructed and prepared what are called the Hanging Gardens[41] for his wife, who had a love of the mountains since she had grown up in Media.

(142) Thus Berossos gave his account about the kings mentioned above and about many other things besides in the third book of his Chaldean history, in which he also blames the Greek writers for their silly mistake in saying that Semiramis of the Assyrians founded Babylon and in ascribing to her its wondrous buildings.[42] (143) The Chaldean writings must be believed. For the written records of the Phoenicians (*FGrHist* #790 F1) on the kings of the Babylonians confirm Berossos's statements because they say that he conquered all of Syria and Phoenicia.

(144) Also others agree with Berossos—Philostratos (*FGrHist* #789 F1) in his histories, when he relates the siege of Tyre and Megasthenes[43] (*FGrHist* #715 F1) in the fourth book of his Indian history, when he tries to prove that the aforementioned king of the Babylonians surpassed Herakles in strength and in the glory of his accomplishments, as he says the king conquered all of Libya and Spain.

F9b

Eusebius *Praeparatio Evangelica* (*Preparation for the Gospel*) 10.10.3: The exile of the Jews, taken prisoners by the Babylonians under Naboukhodonosoros, lasted seventy years, just as Jeremiah prophesied.[44] Berossos the Babylonian recorded Naboukhodonosoros in his history ... (5) Cyrus in the

---

41. The Hanging Gardens of Babylon were one of the seven wonders of the ancient world. In addition to the Hanging Gardens, there were the Colossus of Rhodes, the Lighthouse at Alexandria, the Egyptian Pyramids, the Tomb of Mausolos at Halicarnassus, the Temple of Artemis at Ephesus, and the Statue of Zeus at Olympia. The cuneiform records do not mention the Hanging Gardens of Babylon. On Naboukhodonosoros's (Nebuchadnezzar II's) wife, Amytis, see F8b.

42. Ktesias originally recorded this, which Diodorus Siculus 2.7.2–11 preserves.

43. Megasthenes was an ethnographer, who wrote around 300 B.C. on India. Quite obviously, his history was rather fanciful, if he had a Babylonian king conquer Spain. We know practically nothing more about this Philostratos than what Josephus tells here.

44. On the length of the Babylonian captivity, see T7 n.9.

first year of his reign, which was in the first year of the fifty-fifth Olympiad (559 B.C.), because of Zorababel ... caused the first and most celebrated return of the people, after seventy years had passed, as was recorded in Esdras (Ezra 1–6) for the Hebrews.

F9c

Theophilus *ad Autolycum* (*To Autolycus*) 3.22: Berossos ... who related many things in agreement with Moses, wrote about the Great Flood and many other events. He also told many of the same things as the prophets Jeremiah and Daniel, most especially what happened to the Jews under the king of Babylon, who was Abobassaros, called by the Hebrews Naboukhodonosoros. He records how the temple in Jerusalem was destroyed by the Chaldean king (cf. 2 Kings 25.8), that in the second year of Cyrus's kingship the foundations of the temple were laid, and again that in the second year of Dareios's (Darius's) kingship the temple was completed (cf. Ezra 5–6).

F10a

Josephus *contra Apionem* (*Against Apion*) 1.145–53: Concerning the things mentioned before about the temple in Jerusalem—that it was destroyed by the Babylonian army and that it was rebuilt after Cyrus had taken the kingship of Asia—all this can be proven from what Berossos says. For he says the following in his third book.

(146) Naboukhodonosoros, after he had begun the building of the walls mentioned above, fell sick and died. He had reigned forty-three years. His son Euilmaradokhos succeeded to the kingship. (147) He ruled capriciously and had no regard for the laws. His sister's husband, Neriglisaros, plotted against him and killed him. Euilmaradokhos had ruled two years. After the successful plot and assassination, Neriglassaros ruled four years. (148) His son Laborosoardokhos, still a child, succeeded to the throne and ruled for nine months. Because of his evil ways, his friends plotted against him, and he was beaten to death.

(149) After Laborosoardokhos had been killed, the plotters came to an agreement that a certain Nabonnedos from Babylon should rule. He was one of the plotters. Under his rule, the walls of Babylon along the river were reinforced with baked brick and bitumen. (150) In the seventeenth year of his reign Cyrus marched against him from Persia with a great force, captured the rest of his kingdom, and moved against Babylon.

(151) Nabonnedos learned of Cyrus's coming attack and ordered his army to assemble and meet him, but he lost the battle and had to flee with a few followers to Borsippa, where he barricaded himself in. (152) Cyrus captured Babylon and had the walls of the outer city razed, because they presented too strong a defense for the city. Cyrus went to Borsippa to besiege Nabonnedos. (153) Nabonnedos did not wait for the siege to begin but surrendered almost immediately. Cyrus received him graciously, exiled him from Babylonia, but gave him Karmania[45] instead. Nabonnedos spent the rest of his life in that country and died there.[46]

F10b

Eusebius *Chronicon* (*The Chronicle*) p. 15, lines 5–10 Karst, in an Armenian translation: Polyhistor (*FGrHist* #273 F79), following Berossos, reports that after Naboukhodonosoros his son, Amelmarudokhos, reigned twelve years. The Hebrew scripture calls him Ilmarudochos (2 Kings 25.27). After him, says Polyhistor, Neriglisaros reigned over the Chaldeans four years. Then Nabodenos (Nabonnedos) reigned seventeen years. While he was king, Cyrus, son of Kambyses, conquered in battle the land of the Babylonians. Nabodenos (Nabonnedos) tried to resist but suffered defeat and became an exile.

F11

Eusebius *Chronicon* (*The Chronicle*) p. 15, lines 11–20 Karst, in an Armenian translation: Cyrus ruled Babylonia for nine years. Then, after having been engaged in another war on the Daas Plain,[47] he died. After him Kambyses ruled eight years, and after him Dareios (Darius) for thirty-six years. Then Xerxes ruled and the rest of the Persian kings. Just as Berossos records

---

45. Karmania is in south central Iran, the region called Kerman today.

46. According to the Nabonidus Chronicle (Grayson, *Assyrian and Babylonian Chronicles*, 110, line 16 = BM 35382), however, Nabonnedos (Nabonidus) was captured in Babylon, whereas Xenophon in his *Cyropaedia* (*The Education of Cyrus*) 7.5.29–30 reports that the king of Babylon was killed when the Persians took the city. For an account of individual kings of Babylon, see, on the reign of Nebuchadnezzar II, D. J. Wiseman, *Nebuchadressar and Babylon* (Oxford, 1983); and, on the reign of Nabonidus, Paul-Alain Beaulieu, *The Reign of Nabonidus, King of Babylon 556–539 B.C.* 3d ed. (New Haven, 1989).

47. See Herodotus 1.214 for an account of Cyrus's death, as he was trying to expand the Persian Empire beyond the Araxes River. According to Herodotus 1.202, the Araxes was another name for the Oxus River (modern Amu-Dar'ya), which flows into the Aral Sea but in antiquity seems to have had a branch that flowed into the Caspian Sea.

events in the context of his condensed version of the Chaldean kingship, so Polyhistor (*FGrHist* #273) records the same things. From this it is clear that it was Naboukhodonosoros who captured the Jews and that from him to Cyrus was about seventy years—which figure agrees with that given by the history of the Jews.[48]

F12

Clemens of Alexandria *Protrepticus* (*Exhortation*) 5.65.2–3: The Persians, Medes, and Magoi[49] do not make statues of their gods from wood or stone but honor fire and water as the philosophers do. ... (3) Berossos, however, says in the third book of his Chaldean history that later, after the passage of many years, the Persians did have statues of human figures. This began under Artaxerxes Okhos, son of Dareios (Darius),[50] who first set up the statue of Aphrodite Anaitis[51] and showed respect to it at Babylon, Susa, and Ekbatana, in Persia and Bactria, and at Damascus and Sardis.

F13

Agathias, *Historiae* (*Histories*) 2.24: At the time when Zoroaster-Zarades flourished,[52] he was the Persian leader and guide of the holy rites of the Magoi. He changed the former rituals and established beliefs that were blended and varied and mixed. For of old he honored Zeus and Kronos and all the other gods commonly found among the Greeks, except that he did not preserve their names, but Zeus was Bel, Herakles was Sandes, Aphrodite

---

48. On the seventy-year period of the exile, see T7 n. 9.

49. According to Herodotus 1.140, which is our only source for this, the Magoi were originally a subgroup or tribe of the Medes. One of the Medes then tried to usurp the Persian throne (Herodotus 3.61–87). Whether from the same group or simply bearing the same name, Magoi became the priestly caste for the native Iranian religion, but among the Greeks they were mistakenly identified as skilled practitioners of magic, as Origen *contra Celsum* (*Against Celsum*) 6.80 says.

50. Clemens is mistaken here, as Artaxerxes III Okhos is not a son of a Dareios (Darius) but the son of Artaxerxes II Memnon. Most likely Berossos meant Artaxerxes II Memnon, who was the son of a Dareios, Dareios II.

51. The Persian goddess Anaitis (Anahita in the *Avesta*, the sacred poem of ancient Iranian religion) was also identified with the Greek virgin goddess Artemis (Plutarch *Artaxerxes* 27.3). Both were fertility godesses, but because temple prostitutes played a part in Anaitis's worship, her identification with Aphrodite is understandable.

52. When Zoroaster lived is a matter of great debate, but he was a prophet and devotee of the worship of Ahura-Mazda. The Magoi, whatever their origin, became the priestly class for the worship of Ahura-Mazda.

was Anaitis,[53] and others are called by other names as is told by all those who wrote of the ancient history of the Assyrians and the Medes, as Berossos the Babylonian and Athenokles (*FGrHist* #682) and Simakos (*FGrHist* #683).[54]

History of Babylonia, Unplaced Fragments

F14

Hesychius *Lexicon* (*Dictionary*), s.v. "Sarakhero": In Berossos's history, the personal maid of Hera.[55]

F15a

Pliny *Naturalis Historia* (*Natural History*) 7.160: Epigenes[56] denies that man can live to be 112 years old, Berossos that man can live longer than 116 years.

F15b

Censorinus *de Die Natali* (*The Birthday Gift*) 17.4: Epigenes says the longest life is 112 years, Berossos, however, 116. Others says that it is possible to exceed 120 years.

F15c

Josephus *Antiquitates Judaicae* (*Jewish Antiquities*) 1.107: All the historians, Greek and non-Greek, who wrote foundation stories, support me in this. Manetho, who wrote Egyptian history, Berossos, the compiler of Babylonian history, and Mokhos[57] (*FGrHist* #784 F3), and Hestiaios (*FGrHist* #786

---

53. On Anaitis, see F11 n. 52. Sandes was another name for Herakles, but Nonnus *Dionysiaca* 34.192 says Sandes is a Cilician god.

54. Nothing further is known about these two historians, Athenokles and Simakos.

55. Sarakhero appears only here in Greek literature and has no counterpart in Sumerian and Babylonian literature or religion.

56. Epigenes from Byzantium was an astrologer of the second century B.C.

57. Josephus is justifying the biblical account of the long lives of the patriarchs given in Genesis and cites a number of historians who support his contention that such long lives are possible. Josephus names three writers of Phoenician history:

F2), and besides them the Egyptian Hieronymos (*FGrHist* #787 F1), writers of Phoenician history—they agree with what I am saying, and also Hesiod, Hekataios (*FGrHist* #1 F35), Hellanikos (*FGrHist* #4 F202), Akousilaos (*FGrHist* #2 F46), Ephoros (*FGrHist* #70 F238), and Nikolaos (*FGrHist* #90 F141)—their judgment is that the ancients lived a thousand years.

Astronomical or Astrological Information—Probably from Book 1, On the Moon

F16

Vitruvius *de Architectura* (*On Architecture*) 9.2.1–2: Berossos taught as follows about the moon. It is a sphere, one half of which emits a white, glowing heat, while the other half has a dark blue color. When, however, it passes in its orbit under the orbit of the sun, the moon is overcome by the sun's rays and the force of its heat, and the half of the moon that emits a white, glowing heat turns back to the light of day because of the attraction of light to light. But when the upper parts of the moon face the sun's orbit, then the moon's lower part, which does not give off a white, glowing heat, seems to be obscured because of its resemblance to air. When the moon is perpendicular to the sun's rays, all the light of day is retained on its upper part and is then called the first moon (new moon).

(2) When the moon in its orbit is in the eastern part of the sky, it has more freedom from the force of the sun, and the furthest part of the moon's half that emits a white glowing heat sends its glow to the earth in an exceedingly fine line. This state of the moon is called the second moon. By the daily retardation of its orbit, the third and fourth moon are numbered on the successive days. On the seventh day, since the sun is in the west and the moon, halfway between the eastern and western horizons, holds the middle areas of the sky, the half of the moon that emits a white, glowing heat is

---

Mokhos or Laitos, who lived before the first century B.C.;

Hestiaios, who lived before A.D. 90; and

Hieronymos the Egyptian (see T6).

Very little is known about any of them. There does not survive any fragment of their works to prove Josephus's assertion about their views on long life.

Hesiod was a Greek poet of the late eighth or early seventh century. Hekataios, Hellanikos, and Akousilaos were early Greek historians, mythographers, and geographers. Ephoros was a Greek historian who lived in the fourth century B.C. On Nikolaos of Damascus, see F4b.

Most likely all these historians never asserted what Josephus claims but are names Josephus added merely to give authority to his argument.

turned toward the earth because the moon is half the distance between the earth and the sun. When there is the entire space of the world between the sun and the moon and when the sun in the west is opposite to the rising moon, the moon, where it burns most brightly, is freed from the sun's rays and on the fourteenth day sends forth its total light. During the following days, the moon decreases daily to bring the lunar month to a close. In its revolutions and orbit, the moon feels the sun's wheel and rays, and then the order of the days of the month is complete.

F17a

Aetius *de Placitis Reliquiae* (*Philosophers' Views of Nature*) 2.25.12 Diels *Doxographi Graeci* p. 356: Berossos says that the moon is a sphere half consumed in fire.

F17b

Aetius, *de Placitis Reliquiae* (*Philosophers' Views of Nature*) 2.28.1 Diels *Doxographi Graeci* p. 358: Anaximander, Xenophanes,[58] and Berossos say the moon has its own light.

F17c

Aetius, *de Placitis Reliquiae* (*Philosophers' Views of Nature*) 2.29.2 Diels *Doxographi Graeci* p. 359: Berossos says that the moon has turned its unfired side towards us.

F18

Cleomedes *de Motu Circulari Corporum Caelestium* (*On the Circular Motion of the Heavenly Bodies*) 2.4: Berossos says that the moon is half fire and has numerous different movements. One is along its length in accordance with the earth; another is along its width, breadth, and depth in accordance with the other five planets; and another is in its own center. In this last movement, Berossos thinks that the moon waxes and wanes as it turns

---

58. Both Anaximander of Miletos and Xenophanes of Kolophon were early Greek natural philosophers of the sixth century B.C.

toward the sun and that the revolution is done in equal parts of time in conjunction with the sun. This view, though, is easy to refute.

Miscellaneous

F19

Seneca *Naturales Questiones* (*Questions About Science*) 3.29.1: Berossos, who interpreted the prophecies of Bel,[59] attributes these disasters (the end of the world and its aftermath) to the movements of the planets. He is so certain of this that he can determine a date for the Conflagration and the Great Flood. He maintains that the earth will burn whenever all the planets, which now have different orbits, converge in Cancer and are so arranged in the same path that a straight line can pass through all their orbs, and that there will be a further great flood, when the same planets so converge in Capricorn. For under the sign of Cancer occurs the change to summer, under Capricorn the change to winter. They are signs of great power, occurring when there are movements in the change of season.[60]

F20

Pliny *Naturalis Historia* (*Natural History*) 7.193: Epigenes,[61] a most important author, teaches that among the Babylonians, observations about the movements of the stars have been preserved on baked clay tablets for 720,000 years. Berossos and Kritodemos, however, give a shorter period, 490,000 years. Nevertheless, even with this disagreement, it is apparent that the knowledge of writing is very, very ancient.

F21

Commentariorum in Aratum Reliquiae (*Commentary on Aratus*) pp. 142–43 Maass: God created and placed the stars. Afterward the most knowledgeable

---

59. Bel (Marduk) is not normally associated with prophecy, and Seneca may have garbled the information he is transmitting. See W. G. Lambert, "Berossus and Babylonian Eschatology," *Iraq* 38 (1976): 171–172.

60. Stoics, such as Seneca, believed in recurring cataclysms. Here it seems Berossos believes only that the world will end in a grand cataclysm. There is no cuneiform text that expresses any belief in a general cataclysm that will end the world. See Lambert, "Berossus and Babylonian Eschatology," 172–173.

61. On Epigenes, see F15a–b.

men gave them their proper names and signs and established the laws of their movements. ... These names and placings of the stars in constellations even Berossos in his *Creation*[62] admits have nothing to do with the actual creation of the universe by Jupiter.

F22

Palchus 135 (Cumont, ed. *Catalogus Codicum Astrologorum Graecorum* [*Catalogue of the Manuscripts of the Greek Astrologers*], vol. 5, pars prior [1904] p. 204): Therefore, we, as followers of the teachings of the divine Ptolemy,[63] have had the courage to disagree about the energy and the quality of the thirty bright stars. So that we may be mindful of those who wrote before he did about the appearance of the fixed stars and about the power of the rising stars, let us set the record straight. The Babylonians and then the Chaldeans were practically the first ones to have knowledge about astronomical phenomena, just as we have recognized from those who went before us. For they tell of Apollonios the Myndian and Artemidoros[64] (lac.), and about all these Berossos has written and others after him.

---

62. On the meaning of this title, see Berossos's Life and Work in chap. 1.

63. Ptolemy is the famous Claudius Ptolemy of the second century A.D. who wrote numerous mathematical, astronomical, and astrological works.

64. Both Apollonios and Artemidoros are otherwise unknown.

CHAPTER 4

Berossos—Tables

Table A. Time Outline—Mesopotamia

Early Bronze Age, ca. 3100–2100 B.C.
    Sumerian Kingdoms, ca. 3100–2350 B.C.
    Empire of Akkade, ca. 2300–2100 B.C.
Middle Bronze Age, ca. 2100–1600 B.C.
    Third Kingdom of Ur, ca. 2100–2000 B.C.
    Old Babylonian Period, ca. 1900–1600 B.C.
Late Bronze Age, ca. 1600–1200 B.C.
    Kassite Dynasty, ca. 1500–1150 B.C.
Early Iron Age, ca. 1200–1000 B.C.
Late Iron Age, ca. 1000–539 B.C.
    Assyrian Empire, 934–609 B.C.
    Neo-Babylonian Empire, 609–539 B.C.
Persian Period, 539–330 B.C.
Alexander's Reign, 330–323 B.C.
Struggle for the Succession, 323–301 B.C.
Seleucid Empire, 311–64 B.C.
Parthian Empire, 247 B.C.–A.D. 227
    Parthian rule of Babylonia begins, ca. 140 B.C.
    Roman rule of Babylonia, A.D. 115–117
Sassanid Empire, A.D. 227–637
Arab Conquest, A.D. 637

Table B. Mesopotamian Ruler-Lists

1a. Antediluvian Kings in Berossos (F3)		1b. Antediluvian Kings from the *Sumerian King-List*[1]	
Aloros of Babylon	10 *saroi* (36,000 years)	Alulium of Eridu	28,800 years
Alaparos of Babylon	3 *saroi* (10,800 years)	Alalgar of Eridu	36,000 years
Amelon of Pautibiblon	13 *saroi* (46,800 years)	En-men-lu-Anna of Bad-tibira	43,200 years
Ammenon of Babylon	12 *saroi* (43,200 years)	En-men-gal-Anna of Bad-tibira	28,800 years
Amegalaros of Pautibiblon	18 *saroi* (64,000 years)	Dumu-zi of Bad-tibira	36,000 years
Daonos of Pautibiblon	10 *saroi* (36,000 years)	En-sipa-zi-Anna of Larak	28,800 years
Euedorankhos of Pautibiblon	18 *saroi* (64,800 years)	En-men-dur-Anna of Sippar	21,000 years
Amempsinos of Larankhos	10 *saroi* (36,000 years)	Ubar-Tutu of Shuruppak	18,600 years
Otiartes of Larankhos	8 *saroi* (28,800 years)		
Xisouthros of Larankhos	18 *saroi* (64,800) years		
total	120 *saroi* (432,000 years)		241,200 years

---

1. Thorkild Jacobsen, *The Sumerian King List* (Chicago, 1939), 70–77.

2a. Berossos's Wise Monsters		2b. Abydenus's Wise Monsters[2]		Tablet W 20030,7[3]	
Kings	**Monsters**	**Kings**	**Monsters**	**Kings**	**Apkallu (Monsters)**
Aloros (F3)	Oannes (F1)	Aloros	Oannes (presumed)	Aialu	U An
Alaparos (F3)		Alaparos		Alalgar	U Anduga
Amelon (F3)		Amillaros	2nd Annedotos	Ammelu Anna	Enmeduga
Ammenon (F3)	Annedotos (F3)	Ammenon		Ammegal Anna	Enmegalamma
Amegalaros (F3)		Megalanos		Enme Ushumgal Anna	Enmebulugga
Daonos (F3)	4 monsters (F3)	Daos	Euedokos Eneugamos Eneuboulos Anementos	Dumuzi	Anenlilda
Euedorankhos (F3)	Odakon (F3)	Euedoreskhos	Anodaphos	Enmeduranki	Utuabzu

---

2. Syncellus *Ecloga Chronographica* 68; Eusebius *Chronicon* p. 18, line 18–p. 16, line 8 Karst = *FGrHist* vol. III C 1 (1958), Abydenos #685, F2

3. Jan van Dijk, "Die Inschriftenfunde: II Die tontafeln aus dem res-Heiligtum" in *XVIII. vorläufiger Bericht über die von dem Deutschen Archäologischen Institut und der Deutschen Orient-Gesellschaft aus Mitteln der Deutschen Forschungsgemeinschaft unternommenen Ausgrabungen in Uruk-Warka (1959/1960)*, Heinrich J. Lenzen (Berlin 1962), 43–61.

3a. Postdiluvian Kings mentioned by Berossos to Tiglath-pileser III

First Two Kings After the Flood according to Berossos	
Euekhoios (F5)	4 *neroi* (2,400)
Khomasbelos (F5)	4 *neroi* and 5 *sossoi* (2,700)

3b. Postdiluvian Kings Mentioned by Other Sources to Tiglath-pileser III

First Two Kings after the Flood from the *Sumerian King-List*[4]		Modern Reference[5]
Ga(lac.)ur of Kish	1,200 years	
(lac.)	960 years	

Dynasties (Kings' Names omitted) Listed in the *Sumerian King-List*			Modern Reference[5]
First Kingdom of Kish	23 Kings	24,510 years, 3 months, 3 and one-half days	2900–2700 B.C. Early Dynastic I
Kings of Uruk	12 Kings	2,310 years	

4. Jacobsen, *The Sumerian King List* (Chicago, 1939), 77. On its use as a historical source, see "Berossos's History of Babylonia—Sources, Methods, and Reliability" in chap. 1, and see F5.

5. Dates and modern names are based on William Hallo and William Simpson, *The Ancient Near East: A History* (New York, 1971) and J. A. Brinkman, "Appendix: Mesopotamian Chronology of the Historical Period," in *Ancient Mesopotamia: Portrait of a Dead Civilization*, ed. A. Leo Oppenheim, rev. Erica Reeves (Chicago, 1977), 335–40.

Numbers of Kings mentioned by Berossos	Dynasties (Kings' Names omitted) Listed in the Sumerian King-List			Modern Reference
No correspondences between the dynasties Berossos lists and the dynasties given by the king-lists are possible. [6]	First Kingdom of Ur	4 Kings	177 years	2700–2500 B.C. Early Dynastic II
	Kings of Awan	3 Kings	356 years	
	Kings of Kish	8 Kings	3,195 years	
	Kings of Hamazi	1 (?) King	360 (?) years	
	Kings of Uruk	? Kings	? years	
	Kings of Ur	4 Kings	116 years	
	Kings of Adab	(?) Kings	90 (?) years	
	Kings of Maeri	6 Kings	136 years	
	King of Kish	1 King	100 years	2500–2300 B.C. Early Dynastic III
	Kings of Akshak	6 Kings	99 years	
	Kings of Kish	7 Kings	491 years	
	King of Uruk	1 King	25 years	
	Kings of Akkade	11 Kings	181 years	2334–2154 B.C. Sargonid Dynasty
	Kings of Uruk	5 Kings	30 years	
86 Kings and 33,091 years from Xisouthros to the Medes (F5)		92+ Kings	31,776 years	minimum numbers of kings and years from the Sumerian King-List

6. It is impossible to find any correspondences between what has survived in Berossos's text and the king-lists. J. A. Brinkman, *A Political History of Post-Kassite Babylonia 1158–722 B.C.*, vol. 43 of *Analecta Orientalia* (Roma, 1968), 21 writes: "His (Berossos's) convoluted chronological scheme of the dynasties from the time of the flood to the accession of Phul(os) defies unravelling even in the manuscript tradition."

Numbers of Kings mentioned by Berossos	Dynasties (Kings' Names omitted) Listed in the *Sumerian King-List*			Modern Reference
8 Kings of the Medes[7] (F5) 244 years	Gutians	21 Kings	91 years and 40 days	
	King of Uruk	1 King	7 years, 6 months, 15 days	
No correspondences between the dynasties Berossos lists and the dynasties given by the king-lists are possible.	Kings of Ur	5 Kings	108 years	2112–2004 B.C. Third Kingdom of Ur
	Kings of Isin	14 Kings	203 years[8]	2017–1794 B.C. First Dynasty of Isin
	Dynasties (Kings' Names omitted) Listed in *King-List A*[9]			**Modern Reference**
11 Kings (F5) 28 years	Kings of Babylon	11 Kings	?[10]	1894–1595 B.C. First Dynasty of Babylon
49 Kings of the Chaldeans (F5) 458 years	Kings of Uruku	11 Kings	368 years	First Dynasty of the Sealand
9 Kings of the Arabians (F5) 245 years	Kings of ???	36 Kings	576 years, 9 months	????–1155 B.C. Kassite Dynasty

7. On the identification of the Medes of Berossos's text with the Gutians, see F5 nn. 25 and 27.
8. This marks the end of the *Sumerian King-List*.
9. *ANET*[3] 272 and Brinkman, *A Political History of Post-Kassite Babylon*, 38.
10. Brinkman, "Appendix: Mesopotamian Chronology of the Historical Period," lists the names of the eleven kings and gives their total regnal years as three hundred.

Numbers of Kings mentioned by Berossos	Dynasties (Kings' Names omitted) Listed in King-List A			Modern Reference	
	Kings of Isin	11 Kings	132 years, 6 months	1157–1026 B.C	Second Dynasty of Isin
No correspondences between the dynasties	Dynasty of the Sea Country	3 Kings	21 years, 5 months	1025–1005 B.C	Second Dynasty of the Sealand
Berossos lists and the dynasties given by the king-lists are possible.	Bazi Dynasty	3 Kings	20 years, 3 months	1004–985 B.C.	Bazi Dynasty
	Elamite Dynasty	1 King	6 years	984–979 B.C	Elamite Dynasty
	?	3 Kings (?)	?		
Semiramis (F5, F9a)[11]	E Dynasty	5 Kings (?)	?		
	?	3 Kings (?)	10 years		
45 Kings, 526 years (F5) to Phulos (Tiglath-pileser III)	The text of King-List A is incomplete, as it is missing kings, dynasties, and regnal years until Nabushumishkun (see next table).				

---

11. If Semiramis was an historical figure, she was most likely Sammuramat, wife of Samshi-Adad V (824–811) and mother of Adad-Nirari III (810–782), kings of Assyria.

4. Kings of Babylon from Nabu-nashir to Assurbanipal

Kings listed by Berossos	King-List A[12]	Synchronistic King-List[13] Kings of Babylon	Kings of Assyria
	Nabushumishkun	(lac.)	(lac.)
Nabonassaros (F7)	Nabunasir		
	Nabunadinzeri: 2 years		
	Nabushumukin: 1 month, 12 days		
	Ukinzer: 3 years		
Phulos (F5)	Pulu: 2 years		
	Ululaia: 5 years		
	Mardukaplaiddin: 12 years		
	Sargon: 5 years		
Senakheirimos (F5, F8a, F8b)	Sennacherib: 2 years	Sennacherib	Sennacherib Nabulaplaiddin (vizier)
brother of Senakheirimos (F8b)			

12. *ANET*[3] 272.
13. *ANET*[3] 272–73, there called the *Synchronistic Chronicle*.

Chronicle 1[14]	Ptolemaic Canon[15]	Kings of Babylon	Kings of Assyria[16]
		Nabu-sama-iskum (760?–748)	Assur-nirarir (754–745)
Nabu-nasir: 14 years	Nabonassaros: 14 years	Nabu-nashir (747–734)	Tiglath-pileser III (744–727)
Nabu-nadin-zeri: 2 years	Nadios: 2 years	Nabu-nadin-zer (733–732)	
Nabu-shuma-ukin: 1 month, 2 days	Khinzetros and Poros: 5 years	Nabu-shumaukin II (732)	
Nabu-mukin-zeri: 3 years		Nabu-maukinzeri (731–729)	
Tiglathpileser (III): 2 years		Tiglathpileser III (728–727)	
Shalmaneser (V): 5 years	Iloulaios: 5 years	Shalmanesser V (726–722)	Shalmanesser V (726–722)
Merodach-baladen II: 12 years	Mardok-empados: 12 years	Marduk-Baldan (721–710)	Sargon II (721–705)
Sargon (II) (lac.)	Arkeanos: 5 years	Sargon II (709–705)	
	without a king: 2 years	Sennacherib (704–703)	Sennacherib (704–681)

---

14. A. K Grayson, *Assyrian and Babylonian Chronicles* (Locust Valley, N.Y., 1975), 69–87.

15. The *Ptolemaic Canon* exists in several copies and was much used in Byzantine times. Our list is based on the copy of the canon that appears in Kurt Wachsmuth, *Einleitung in das Studium der alten Geschichte* (Leipzig, 1895), 305–06. Two lists, which appear in Syncellus *Ecloga Chronographica* 390–396, seem to be based on the *Ptolemaic Canon*, but, nevertheless, contain some spellings and some lengths of regnal years different from those of the *Ptolemaic Canon*.

16. These lists of the kings of Babylon and Assyria are based on Brinkman, "Appendix: Mesopotamian Chronology of the Historical Period," 335–340 and on the lists in *CAH*².

Kings listed by Berossos	*King-List A*	*Synchronistic King-List* Kings of Babylon	Kings of Assyria
Akise: 30 days (F8b)	Mardukzakir-shumi:1 month		
Beladas: 6 months (F8b, F8c)	Marduk-aplaiddin: 9 months		
Belibos: 3 years (F8b)	Belibini: 3 years		
	Ashur-nadin-shumi 6 years	Ashurnadinshumi	
	Nergalushezib: 1 year	Nergalushezib	
	Ushezib-Marduk: 5 years	Mushezib-Marduk	
Senakheirimos: 18 years (F8b)[17]	Sennacherib: 8 years	Sennacherib Kalbu (vizier)	Belupahhir (vizier)
Asordanios: 8 years (F8b)	Esarhaddon (lac.)	Esarhaddon	Esarhaddon
		Ishtarshumersch (vizier)	Nabuzerlishir (vizier)
Samoges (F8b)	Shamashshum (lac.)	Shamashshu-mukin	Assurbanipal
Brother of Sam-oges: 21 years (F8b) = Sarda-napallos[18]	Kandal (lac.)	Kandalanu	Ishtarshumersch (vizier)

---

17. See F8b n. 33 on the mistake over the number of years Senakheirimos reigned and the confusion of Senakheirimos's two sons, Ashur-nadin-shumi and Esarhaddon (Asordanios).

18. On the mistaken identification of Sardanapallos as the son of Assurbanipal, see F8b n. 37.

Chronicle 1	Ptolemaic Canon	Kings of Babylon	Kings of Assyria
		Marduk-zaki-shumi (703)	
Merodachbal-adan II (lac.)		Marduk-Baldan (703)	
Belibni: 3 years	Bilibos: 3 years	Bel-ibni (702–700)	
Ashur-nadin-shumi: 6 years	Aparanadios: 6 years	Ashur-nadin-shumi (699–694)	
Nergal-ushezib: 1 year, 6 months	Rhegebelos: 1 year	Nergal-ushezib (693)	
Mushezib-Mar-duk: 4 years	Mesesimordakos: 4 years	Mushezib-Mar-duk: (692–689)	
without a king: 8 years	without a king: 8 years	Sennacherib (688–681)	
Esarhaddon: 12 years	Asardinos: 13 years	Esarhaddon: (680–669)	Esarhaddon: (680–669)
Nabu-zer-kitti-lishim			
		Assurbanipal (668)	Assurbanipal (668–629)
Shamash-shuma-ukin	Saosdoukhinos: 20 years	Shamash-shum-ukin: (667–648)	
	Kineladanos: 22 years	Kandalanu (647–627)	

5. Kings of Babylon Listed by Berossos Compared to the *Uruk King-List*, the *Ptolemaic Canon*, and a Modern List.

Berossos's Kings	*Uruk King-List*[19]	*Ptolemaic Canon*[20]
Samoges (F8b)	(lac.)	Saosdoukhinos: 20 years
Sardanapallos: 21 years (F8b)[21]	Kandalan: 21 years	Kineladanos: 22 years
	Sin-shum-lishin and Sin-shar-ishkun: 1 year	
Nabopalassaros: 21 years (F8b, F9a)	Nabopalassar: 21 years	Nabopolassaros: 21 years
Naboukhodonosoros: 43 years (F8b, F9a, F9b, F9c, F10a, F10b, F11)	Nebuchadnezzar (II): 43 years	Nabokolassaros: 43 years
Euilmaradokhos: 2 years (F10a), but Amelmarudokhos: 12 years (F10b)	Amel-Marduk: 2 years	Illoaroudamos: 2 years
Neriglisaros: 4 years (F10a, F10b)	Neriglissar (lac.): > 2 years, 8 months	Nerigasolassaros: 4 years
Laborosoardokhos: 9 months (F10a)	Labashi-Marduk (lac.): > 3 months	
Nabonnedos (F10a) or Nabodenos (F10b): 17 years	Nabonidus (lac.): > 15 years	Nabonadios: 17 years

---

19. *ANET*[3] 566.

20. The *Ptolemaic Canon* exists in several copies and was much used in Byzantine times. Our list is based on the copy of the canon that appears in Wachsmuth, *Einleitung in das Studium der alten Geschichte*, 305–306. Two lists, which appear in Syncellus *Ecloga Chronographica* 390–396, seem to be based on the *Ptolemaic Canon*, but, nevertheless, contain some spellings and some lengths of regnal years different from those of the *Ptolemaic Canon*.

21. On the mistaken identification of Sardanapallos as the son of Assurbanipal, see F8b, n. 37.

Kings of Babylon	Kings of Assyria[22]
Shamash-shum-ukin (667–648)	Assurbanipal (668–629)
Kandalanu (647–627)	
interregnum	Ashur-etil-ilami
Nabu-apal-usur (625–605)	Senshumu-liser Sin-shar-ishhur (??? –612) Ashur-uballit II (611–609)
Nebuchadnezzar II (604–562)	
Evil-Merodach (561–560)	
Neriglissar (559–556)	
Labashi-Marduk (556)	
Nabonidus (555–539)	

22. Lists of the kings of Babylon and Assyria are based on Brinkman, "Appendix: Mesopo-tamian Chronology of the Historical Period," 335–340 on the lists in *CAH²*.

Berossos's Kings	*Uruk King-List*	*Ptolemaic Canon*
Kyros: 9 years (F9c, F10a, F10b, F11)	Kyros: 9 years	Kyros: 9 years
Kambyses: 8 years (F11)	Kambyses: 8 years	Kambyses: 8 years
Dareios: 36 years (F9c, F11)	Dareios: 36 years	Dareios I: 36 years
Xerxes (F11)	(lac.)	Xerxes: 21 years
		Artaxerxes I: 41 years
		Dareios II: 19 years
		Artaxerxes: 46 years
Artaxerxes Okhos (F12)		Okhos: 21 years
		Arogos: 2 years
	Darius (III): 5 years	Dareios III: 4 years
	Alexander: 7 years	Alexander of Macedon: 8 years
	Philip: 6 years	Philip: 7 years
	Antigonus: 6 years	Alexander II: 12 years
	Seleukos (I): 31 years	(Egyptian kings listed)
	Antiochos (I): 22 years	

Kings of Babylon	Kings of Assyria
Cyrus the Great (538–530)	
Cambyses (529–522)	
Bardija (522)	
Nebuchadnezzar III (522)	
Nebuchadnezzar IV (521)	
Darius I (521–486)	
Xerxes (485–465)	
Bel-shimanni (482)	
Artaxerxes I (464–424)	
Xerxes II (424)	
Darius II (423–405)	
Artaxerxes II Memnon (404–359)	
Artaxerxes III Ochus (359–338)	
Arses (337–336)	
Darius III (335–331)	
Alexander III (330–323)	
Philip Arrhidaeus (323–316)	
Alexander IV (316–307)	
Seleucus I Nicator (305–281)	
Antiochus I Soter (281–261)	

Table C. Jacoby's Numbering for Berossos's Testimony and Fragments with Our Corresponding Numbering

Jacoby[23]		Verbrugghe and Wickersham
T1	Eusebius *Chronicon* p. 6, line 14 Karst = Syncellus *Ecloga Chronographica* 25–27	T11a
T2	Eusebius *Praeparatio Evangelica* 10.11.8–9 = Tatianus *Oratio ad Graecos* 36	T7
T3	Eusebius *Chronicon* p. 21 Karst = Josephus *contra Apionem* 1.128–131	T4
	Theophilus *ad Autolycum* 3.22	F9c
	Josephus *Antiquitates Judaicae* 1.107	F15c
	Tertullian *Apologeticum* 19	T6
	Expositio Totius Mundi et Gentium 2	T9
T4	Moses of Chorene *Historia Armeniae* 1.1	T10
T5a	Vitruvius *de Architectura* 9.6.2	T1a
T5b	Vitruvius *de Architectura* 9.2.1	T1b, F16
T5c	Vitruvius *de Architectura* 9.8.1	T1c
T6	Pliny *Naturalis Historia* 7.123	T3b
T7a	Pausanias *Graeciae Descriptio* 10.12.9	T5
T7b	*Suda* s.v. "The Delphic Sibyl"	T12
T7c	Pseudo-Justinus *ad Gentes* 37	T8
T8a	Josephus *Antiquitates Judaicae* 1.107	F15c
T8b	Syncellus *Ecloga Chronographica* 25	T11a
T8c	Syncellus *Ecloga Chronographica* 390	F7
T8d	Agathias *Historiae* 2.24	F13
T9	Seneca *Naturales Questiones* 3.29.1	T2, F19
T10	Eusebius *Chronicon* p. 6, line 14 Karst = Syncellus *Ecloga Chronographica* 29	T11b
	Tatianus *Oratio ad Graecos* 36	T7
	Josephus *contra Apionem* 1.128–29	T4
T11a	Pliny *Naturalis Historia* 1.7	T3a
T11b	Palchus 135	F22
F1a	Eusebius *Chronicon* p. 6, line 8–p. 9, line 2 Karst =	
F1b	Syncellus *Ecloga Chronographica* 49–53	F1

---

23. *FGrHist*, vol. III C 1 (1958), Berossos #680, pp. 364–397.

Jacoby		**Verbrugghe and Wickersham**
F2	Athenaeus *Deipnosophistae* 14.44 p. 639C	F2
F3a	Eusebius *Chronicon* p. 4, line 8–p. 6, line 8 Karst =	
F3b	Syncellus *Ecloga Chronographica* 71–72	F3
F4a	Eusebius *Chronicon* p. 10, line 17–p. 12, line 6 Karst	not translated
F4b	Syncellus *Ecloga Chronographica* 53–56	F4a
F4c	Eusebius *Praeparatio Evangelica* 9.10.7–9.11.4 = Josephus *Antiquitates Judaicae* 1.93	F4b
F5a	Eusebius *Chronicon* p. 12, line 17–p. 13, line 18 Karst	F5
F5b	Syncellus *Ecloga Chronographica* 147	not translatcd
F6	Eusebius *Praeparatio Evangelica* 9.16.2 = Josephus *Antiquitates Judaicae* 1.158	F6
F7a	Josephus *Antiquitates Judaicae* 10.20	F8a
F7b	Josephus *Antiquitates Judaicae* 10.34	F8c
F7c	Eusebius *Chronicon* p. 13, line 18–p. 15, line 4 Karst	F8b
F7d	Syncellus *Ecloga Chronographica* 396	not translated
F8a	Eusebius *Chronicon* p. 21 Karst = Eusebius *Praeparatio Evangelica* 9.40.1–2 = Syncellus *Ecloga Chronographica* 416–418 = Josephus *Antiquitates Judaicae* 10.220–228 = Josephus *contra Apionem* 1.131–144	F9a
F8b	Clemens of Alexandria *Stromata* 1.122.1 = Eusebius *Praeparatio Evangelica* 10.11.8–9 = Tatianus *Oratio ad Graecos* 36	T7
F8c	Africanus ex Eusebii *Praeparatione Evangelica* 10.10.3	F9b
F8d	Theophilus *ad Autolycum* 3.22	F9c
F9a	Eusebius *Chronicon* p. 23, line 24 Karst = Eusebius *Praeparatio Evangelica* 9.40.3–11 = Josephus *contra Apionem* 1.145–153	F10a
F9b	Eusebius *Chronicon* p. 15, lines 5–10 Karst	F10b
F10	Eusebius *Chronicon* p. 15, lines 11–20 Karst	F11
F11	Clemens of Alexandria *Protrepticus* 5.65.2–3	F12
F12	Agathias *Historiae* 2.24	F13

Jacoby		Verbrugghe and Wickersham
F13	Hesychius s. v. "Sarakhero"	F14
F14	Eusebius *Praeparatio Evangelica* 9.13.5 = Syncellus *Ecloga Chronographica* 78 = Josephus *Antiquitates Judaicae* 1.107	F15c
F15	Palchus 135	F22
F16a	Syncellus *Ecloga Chronographica* 388 (390)	F7
F16b	Pliny *Naturalis Historia* 7.193	F20
F17	*Commentariorum in Aratum Reliquiae* pp. 142–43 Maass	F21
F18	Cleomedes *de Motu Circulari Corporum Caelestium* 2.4	F18
F19a	Aetius *de Placitis Reliquiae* p. 356 Diels	F17a
F19b	Aetius *de Placitis Reliquiae* p. 358 Diels	F17b
F19c	Aetius *de Placitis Reliquiae* p. 359 Diels	F17c
F20	Vitruvius *de Architectura* 9.2.1–2	F16
F21	Seneca *Naturales Quaestiones* 3.29.1	F19
F22a	Pliny *Naturalis Historia* 7.160	F15a
F22b	Censorinus *de Die Natali* 17.4	F15b

Table D. Our Numbering Corresponding to Jacoby's[24]
and Burstein's[25] Numbering for Berossos's Fragments

Verbrugghe/ Wickersham	Jacoby #680	Burstein
F1	F1	Book One, 1.1–2.4 (pp. 13–15)
F2	F2	Book One, 6.1 (p. 17)
F3	F3	Book Two, 1.1–11 (pp. 18–19)
		Book Two, 5.2 (p. 22)
F4a, F4b	F4b, F4c	Book Two, 2.1–4 (pp. 20–21)
F5	F5a	Book Two, 4.1–10 and Book Three, 1 (pp. 21–22, 23)
F6	F6	Book Two, 3 (p. 21)
F7	F16a	Book Two, 5.1 (p. 22)
F8a, F8c, F8b	F7	Book Three, 2.5a and 6a (pp. 25–26) and Book Three, 2.1 and 2.2a (pp. 23–24)
F9a, F9b, F9c	F8	Book Three, 3.1–3 (pp. 26–28)
F10a, F10b	F9	Book Three, 4 (p. 28)
F11	F10	Book Three, 5.1 (p. 29)
F12	F11	Book Three, 5.2 (p. 29)
F13	F12	not translated
F14	F13	Book One, 6.2 (p. 17)
F15a	F22a	not translated
F15b	F22b	not translated
F15c	F14	Book Three, 6.1 (p. 29)
F16	F20	Book One, 4 (p. 16)
F17	F19	not translated
F18	F18	not translated
F19	F21	Book One, 3 (p. 15)
F20	F16b	not translated
F21	F17	not translated
F22	F15	not translated

24. *FGrHist*, vol. III C 1 (1958), Berossos #680, pp. 364–397.

25. Stanley Burstein, *The Babyloniaca of Berossus*, Sources and Monographs: Sources from the Ancient Near East, vol. 1, no. 5 (Malibu, 1978). Burstein does not include in his translation any of the ancient testimony on Berossos.

Burstein includes as part of Berossos's *History* fragments from a later Greek historian, Abydenos,[26] which we do not translate.

Jacoby #685   Burstein

F1	Book One, 5 (p. 17)
F5	Book Three, 2.2b–4 (p. 24)
	Book Three, 2.5b and 2.6b–c (pp. 25 and 26)
F6	Book Three, 3.2b (p. 27)

In addition, Burstein includes as fragments of Berossos's *History* two passages from two other ancient authors, which we do not translate.

Aelian *De natura Animalium* (*On Animals*) 12.21	Burstein—Book Three, 6.2 (p. 29–30)
Damascius *de Principiis* (*On Beginnings*) Vol. 1, p. 322	Burstein—Book Three, 7 (p. 30)

---

26. *FGrHist*, vol. III C 1 (1958), Abydenos #685, pp. 398–410.

Table E. Ancient and Medieval Authors Who Preserve or Mention Berossos with Our Corresponding Numbering of the Fragments

Aetius
   de Placitis Reliquiae 2.25.12   F17a
   de Placitis Reliquiae 2.28.1   F17b
   de Placitis Reliquiae 2.29.2   F17c
Agathias
   Historiae 2.24   F13
Athenaeus
   Deipnosophistae 14.44 p. 639C   F2
Censorinus
   de Die Natali 17.4   F15b
Clemens of Alexandria
   Stromata 1.122.1 = Tatianus *Oratio ad Graecos* 36 = Eusebius   T7
      Praeparatio Evangelica 10.11.8–9
   Protrepticus 5.65.2–3   F12
Cleomedes
   de Motu Circulari Corporum Caelestium 2.4   F18
Commentariorum in Aratum Reliquiae pp. 142–43 Maass   F21
Eusebius
   Chronicon p. 12, line 17–p. 13, line 18 Karst   F5
   Chronicon p. 13, line 18–p. 15, line 4 Karst   F8b
   Chronicon p. 15, lines 5–10 Karst   F10b
   Chronicon p. 15, lines 11–20 Karst   F11
   Josephus *contra Apionem* 1.128–131 = *Chronicon* p. 21 Karst   T4
   Josephus *contra Apionem* 1.131–144 = Josephus *Antiquitates Judaicae* 10.220–228 = *Chronicon* p. 21 Karst = *Praeparatio Evangelica* 9.40.1–2 = Syncellus *Ecloga Chronographica* 416–18   F9a
   Josephus *Antiquitates Judaicae* 1.93 = *Praeparatio Evangelica* 9.10.7–9.11.4   F4b
   Josephus *Antiquitates Judaicae* 1.107 = *Praeparatio Evangelica* 9.13.5   F15c
   Josephus *Antiquitates Judaicae* 1.158 = *Praeparatio Evangelica* 9.16.2   F6
   Josephus *contra Apionem* 1.145–153 = *Praeparatio Evangelica* 9.40.3–12   F10a
   Praeparatio Evangelica 10.10.3   F9b

Eusebius (continued)

Praeparatio Evangelica 10.11.8–9 = Tatianus *Oratio ad Graecos* 36 = Clemens of Alexandria *Stromata* 1.122.1	T7
Syncellus *Ecloga Chronographica* 25–27 = *Chronicon* p. 6, line 14 Karst	T11a
Syncellus *Ecloga Chronographica* 29–30 = *Chronicon* p. 6, line 14 Karst	T11b
Syncellus *Ecloga Chronographica* 32	T11c
Syncellus *Ecloga Chronographica* 50–53 = *Chronicon* p. 6, line 8–p. 9, line 2 Karst	F1
Syncellus *Ecloga Chronographica* 53, 30, 71–72 = *Chronicon* p. 4, line 8–p. 6, line 8 Karst	F3
Syncellus *Ecloga Chronographica* 53–56 = *Chronicon* p. 10, line 17–p. 12, line 6 Karst	F4a
Syncellus *Ecloga Chronographica* 390	F7
Expositio Totius Mundi et Gentium 2	T9

Hesychius

Lexicon s.v. "Sarakhero"	F14

Josephus

Antiquitates Judaicae 1.93 = Eusebius *Praeparatio Evangelica* 9.10.7–9.11.4	F4b
Antiquitates Judaicae 1.107 = Eusebius *Praeparatio Evangelica* 9.13.5	F15c
Antiquitates Judaicae 1.158 = Eusebius *Praeparatio Evangelica* 9.16.2	F6
Antiquitates Judaicae 10.20	F8a
Antiquitates Judaicae 10.34	F8c
contra Apionem 1.128–131	T4
contra Apionem 1.131–144 = Josephus *Antiquitates Judaicae* 10.220–228 = *Chronicon* p. 21 Karst = *Praeparatio Evangelica* 9.40.1–2 = Syncellus *Ecloga Chronographica* 416–18	F9a
contra Apionem 1.145–153	F10a

Moses of Chorene

Historia Armeniae 1.1	T10

Palchus

Catalogus Codicum Astrologorum Graecorum 135	F22

Pausanias

Graeciae Descriptio 10.12.9	T5

Manetho

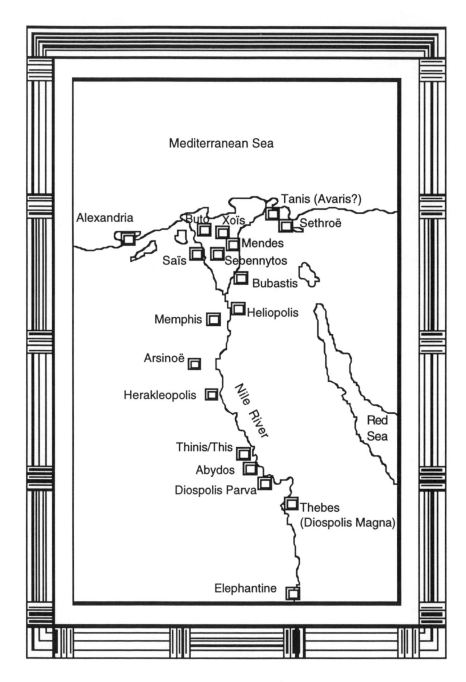

Map 3. Manetho's Egypt

CHAPTER 5

Introduction to Manetho

Manetho was the Egyptian counterpart of Berossos. Like Berossos, he was living and active in the earliest phase of the new Hellenistic rulership—when the successors of Alexander the Great had become kings in their own right and own name. Like Berossos, he was a native and a priest, representative of the most expert and learned class of a most ancient and respected non-Greek nation. Like Berossos, he was most opportunely placed to mediate between his own ancient national traditions and the new influx of Macedonian rulers and Greek immigrants.

Manetho's Life and Work

Manetho's name was Egyptian, but no Egyptian version of it has survived. Conjectures about this original version and its etymology have included "Gift of Thoth,"[1] "Beloved of Thoth," "Beloved of Neith,"[2] "Lover of Neith," and "Truth of Thoth." Among further suggestions, one assumes an original *Myinyu-heter,* meaning "Horseherd," or "Groom," while another advances *Ma'ani-Djehuti,* "I have seen Thoth." We are also offered "Beloved by the Great God" and, most recently, "Temple Guardian." For present purposes, we should ask how Manetho wrote his name in Greek and how we ought to ren-

---

1. The versions involving Thoth are immensely apt, since the ibis-headed Thoth was god of writing and recording. See, for example, the relief from Ramesses's temple at Abydos that shows Thoth painting cartouches and annals, reproduced in D. B. Redford, *Pharaonic King-Lists, Annals, and Day-Books: A Contribution to the Study of the Egyptian Sense of History,* SSEA Publication 4 (Mississauga, Ontario, 1986), plate IV. Also apt would be a version involving the word *menesh,* "cartouche."

2. Neith was an old Egyptian goddess of weapons, worshiped at several places, including Sais. The Greeks equated her with Athena.

der it here in the Roman alphabet. The Greek sources present a fine variety, transcribable as Manethôn, Manethôs, Manethô, Manethos, Manêthôs, Manêthôn, and even the Egyptian-looking Manethôth. The Latin sources offer Manethon, Manethos, Manethonus, and Manetos. We have decided to assume that Manethôn was our author's Greek version of his own name: this is the form preferred in our oldest witnesses—the Carthage inscription (T1), the Hibeh papyrus (T2), and Josephus (T3a, T3b, F9–F12).[3] It has been the convention in English-speaking scholarship to render the names of Greek authors in the Roman alphabet and a classical Latin form (e.g., Platôn —> Plato), so we will refer to Manetho as Manetho.

Manetho came from Sebennytos (T4, T10b, T12, F25), a settlement on the east branch of the Nile in the delta. No ancient source mentions a date of birth or death, but his activities are connected with the reigns of Ptolemy I Soter[4] (323–283 B.C.; T4) and Ptolemy II Philadelphos (285–246 B.C.; T10b). The papyrus of T2 is datable to 241/0 B.C., and if, as is likely, the Manetho mentioned in it is our Manetho, then we find him still active in the reign of Ptolemy III Euergetes (246–222 B.C.).

He was a priest, even a chief priest, and perhaps specifically of the temple of the sun god Ra[5] at Heliopolis (Pseudo-Manetho *Book of Sothis* T1a–b, F1). He acquired influence beyond this, because he became a practical authority in the cult of Sarapis. The name of the god Sarapis came from the Egyptian "Osiris-Apis"; from the time of the New Kingdom, bulls named Apis and kept at Memphis were sacrificed, then mummified and preserved in catacombs in the Memphite necropolis at the modern Saqqara.[6] The cult of Sarapis was a Greco-Macedonian appropriation of this Egyptian cult, preserving at least the name and the victim. The new cult seems to have first begun un-

---

3. Josephus of Judea, born A.D. 37–38, was captured by the Romans in the Jewish War of A.D. 66–73 and was settled in Rome, where he ultimately attained Roman citizenship. His writings include *de Bello Judaico* (*The Jewish War*), *Antiquitates Judaicae* (*Jewish Antiquities*, on the history of the Jews), and *contra Apionem* (*Against Apion*, defending Jewish heritage against a detractor). The last is especially valuable for the study of Manetho.

4. Ptolemy the son of Lagos was a lieutenant of Alexander the Great. After the death of Alexander (323 B.C.), Ptolemy took possession of Egypt (as well as the body of Alexander), declared himself king in ca. 305, and founded the Ptolemaic Dynasty, which ruled Egypt for nearly three centuries until Cleopatra VII and the Roman conquest of Egypt by Octavian (Augustus) in 30 B.C.

5. Ra was the sun god and chief god of the Egyptians from the time of the Old Kingdom on. The Theban god Amon was combined with Ra during the New Kingdom. Amon-Ra was equated by the Greeks with Zeus.

6. For further information on the Apis cult, see Dorothy J. Thompson, *Memphis under the Ptolemies* (Princeton, 1989), 27–31.

der Alexander the Great, in connection with his foundation of Alexandria in Egypt (332/1 B.C.).[7] One central feature—the statue of the god—was lacking for many years. This need was filled in some year between 286 and 278 B.C., when Ptolemy (either Ptolemy I Soter, late in his reign, or Ptolemy II Philadelphos, early in his) arranged to bring an idol from Sinope, a Greek colony far away on the Black Sea.[8] Two men were consulted by Ptolemy throughout the process, the Athenian Timotheus (member of a clan with authority in the cult of Demeter at Eleusis)[9] and our Manetho (T4). The cult of Sarapis, often combined with that of Isis (= Demeter), spread well beyond Egypt. The inscription of T1 connecting Manetho with the cult of Sarapis at Carthage suggests that Manetho continued to act as consultant for new foundations. His involvement here shows him mediating between Egyptian and Hellenic institutions, a role that continues in his literary activities.

All of Manetho's writings were, on the one hand, on Egyptian subjects and, on the other hand, written in Greek. We do not know when he wrote each or in what order. Much of the testimony concerning Manetho quite rightly makes his activities parallel in form and spirit to those of Berossos (T6, T9, T10a). T10b goes farther in asserting that Manetho's work (specifically the *History of Egypt*) appeared at about the same time as or slightly after that of Berossos and was an imitation of Berossos, but we cannot rely on this report, which is more likely to be an inference from the other undoubted parallels than a reflection of solid information. Our sources mention eight separate titles: the *History of Egypt*, *Against Herodotus*, the *Sacred Book*, *On Antiquity and Religion*, *On Festivals*, *On the Preparation of Kyphi*, the *Digest of Physics*, and the *Book of Sothis*.

The *History of Egypt* (T3a–b, T6, T7, T8a–d, T9, T10a–c, F1–F16) is by far the most important of Manetho's writings—not only to us, perhaps, but also to Manetho himself. It was long enough to be divided into three *tomoi* ("scrolls," "volumes," or "books"). We might imagine it as filling up one average-sized volume of an Oxford classical text, nearly as much as one-quarter the bulk of Herodotus's *Histories*.[10]

---

7. Egypt had had many capitals (i.e., the place of the ruler's throne). Alexandria was the seat of the Ptolemies.

8. Sinope was founded by Miletos in the eighth century B.C., destroyed by barbarians, and re-founded by 600 B.C.

9. A sanctuary near Athens, site of the most prestigious mystery cult of the ancient world.

10. Herodotus of Halicarnassus, ca. 484–ca. 430 B.C., known as the "Father of History," wrote nine volumes (the *Histories*) describing the Persian Wars of 490–479 B.C. He included much about the history and culture of many peoples; all of book 2 and the beginning of book 3 are devoted to Egypt.

It had a clear chronological organization, proceeding in order from the earliest (the gods) to the latest (just before the conquest by Alexander the Great). The main thread was the succession of rulers: Manetho named every one he could and stated the length of the reign. Manetho further divided the series of rulers into a series of "dynasties." *Dynasteia* was Manetho's Greek word for each grouping, and it appears that this was a new and original move. Outside of Manetho, the Greek word had the abstract sense "governmental power" or denoted the power of a particular ruler. Only in Manetho does it acquire the sense of a sequence of potentates with a common origin or other unifying feature. Manetho did not find this succession of dynasties explicitly so designated in the Egyptian or other sources he may have used.[11] The Turin Royal Canon at some points makes a total of years, and these points are often the same points at which Manetho divides his dynasties, but the thoroughgoing application of the method was in no sense ready-made for him.[12] Whenever he perceived a discontinuity in the locale of the rulers, and also if he saw any other sort of discontinuity, especially of family, he called that a change of "dynasty" (e.g., Dynasty IV from Memphis, Dynasty V from Elephantine). In the outline for his first dynasty, each successor is explicitly noted as "son"; one must infer that this is to clarify at the beginning what he will mean by a continuity of "dynasty."[13] Manetho, therefore, deserves the credit for coining this much-used term of historical discourse.

Interwoven with this outline of rulers and dynasties was a substantial fabric of narrative and other historical exposition. One can get the feel of this component best—if at all—from the excerpts in Josephus's *contra Apionem* (*Against Apion*; F9, F10, F12).[14] As Greek, it is very good *Koinê*,[15] and the pace is indeed worthy of an ancient Greek historian.

---

11. Hekataios of Abdera (late fourth century B.C.) wrote historical works, now lost, dealing with the Jews, the Hyperboreans, and Egypt. The last is suggested by some as a Greek model for Manetho, but the remains (*FGrHist* #264) indicate that Hekataios was a successor to Herodotus rather than a predecessor of Manetho.

12. Further description of the Turin Royal Canon comes later in this chapter.

13. Manetho's reasons for changing dynasties may at times elude us. Dynasties III–VIII are all from Memphis, Dynasties XI–XIII are all from Thebes, while Dynasties XVII and XVIII are from Thebes and from the same family. Jaromir Málek, "The Original Version of the Royal Canon of Turin," *Journal of Egyptian Archaeology* 68 (1982): 93–106, suggests that the original layout of the Turin Royal Canon may have influenced Manetho's divisions.

14. On the need to be cautious about these excerpts, see "Manetho's *History of Egypt*—Reception and Transmission" later in this chapter.

15. *Koinê* means "the common language," the standard international form of Greek in the Hellenistic period.

Volume 1 contained, first, the predynastic reigns of gods, demigods, humans, and "spirits of the dead." Here might have been the quasi-heroic myths involving the divinities of Egypt, especially the struggles of Osiris, Isis, Seth, and the avenging Horus.[16] Rather than transliterate, Manetho gave Greek names for these figures. A set of equivalences was available long before Manetho: Ptah = Hephaistos, Isis = Demeter, Thoth = Hermes, Horus = Apollo, Seth = Typhon, and so forth.[17] Then began the sequence of fully human and mortal rulers whose dynasties would run through the rest of the work. For dynastic Egypt, volume 1 covered Dynasties I through XI. For Manetho as for us, this meant rulers of all Egypt, the pyramid builders (the Old Kingdom), then a period of regnal confusion where Manetho could not specify the names of the rulers (First Intermediate Period), and finally the beginning of a new stability (early Middle Kingdom). Manetho based the coherence of his outline on unity of rulership.

Volume 2 contained Dynasties XII–XIX. Dynasty XII continued the stability established by Dynasty XI (Middle Kingdom). Confusion set in again for Dynasties XIII–XIV, while XV–XVII brought a wave of foreign rulers (Second Intermediate Period).[18] Expulsion of the foreigners, reunited Egyptian rule, and imperial grandeur in Dynasties XVIII–XIX (New Kingdom) brought this volume to a close.

---

16. Isis and Osiris were siblings and mates; Horus was their son. Their evil brother Seth attacked Osiris and tore him limb from limb. Horus avenged his father by vanquishing Seth. Isis collected and reunited the pieces of Osiris, who then passed into eternal life beyond this world and time. Part of this myth's function was to validate the practice of mummification and the rest of Egyptian funeral practices and beliefs.

17. In these equivalences, the "Egyptian" names we use are themselves based on ancient Greek transcriptions. A modern transcription of the ancient Egyptian names (from hieroglyphic, hieratic, or demotic sources) yields different and stranger results. The name of the the god Thoth was spelled in hieroglyphs as

and is nowadays transcribed as Djehuti. Similarly, Horus would be Heru, Isis would be Aset, and Osiris would be Usir or even Wesir—very different from our usual versions.

18. Through Josephus (F9), the Egyptian term for the foreign rulers—"Hyksos"—was reintroduced into our tradition of discussing the episode and is now prevalent in our histories of Egypt. As translations of "Hyksos" Josephus offered "king-shepherds" or "captive-shepherds." It is not certain that Manetho himself gave "Hyksos" or either of these two interpretations. It is just as possible that, as the epitome (F2a at D. XVII, version of Eusebius in the Armenian and in Syncellus) indicates, Manetho translated "Hyksos" into Greek with the meaning "foreign kings," a rendering that accords well with modern Egyptologists' interpretation of "Hyksos" as "Lords of the Foreign Lands": see Alan H. Gardiner, *Egypt of the Pharaohs* (Oxford, 1961), 157; John van Seters, *The Hyksos, a New Investigation* (New Haven, 1966), 187; H. W. Helck and Eberhard Otto, *Kleines Wörterbuch der Aegyptologie* (Wiesbaden, 1987), 156. The Turin Royal Canon calls them *Heka-khasut*, "chieftains of a foreign country."

Volume 3 contained Dynasties XX–XXX (or XXXI). Dynasty XXV consisted of Ethiopian[19] rulers, and we refer to Dynasty XXVI as the Saite Renaissance.[20] Persian conquest interrupted native African rule, and Dynasty XXVII comprises eight stages of Persian rule from Kambyses son of Cyrus to Darius Nothos (father of Cyrus the Younger).[21] Three more native dynasties carried the series through the fourth century B.C., when Manetho considered Persian rule to be in abeyance. Dynasty XXXI has three Persian rulers, bringing Egypt to the eve of Macedonian rule. It is disputed whether Dynasty XXXI was actually included by Manetho or was added by a continuator. F16 and Jerome's Eusebius (see at F2a, D. XXX.3 and D. XXXI) say to stop with Nektanebos, the last king of Dynasty XXX, but otherwise Dynasty XXXI seems as well attested as any other dynasty and as well grounded in Manetho's purpose of showing who held the ruling power (*dynasteia*). Foreign rulers—Ethiopians and Persians—were certainly included by Manetho. Furthermore, it is a fitting ending for Manetho's overall outline in that it is the last complete dynasty: for Manetho Dynasty XXXII, Macedonians, had just begun.

Some have suggested that Manetho's *Against Herodotus* does not actually represent a separate opus but is a part of the *History of Egypt*[22] or perhaps a set of excerpts from it. That Manetho disputed Herodotus in the *History of Egypt* is attested by F1. In any case, Manetho had strong reasons for attacking Herodotus (whose account of Egypt occupies all of his book 2 and the beginning of book 3; the systematic presentation via a ruler-list begins at 2.99). Our one specific reference to Manetho's criticisms concerns the habits of lions (F17), but the disagreement goes much farther and deeper. As to format, Manetho's *History* began with a fairly long list of gods, demigods, heroes, and so forth. (see F2a and chap. 9, table B), but Herodotus had buried this era in the middle of his account (2.146) and named only Osiris, Typhon, and

---

19. Ethiopia here includes Nubia and other territory south of Egypt, the Nile Valley above the first cataract (at Elephantine).

20. The capital of these rulers was at Saïs, in the delta.

21. The sixth and fifth centuries of the Achaemenid dynasty of Persia: the founding by Cyrus the Great (who reigned from 559 to 530 B.C.); his son Kambyses (530–522), who conquered Egypt; the one-year rule by Bardiya, who was probably Kambyses's brother but is described by Darius I as an usurper from the priestly caste of Magoi; the dynasty "continued" by Darius I the Great (522–486; Darius was probably not directly related to Cyrus, but he made use of a genealogy tracing both himself and Cyrus back to an ancestor Achaemenes); Xerxes I (486–465), who attacked Greece in the great Persian War of 481–479; Artaxerxes I (464–424); Darius II Nothos (424–405). Egypt was in revolt under Artaxerxes II (404–358).

22. As part of *Iliad* 2 was called the "Catalog of Ships," and part of book 1 of Thucydides was referred to as the "Archaeology" and another part as the "Half-Century."

Horus. As to judgment, Herodotus, who had learned about 348 rulers from
Min,[23] the first king, up to the conquest by the Persian Kambyses, had decided that the first 330 who came after Min were not worth mentioning by
name, except for Nitokris[24] and Moiris.[25] As to chronological accuracy, although Herodotus and Manetho are close in the number of kings from
Min/Menes until Kambyses (Herodotus 348, Manetho 333), Herodotus's
count of years in that interval (ca. 11,500) is vastly discrepant with
Manetho's (ca. 5,100). Furthermore, Herodotus had excluded the Ethiopian
ruler Sabakos[26] from his count of rulers, but Manetho included him and other
rulers, although of "foreign" origin, in his ordering and reckoning. Also,
Manetho found that the Great Pyramid and its neighbors had been built by the
Fourth Dynasty and 4,300 years before Kambyses; Herodotus had dislocated
the whole dynasty and put it only twelve kings, about four hundred years, before the Persian conquest. This must have infuriated Manetho—certainly it
still astounds readers of Herodotus.

That the *Sacred Book* was about Egyptian theology is all that we can say
(T7). Of *On Antiquity and Religion*, one brief excerpt, concerning the re-
placement of human sacrificial victims with wax mannequins by Amosis, is
all that survives (F18). Of *On Festivals*, one incidental remark is preserved
(F19). *On the Preparation of Kyphi* dealt with the preparation of a mixture
and its uses as incense and balm. It is hard to imagine that the whole treatise
can have been much longer than the excerpts we possess (F20–F22). In the
Digest of Physics (F23), Manetho claimed that Egyptian science and philosophy were encoded in certain symbolic animals. Apart from this, it is hard to
separate Manetho from other writers whether they are named in this citation
or not. The *Physiologica (On Nature)* mentioned in T12 may be the same
work. F24–F29a, which mention Manetho but no title, could also derive from
this book; the subject matter sounds similar.

The medieval monk George Syncellus rescued the outline of the *History of
Egypt* for us by objectively quoting the entire versions of it that he found in

23. *Min* is Herodotus's version of the name of the ruler called Menes by Manetho (Dynasty
I.1).

24. Herodotus 2.100 describes the vengeance Nitokris took on her brother's killers. In
Manetho F2a, see D. VI.6.

25. Herodotus 2.101 describes Moiris's building activities and the creation of Lake Moiris. In
Manetho F2a, see D. XII.4 (Moiris = Lamares).

26. Herodotus 2.137 notes Sabakos's conquest of Upper Egypt. In Manetho F2a, see D.
XXV.2 (Sabakos = Sebikhos).

Africanus and Eusebius (F2a).[27] At another point, however, he vilified Manetho for presenting Egyptian history from a native Egyptian stance, and he quoted yet another version, which he said was called the *Book of Sothis*, and which he regarded as the genuine Manethonian history of Egypt, to be ranked ahead of Africanus's and Eusebius's versions. We are not to believe these claims of Syncellus. *Sothis*'s dedicatory letter to Ptolemy Philadelphos calls him "Augustus,"[28] a title that is plainly anachronistic and marks the piece as a forgery (Pseudo-Manetho *Book of Sothis* F1). It indeed seems to show some knowledge of the genuine *History of Egypt* by Manetho, and it may be of some interest or even use, especially in regard to the predynastic dynasties of gods and demigods. It does not, however, preserve the division into dynasties (although Syncellus says that it does), and the list of rulers is but a selection of 86 (versus the 129 named and more than 500 enumerated in the Africanus-Eusebius versions), beginning with the first ruler, but stopping at what would be the Twenty-sixth Dynasty—it is incredible that the genuine Manetho would have so amputated the Saite Twenty-eighth Dynasty or the Twenty-ninth Dynasty from Mendes and the Thirtieth Dynasty from Sebennytos, all three so close to Manetho's home. *Sothis* calls the first human ruler Mestraim[29] as well as Menes, and in many other ways as well it is so contaminated by Judaic or Judeo-Christian chronographic material that this element is dominant, while what may be Manethonian is a small part of its thrust. The texts preserving this hoax are sequestered as chapter 8 in this book, after the genuine Manetho fragments in chapter 7.

One other spurious work, the *Apotelesmatika* (*Astrological Influences*), attributed itself to Manetho or a Manetho. This work, six books of hexameter verse, survives complete and deals with astronomy and astrology. It dates, most likely, from the fourth century A.D. and so cannot be by our Manetho. Illustrative excerpts from it are included with the *Book of Sothis* excerpts in chapter 8 in this book. Some scholars have suggested that it belongs to a writer genuinely named Manetho. The preambles, however, with their dedications to "King Ptolemy" and their flourishes about "unenterable sacred books" and "secret inscriptions" seem a plain attempt to trade on our Manetho, his name, and the true and false lore about his sources and methods. There was only one Manetho.

---

27. On Africanus, Eusebius, and Syncellus, see "Berossos's *History of Babylonia*—Reception and Transmission" in chapter 1.

28. No ruler was called Augustus until the first Roman emperor, two centuries later than Manetho.

29. Mestraim (more familiarly Mizraim) is the Judaic, biblical name for Egypt.

Manetho's *History of Egypt*—Sources, Methods, and Reliability

As to how and where Manetho gathered his materials, we can be grateful to Josephus, who assures us that Manetho himself claimed to have translated from the "priestly writings" (F1), supplemented by "myths and legends," "nameless oral tradition" (F10). By "priestly writings" we may understand documents in either hieroglyphs—these would chiefly be inscriptions—or hieratic, the form of writing usual for brush and papyrus. As it happens, we have preserved examples of ancient Egyptian documents that harmonize with Manetho's outline based on a king-list. Examples of king-lists from the Old Kingdom and the New Kingdom are available for comparison with Manetho.

From the Old Kingdom, we have the Old Kingdom Annals, which were on a slab of diorite stone, originally perhaps seven feet long by two feet high, and which were inscribed and erected in the Fifth or Sixth Dynasty (ca. 2500–2200 B.C.) In hieroglyphs, this is the earliest of the Egyptian documents to be compared with Manetho in scope and format. It was inscribed on both sides with horizontal rows divided vertically into compartments. The first row dealt with predynastic rulers, and each compartment of that row contained only the name of one ruler. Thereafter each compartment contained a record for one year, the series continuing year by year through several rulers until the end of the monument and the Fifth Dynasty. It is not known where this inscription was originally erected. This slab was broken and now survives in fragments as the Palermo Stone, with the largest fragment now in the museum in Palermo, Sicily; four fragments now in Cairo; and one piece in the Petrie Museum, University College, London.

The Old Kingdom Annals do not seem to have been Manetho's immediate source. As far as we know, this was a unique object, whose original location is unknown, and we cannot say that Manetho would have had access to it. It is, however, the differences in content and format that are decisive. In the first place, the Old Kingdom Annals reached only to Dynasty V. Furthermore, whereas Manetho has predynastic deities and demigods, the Old Kingdom Annals have (presumably human) kings of Lower Egypt and kings of Upper Egypt (see chap. 9, table B).[30] Finally, and chiefly, the Old Kingdom Annals gave year-by-year accounts for the dynastic reigns, whereas we see no

---

30. Lower Egypt includes the delta. Upper Egypt includes the area from the delta to the first cataract (at Elephantine).

sign that Manetho's *History of Egypt* employed this degree of chronological detail.[31]

From the New Kingdom, we have Thutmose's list at Karnak, Seti's list at Abydos, the Saqqara list, and Ramesses's list at Abydos. Thutmose's[32] list at Karnak presented three walls of inscribed hieroglyphic cartouches[33] with a selection of sixty-one royal names, arranged in an order that is to us difficult to follow. In his list at Abydos Seti I (father of Ramesses II the Great) inscribed seventy-six hieroglyphic royal cartouches from Dynasty I to Dynasty XIX, in order, ending with Seti himself. Seti and his son are depicted making offerings to the rulers named in the cartouches. Omitted were rulers from the Second Intermediate Period, the Hyksos,[34] and those rulers of the dynasty just before Seti who had been close to the heretic Akhenaten.[35] The Saqqara list was found in the tomb of a scribe and priest named Tenry. Dating from the reign of Ramesses II, this is also a hieroglyphic inscription, similar to the preceding, with fifty-eight names, in order, and with the same omissions as the preceding. As with Seti and Ramesses in the Abydos list, Tenry is depicted making prayers to the named rulers. Ramesses's list at Abydos duplicated his father Seti's Abydos list, but brought it up to date with himself.

All of the preceding king-lists from the New Kingdom differ from each other in arrangement and elaborateness, but they have one feature that disqualifies them all from being Manetho's immediate source: to one extent or another, each is selective by comparison with Manetho. In other words, Manetho could not have gotten the comprehensive and orderly outline that is plain to see in the fragments (especially F2a) by using any or all of these Pharaonic lists.

---

31. Between the Old Kingdom Annals and Manetho, there also appears a difference in the kind of event noted. The Annals recorded Nile heights and cultic acts by the king, while Manetho mentioned events of more interest to a Greek historian.

32. Thutmose III, ca. 1490–1440 B.C. (Dynasty XVIII). The modern Karnak is in ancient Thebes.

33. From the Old Kingdom on, it became the custom to enclose two of the pharaoh's names (specifically the throne name and the personal name) within a lozenge-shaped design: ▭. We call this enclosure by the French word *cartouche*. See Jürgen von Beckerath, *Handbuch der ägyptischen Königsnamen* (Munich and Berlin, 1984), 34–37, which discusses the significance of this practice and dates its introduction to the reign of Sneferu (first king of the fourth Dynasty). This practice makes it easy to spot a royal name in a text, and it was immensely helpful to the modern decipherers of ancient Egyptian writing (e.g., Champollion).

34. The Hyksos were invaders from Asia who dominated Egypt during the Second Intermediate Period, ca.1640–1532 B.C. (Dynasties XV–XVI).

35. Akhenaten (Dynasty XVIII) attempted to replace Amon-Ra with Aten, the solar disc that is a specific aspect of the sun god. His reform hardly survived his own reign.

Furthermore, the purpose of these lists was to cover the walls of a sacred room in which the reigning Pharaoh (or other worshiper, as in the case of Tenry and his Saqqara list) made offerings or prayers to his or her predecessors, imagined as ancestors. Each royal house had a particular traditional list of these "ancestors," different from that of other houses. The purpose of these lists is not historical but religious. It is not that they are trying and failing to give a complete list. They are not trying at all. Seti and Ramesses did not wish to make offerings to Akhenaten, Tutankhamen, or Hatshepsut, and that is why they are omitted, not because their existence was unknown or deliberately ignored in a broader historical sense. For this reason, Pharaonic king-lists were generically wrong for Manetho's purposes, and we should commend Manetho for not basing himself on them.

Of course, we must not assume that Manetho took the trouble to travel and study these immovable lists, some of which lay far up the Nile. If Manetho preferred to base himself on something near to hand in the library, this would be quite in accordance with the dominant methods of Hellenistic Greek historiography, Manetho's new adoptive métier. Manetho's main source is most likely, therefore, to have been something both comprehensive, orderly, and portable or on hand.

The right sort of thing is exemplified by the Turin Papyrus, containing the Turin Royal Canon, a papyrus written in the hieratic script. The papyrus itself, now in the Museum of Torino, Italy, dates from about the time of Ramesses II (ca. 1290–1224 B.C., Dynasty XIX). When complete, it contained, in order, the names of over three hundred kings with the lengths of the life and reign of each. Its special importance for illuminating Manetho lies in the fact that it is the only one of these Egyptian documents to begin with the very earliest time, that of the gods. Furthermore, it presents "the remains of a genuine chronicle remarkably like the Manetho of Africanus and Eusebius,"[36]—that is, in epitome. It may originally have extended its records down to contemporary kings. It occasionally gave totals of the number of kings and years elapsed; the number of kings is close to that given by Manetho. Much of it is now imperfect or missing, especially toward the end of what survives, which comes almost to the Eighteenth Dynasty.

This Turin Royal Canon was not identical with Manetho's main source, since there is considerable difference of content in the overlapping portions.[37] It proves, nevertheless, the existence of materials well suited to provide a ba-

---

36. Gardiner, *Egypt of the Pharaohs*, 47.
37. For further discussion of the relationship between Manetho and the Turin Royal Canon, see Málek, "The Original Version of the Royal Canon of Turin."

sis for the overall plan of Manetho's historical project. Furthermore, it should be noted that the other side of the papyrus contains accounts from, apparently, a government office. There is a connection between the two sides in that certain governmental records would require a complete and orderly catalog of rulers, in order to date contracts, leases, debts, titles, and other instruments. Such a list could not afford the selectivity of, for example, Seti's offering list. Just as there was a strong reason why royal king-lists were not suitable for Manetho, there was a strong reason why a bureaucratic office would have a list that was suitable.

We do not need to imagine, however, that Manetho first conceived of his project to write a history of Egypt and only then began to search for suitable materials, such as the king-list with regnal lengths. Because Manetho was an Egyptian priest and therefore received the highest class of literate education, it is far more likely that he grew up among such documents, standard equipment for the priestly establishments that were his homes and schools. Because priestly establishments had a considerable economic aspect involving produce, manufactures, and rents with the pertinent titles and contracts, a priesthood was likely to have possessed a complete king-list. It was not necessary for Manetho to comb other bureaus.[38]

That Manetho's materials were already known to him well before he executed his project should be true not just for his basic outline (the king-list with lengths of reign) but also for the narrative sections. The priestly libraries could also possess written accounts of legendary or historical events, and these accounts would also have been a part of Manetho's education and his life well before he became a Greek historian. Many such narratives from ancient Egypt have survived. They comprise divine myths; quasi-epic material; tales about rulers, priests, and other dignitaries; and also accounts of historical events.[39] Not enough of Manetho has survived to allow a specific comparison with any of them. In general, however, they prove the plentiful existence of relevant material for Manetho to translate. Added to the outline, this narrative element made Manetho's *History of Egypt* nearly complete. Josephus's statement (F1) that Manetho translated the priestly writings into Greek would therefore be true not merely as to the nature of the language and form of the writings—the hieroglyphic or hieratic writing, in which the priests were the

---

38. It is, of course, possible that Manetho used more than one list, as is concluded by H. W. Helck, *Untersuchungen zu Manetho und den ägyptischen Königslisten, Untersuchungen zur Geschichte und Altertumskunde Aegyptens* 18 (Berlin, 1956), 15–16.

39. Examples can be read in *ANET*[3] 3–10, 227–263.

most literate and authoritative—but also as to the content, which was furnished precisely by priestly libraries.

Josephus also mentioned that Manetho used nonwritten sources as well (F10: "nameless oral tradition"; F12: "myths and legends"), and Josephus claims that this declaration, as for the written sources, was made by Manetho himself. We can certainly accept this claim and understand it as a component of Manetho's methods. We must beware of the modern historian's avoidance of oral tradition as unsupported rumor. It was actually one of the main tasks for historians in antiquity to record and preserve the traditions of the community. They did not see why an account would be made more credible merely by being in writing, or why a written tale would be truer than a tale with generations of oral transmission behind it. On the contrary, age and traditional status gave a tale more claim to be believed, not less. To put it in writing made it more widely portable but did not change its truth.[40] In treating history as vulgate, Manetho is upholding the same standards as the rest of the mainstream of ancient Greek historiography, as it was conceived and practiced by Herodotus and onward. Josephus, to be sure, mentions Manetho's oral source to attack it as false while the part that comes from the "priestly writings" is regarded as acceptable. This is, however, because Josephus disgrees with the *content* of the oral material. It is offensive to Josephus's own findings as to Jewish history. If the situation were reversed— if, that is, Manetho's written sources had said that the Jews originated from a rabble of Egyptian misfits and pariahs (F12)—then Josephus would still have refuted the account, regardless of its status as "written."

Manetho's lifelong intimacy with his Egyptian material is simple to imagine. It is more difficult to conjecture how Manetho became learned in Greek language and literature. It is at least certain that he knew Greek literature well enough to know Herodotus's writings on Egypt and to make it one of his goals to correct what he considered Herodotus's mistakes (F1).[41] One may also catch some impression of Manetho's command of Hellenic lore, if one peruses the condensed version of the *History of Egypt* that appears in F2a. It contains a few cases where an Egyptian reign is synchronized with Greek matters. These cases are as follows:

---

40. See Paul Veyne, *Did the Greeks Believe in Their Myths?* trans. P. Wissing (Chicago, 1987), chap. 2.

41. Manetho's possible complaints about Herodotus are discussed earlier in this chapter.

Dynasty	Ruler	Comment in the Condensed Version
XVIII.8	Amenophis	It is believed that Memnon, the talking statue, is this king.
XVIII.14	Armesis (Armais, Armaios)	This king is also known as Danaos. Persecuted by his brother Aigyptos, he fled Egypt and came to Greece, where he became king of Argos.[42]
XIX.6	Thouoris	This is the king called Polybos, the husband of Alkandra, by Homer.[43] Troy was captured in his reign.
XXIII.2	Osorkho	The Egyptians called him Herakles.

Some have assumed that these synchronisms were added by later editors of this condensed version of Manetho. This is quite possible, but it is also still possible that they stood in the original. If one accepts them as authentic, then one could infer that Manetho was familiar with the Epic Cycle (in which the Ethiopian hero Memnon comes to the Trojan War and is slain by Achilles),[44] with the myths regarding the prehistory of Argos (Danaos and Aigyptos; see Aeschylus *Suppliants*), and with Homer (Polybos and Alkandra are mentioned in *Odyssey* 4.126.) This evidence, slim and debatable though it is, hints at a solid grounding in Hellenic lore.[45]

How did Manetho translate his Egyptian materials into Greek? For some matters, specifically the names of gods, the Greeks already had standard translations, and Manetho accepted them. For most names, however, Manetho

42. According to the Greek myth, Zeus dallied with the Argive princess Io. To fool Hera, he turned Io into a hiefer. Hera, not fooled, sent a gadfly to torment Io, who was driven in pain all around the world, finally reaching Egypt, where Zeus turned her back into a woman, and she gave birth to Epaphos. Some generations later, Epaphos's descendant Aigyptos sought to marry his fifty sons to his brother Danaos's fifty daughters. Unwilling, they fled and were pursued back to Greece and Argos, where, forced to marry, all of the daughters killed their husbands, except for Hypermestra, who spared her husband Lynkeus. Hypermestra and Lynkeus were the ancestors of Perseus and, most famously, of Herakles.

43. *Odyssey* 4.126: "Alkandra, the wife of Polybos, who lived in Egyptian Thebes, with a palace full of wealth."

44. The Greeks had identified their Memnon with the Amenophis of the colossus. For the talking statue, see further ch. 7, footnote on F2a, D. XVIII.8 n. 11.

45. It must be observed that the order of the myths is wrong: Aigyptos and Danaos, figures of the deep prehistory of Argos, should come much earlier than Memnon, a figure of the Trojan War. Herakles also should be before the Trojan War. This anachronism does not, however, mean that Manetho was ignorant of the proper order: the notices merely make a statement about Egyptian popular belief.

was completely on his own. In fact, even where Greek versions existed, Manetho sometimes preferred to produce an original transcription. For example, the fourth ruler of Dynasty IV had a name that we would now transcribe as Men-kau-re. Herodotus had already made Mykerinos current as the Greek version, but Manetho ignored that version and Hellenized Men-kau-re as Menkheres, and we now would agree that Manetho's version seems more accurate.

It would be interesting to observe Manetho's methods for transcribing the names of rulers and other personages. We could do this if we could compare ancient Egyptian versions of the names (hieroglyphic, hieratic, or demotic) with the Greek versions of Manetho. The best situation would of course be to compare the original king-list(s) that Manetho used, but this is not possible. As noted above, the Turin Royal Canon is likely to be the closest available parallel to Manetho's original, but it is not the very thing. Modern Egyptology, however, does have knowledge of the rulers' Egyptian names that is independent of Manetho and invites comparisons. This knowledge has been gathered from various sources. The sources include the retrospective king-lists already described (the Old Kingdom Annals, the Karnak list, the Saqqara list, the two Abydos lists, and the Turin Royal Canon). Also available are contemporary documents: inscriptions on buildings—pyramids or other forms of tomb, royal temples, and sanctuaries—and on statues, jar seals, private letters, and so forth. Being contemporary, these inscriptions are of greater historical value while at the same time less likely to match Manetho's original. Taken altogether, however, they give a fuller and clearer picture of the complexity of royal nomenclature than either Manetho's list or the other retrospective lists.

From these documents comes the striking fact that the rulers had more than one name each. By as early as the Fourth Dynasty they had five separate names:

1. The Horus name, preceded by the sign ![Horus sign] *Hor*, "Horus,"[46] or enclosed in a *serekh* ![serekh sign], with Horus on top.

2. The Two Ladies name, preceded by ![Nebty sign] *Nebty*, representing the goddesses Nekhbet (Upper Egypt) and Wadjet (Lower Egypt).

3. The Gold Horus name, preceded by ![Bik Nebu sign] *Bik Nebu*, "Falcon of Gold."

---

46. Horus was always pictured as a falcon.

4. The throne name, also called the praenomen. This name was taken by the ruler on coronation. It was preceded by either ✦🦅 ⌂ ⌂ *Nesubit* (also read *insibya*), "Ruler of Upper and Lower Egypt," or ⌐🕯*Netjer Nefer*, "the Good God." It was enclosed in a cartouche ⬭.

5. The personal name, also called the nomen, given at birth, preceded by 🦆 ☉ *Sa Re'*, "Son of Ra," and, like the throne name, enclosed in a cartouche ⬭.

The names themselves are significant and could be translated, although this is not the usual approach. So a full titulature for Thutmose III (D. XVIII)[47] is

Horus	Two Ladies	Gold Horus	Throne	Son of Ra
Ka-nakht Khai-em-Waset	Wah-mesut-mi-Re'-em-pet	Sekhem-pehti Djeser-khau	Men-kheper-Re'	Djehuti-mesu Nefer-kheperu
Mighty Bull Arising in Thebes	Enduring of Kingship like Ra in Heaven	Powerful in Strength, Holy of Crowns	The Form of Ra Abides	Thoth is Born, Beautiful of Forms

One sees the immense scale of the situation: modern Egyptology has identified approximately 375 rulers of ancient Egypt from the predynastic period until the Macedonians; if each one had five names, there would be 1,875 names to examine. There are not in fact that many, because rulers before the Fourth Dynasty did not have all five names and because a full set of names has not been discovered for all. However, some rulers, especially after Dy-

---

47. For this ruler there is actually more to each of the names, but we simplify here for the sake of clarity. The example is taken from A. H. Gardiner, *Egyptian Grammar*, 3d ed. (Oxford, 1982), 72.

nasty XVIII, had more than one version of each name—Ramesses II, for example, had over six Horus names.

Manetho, to judge from F2a, enumerated more rulers than this—about 473. We assume that he also gave a name for each, but only one (in most cases). Of these 473, 114 names are preserved. Of these 114, 84 are comparable with the names discovered independently by modern Egyptology. In other words, a ruler with a name preserved from Manetho has been identified with a ruler in the modern list with some form of name attested.

When one examines the Manethonian names with the recently discovered ancient names, one sees a spectrum of clarity with some items showing easily which name Manetho transcribed; others are not so easy, others are difficult and involve unexpected techniques, and others are still unexplained. Some examples for each level of difficulty follow.

Level 1. In these examples, it is easy to see which name Manetho was dealing with, and there are no great puzzles about his handling—that is, we would transcribe it into Greek in the same way or nearly so.

Dynasty I.1 Menes (Here we give the number and name as they appear in the representations of Manetho's results in F2a.)

I.1 Aha						
(Here we give the number and name as given in a standard modern listing.)						
Horus	*Two Ladies*	*Gold Horus*	*Throne Name*	*Son of Ra*	*King-Lists*[48]	*Manetho*
Aha				**Men**	**Meni**	**Menes**

II.3 Binothris

II.3 Ninetjer						
Horus	*Two Ladies*	*Gold Horus*	*Throne Name*	*Son of Ra*	*King-Lists*	*Manetho*
Ni-netjer (Netjer-en)	Nebty-Ni-netjer				**Ba-netjer-en**	**Binothris**

The sound *tj* in *netjer* did not exist in Greek. *Th* is a reasonable substitute.

II.7 Nepherkheres

II.6 Neferkare

---

48. From the Old Kingdom Annals, the Abydos and Saqqara lists, and the Turin Royal Canon (see chap. 9, table B.)

Horus	Two Ladies	Gold Horus	Throne Name	Son of Ra	King-Lists	Manetho
					Nefer-ka-Reʻ	Nepher-kheres

V.7 Menkheres

V.7 Menkauhor						
Horus	Two Ladies	Gold Horus	Throne Name	Son of Ra	King-Lists	Manetho
Men-khau			Men-kauhor	Kaiu/ Hor-kaiu (?)	Men-kauhor / Men-kahor	Men-kheres

V.9 Onnos

V.9 Unas						
Horus	Two Ladies	Gold Horus	Throne Name	Son of Ra	King-Lists	Manetho
Wadj-tawi	Wadj-em-Nebty	Wadj-bik-nebu		Unis	Unis/ Unas	Onnos

Other problem-free examples include Dynasties XVIII.1 Amosis, XVIII.7 Thoutmosis, and XIX.4 Ramesses I.

Level 2. Some items allow confident identification but with puzzling differences, as in the next two examples.

II.5 Sethenes

II.5 Sened						
Horus	Two Ladies	Gold Horus	Throne Name	Son of Ra	King-Lists	Manetho
				Sened	Senedi/ Senedj	Sethenes

We would expect Manetho's version to be Senethes rather than Sethenes; consonants have been exchanged, as also occurs in the next example.

XIX.6 Thouoris

XIX.8 Twosre/Tausret						
Horus	Two Ladies	Gold Horus	Throne Name	Son of Ra	King-Lists	Manetho

			Sat-Re' Merit-Amen	**Ta-usre(t)**		**Thouoris**

As with the preceding example, there is a switching of consonants, and Manetho has Thouoris instead of the expected Thouser-.

Level 3. Some equivalences have a "trick" to them:

XVIII.2 Khebron

XVIII.4 Thutmose II						
Horus	*Two Ladies*	*Gold Horus*	*Throne Name*	*Son of Ra*	*King-Lists*	*Manetho*
Ka-nakht-User-pehti	Netjeri-nesut	Sekhem-kheperu	A'a-**kheper-en-Re'**	Djehuti-mesiu (+ Nefer-kau/ Iri-en-Amen/ Meri-Amen/ Tit-Amen/ Tit-Re')	A-**kheper-enre**	**Khebron**

Here it appears that Manetho has abbreviated and given just the middle syllables of the throne name, omitting the first and last syllables.

I.4 Ouenephes has puzzled scholars. The Son of Ra name *Itti* was seen as the basis of Manetho's I.2 Athothis (also identified by the modern list as I.3 Horus Djer), but the alternate Manethonian name (Ouenephes) is unexplained until one observes that it may be a version of the Gold Horus name En-nebu.

I.3 Djer						
Horus	*Two Ladies*	*Gold Horus*	*Throne Name*	*Son of Ra*	*King-Lists*	*Manetho*
Djer		**En-nebu**[49]		Itti		Athothis/ **Ouene-phes**

---

49. From Beckerath, *Handbuch der ägyptischen Königsnamen.*

XVIII.4 Amensis

XVIII.5 Hatshepsut						
Horus	*Two Ladies*	*Gold Horus*	*Throne Name*	*Son of Ra*	*King-Lists*	*Manetho*
Userit-kau	Wadjet-renep-ewet	Netjerit-kheperu	Ma'at-ka-Re'	Hat-shepsut/ **Amen-**(khnum)-et hat-**shepsi**[50]		**Amensis**

Manetho's name for Hatshepsut is apparently another abbreviation (using her Son of Ra name), but instead of using a continuous section of the fuller name, as with XVIII.2 Khebron, he has "leapfrogged," skipping the beginning, giving *Amen*, and then cutting to the final syllable *si* and adding a final -*s* to make it Greek. This sort of truncation or syncopation is, as a matter of fact, paralleled elsewhere in the ancient Egyptian treatment of proper names, even royal names. For example, the name Meriamoun (which means "Beloved of Amon") is found shortened to Miamoun (see in F10, Ramesses Miamoun). Compare also Manetho's Dynasty I.6, where the Merbiape(n) of the lists appears as Miebidos

Level 4. There are, lastly, cases in which one cannot as yet see how the Manethonian name reflects any of the independently attested names. We should perhaps infer that in fact some rulers were generally known by a name that was not any of the usual five.

V.6 Rhathoures

V.6 Niuserre						
Horus	*Two Ladies*	*Gold Horus*	*Throne Name*	*Son of Ra*	*King-Lists*	*Manetho*
Set-ib-tawi	Set-ib-Nebty	Netjeri-bik-nebu	Ni-user-Re'	Ini	Ni-user-Re'	Rhathou-res

The above is merely a sample of the picture that emerges from comparing the ruler-names given by Manetho with those gained from independent ancient documents. It is plainly not a simple matter: Manetho had several different approaches, and it is not possible to give a one-to-one formula for predicting how Manetho would have transcribed a given name, nor can one say,

---

50. Supplied by Beckerath, *Handbuch der ägyptischen Königsnamen.* H. W. Helck, *Untersuchungen zu Manetho und den ägyptischen Königslisten*, 40, had also hinted at this solution.

given Manetho's version, what the original Egyptian form of it must have been.

Manetho's *History of Egypt*—Reception and Transmission

Manetho's *History of Egypt* is a lost work, in that it has not been preserved through its own tradition of copying and recopying in manuscript. Instead we have the references to Manetho and citations from Manetho made by other writers in their own works, which have indeed been transmitted through a manuscript tradition (see chap. 9, table D.) These are the texts presented in translation here (in chaps. 6 and 7), and we are totally dependent on these for our knowledge of Manetho and his writings.

We say that our knowledge of what Manetho wrote depends on *indirect* tradition. All of the remains of Manetho's writings come to us indirectly, and the fact that none of it has been transmitted directly must warn the student to be on the alert for errors and distortions that might give a false picture of what Manetho actually wrote.

There are in fact severe difficulties with the fragments. In the first place, Manetho's work became involved in a serious polemic that occurred during the Hellenistic period: various barbarian cultures of the newly Hellenized kingdoms made claims to being older than Greek civilization and to having contributed significantly to the formation of Greek culture. Hellenes were on the whole not averse to viewing their culture as an import from some venerable non-Greek source—lawgivers, for example, were normally said to have gained wisdom abroad, as the Athenian Solon was supposed to have visited Egypt and stayed at Sebennytos (which was, by coincidence, Manetho's birthplace).[51] Leading contestants in this battle to appropriate the origins of the ruling Hellenic civilization were the Egyptians and the Jews, and there is a body of literature representing the claims of one party or attacking the claims of the other.[52] The consequence for Manetho was that his work as a whole was lost in antiquity—one cannot say just how early—and replaced by sets of excerpts designed to be used in the polemic.

---

51. Solon was an Athenian legislator of the early sixth century B.C. who gave Athens a new constitution and then, for ten years, left the Athenians to apply the new laws while he journeyed abroad, to Cyprus, Asia Minor, and Egypt (Plutarch *Life of Solon*).

52. For examples of how Hellenism was appropriated by Judiasm, see Erich S. Gruen, "Cultural Fictions and Cultural Identity," *Transactions of the American Philological Association* 123 (1993): 9–13.

The excerpts from Josephus's counterpolemic *contra Apionem* (*Against Apion*) found in F9–F12 are not in fact a genuine quotation from Manetho's whole work but citations from a set of altered and distorted excerpts. We cannot give a thorough discussion here, but the reader can easily see problems in Josephus's text: the foundation of Avaris is described twice (F9 §§78, 86–87); Osarsephos is introduced twice (F12 §§238, 250); the citation at the beginning of F10 gives a mere list of seventeen rulers and their lengths of reign, with no narrative for any—only with the eighteenth does narrative begin; furthermore, this same ruler-list gives no indication of which dynasty is meant, and it actually runs two of Manetho's dynasties (Dynasties XVIII and XIX) together without a break. Certainly this is not genuine Manetho. It is truly unfortunate that this sort of material bulks so large in the supposed quotations from Manetho. It is also unfortunate that Josephus, who furnishes these texts, is the earliest to cite from "Manetho."

Several scholars have attempted to analyze the citations in Josephus, attributing some portions to pro-Jewish publicists, others to anti-Jewish writers, others to a Greek whose interest was academic rather than polemical—and even some sections to Manetho. But the different scholars have offered different allocations, and none has proven authoritative. The problem of seeing genuine Manetho in these fragments has been called the most difficult problem in Classics, and so it remains.[53]

The student must not, therefore, be quick to accept the anti-Jewish material (such as in F12 §§232–51) as Manetho's writing. Similar material (the unclean lepers and misfits) is found in other writers, such as Lysimakhos of Alexandria,[54] and it may have been injected into Manetho from outside. Manetho, writing his *History of Egypt* in the early third century B.C., was perhaps too early for the rising wave of polemic. He may or may not have mentioned the Jews and the Exodus; and, if he did, we cannot be certain as to his point of view.[55]

Besides being embellished, altered, and excerpted, Manetho's work was also converted—probably from the altered version—into a condensed version, an epitome, in at least one edition. Again, we cannot say when the epitomizing was done or who did it. The results can be seen in F2a: the narrative was almost entirely cut out, leaving the succession of dynasties with the

---

53. The problem was so ranked by Augustus Boeckh in 1845 (quoted by W. G. Waddell, *Manetho* [Cambridge, Mass., and London, 1940], vi).

54. *FGrHist* #621; his date and identity are controversial.

55. If Manetho was indeed influenced by Hekataios of Abdera, then his view of the Jews would have been favorable.

names of the rulers and the lengths of their reigns—an outline very similar to what Manetho may have begun with.

Besides the bare outline of the dynasties, with the names of the rulers and the years involved, the epitome of Manetho also preserved a selection of remarkable facts, about two dozen of them, to go with the sequence. Examples of Manetho's remarks follow:[56]

Dynasty	Ruler	Remark
I.1	Menes	Menes was the first king. He was snatched and killed by a hippopotamus.
I.2	Athothis	Athothis built the palace at Memphis. He practiced medicine and wrote books on anatomy.
I.4	Ouenephes	A great famine seized Egypt. Ouenephes built the pyramids around Kokhome.[57]

The student needs to be careful in using the epitome, no less than with the excerpts from Josephus in F9–F12. As our presentation in F2a shows, there are many serious discrepancies in the different versions we have received. The version that comes by way of Africanus is considered by most to be generally better than the one used by Eusebius, but this is no guarantee that it is better in all cases, and there are many spots where we remain unsure what Manetho actually wrote.

To summarize and illuminate these warnings, we present figure 1, showing the history of Manetho's *History of Egypt*, how it was adapted rather than

---

56. The rest of these remarks are listed in the next note. We give the rulers' names and numbering from Syncellus's version of Africanus. We have chosen the items that, according to Syncellus, appear in both Africanus and Eusebius and that possess character appropriate to Manetho as a mediator of Egyptian history to Greco-Macedonian culture. We have omitted items that are likely to be additions by editors with Judeo-Christian interests (such as the comment in D. XXVI.5 that Nekhao II captured Jerusalem and brought its king "Ioakhaz" [= Jehoahaz] back to Egypt as a prisoner. We have included D. XVIII.14, even though it is absent from Syncellus's Africanus, because, as a crucial synchronism with Greek myth, it seems appropriate to regard it as genuinely Manetho's (compare D. XIX.6, where Thouoris = Homer's Polybos.)

57. The other remarks concern I.7 Semempses, II.1 Boethos, II.2 Kaiekhos, II.3 Binothris, II.7 Nepherkheres, II.8 Sesokhris, III.1 Nekherophes, III.2 Tosorthros, IV.2 Souphis, VI.6 Nitokris, IX.1 Akhthoes, XII.3 Sesostris, XII.4 Lamares, XV Shepherds, XV.1 Saites, XVIII.8 Amenophis, XVIII.14 Armesis, XIX.6 Thouoris, XXIII.2 Osorkho, XXIV Bokhkhoris, and XXV.1 Sabakon.

preserved and transmitted. The bulk of what remains for us to examine has come the route illustrated in figure 1.[58]

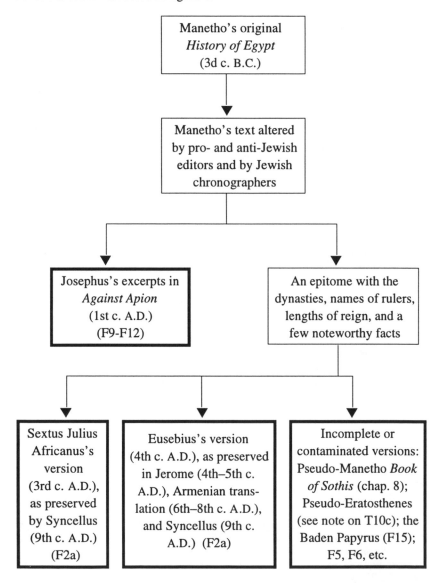

58. Figure 1 is based on H. W. Helck, "Manethon (1)," in *Der kleine Pauly*, ed. K. Ziegler and W. Sontheimer (Munich, 1975), 3:952–953. Surviving stages are in boxes with darker borders; lighter borders enclose lost stages.

Manetho's *History of Egypt*—Goals and Accomplishments

Why did Manetho write, and what did he hope to achieve? The claim is often made that Manetho wrote at the request of Ptolemy (I or II) and that Ptolemy's aim was to inform the Greek and Macedonian ruling class about the history of Egypt from an authentic native point of view. This claim is total conjecture; there is no statement from Manetho about the occasion for his project, and there is not any other sort of reliable evidence for it. Nor was such an aim achieved, since the Hellenic class continued to prefer other writers, such as Herodotus, for basic reading about Egypt.[59]

It is just as plausible to believe that the project was Manetho's own idea and that his purpose was indeed to serve patriotic truth and in the process correct Herodotus on Egypt. As we have said, he did not supersede Herodotus, but he certainly met with another sort of success, because his version of Egypt was regarded as the one to use in the polemics between Jews and Egyptians during the centuries after Manetho. That his *History* was complete, systematic, and written by a native Egyptian gave it an authority that no other source—not the Greek Herodotus, a mere tourist self-admittedly ignorant of the language—could claim. Manetho's text did achieve first place, even though it was being put to unfortunate use and distorted in the process. There was lively heated interest in Manetho's work, or in what passed for his work, down through the time of Josephus.[60]

Manetho was picked up by Jewish chronographers and passed on, especially in epitome, to Christian chronographers, who regarded him as a challenge (since his chronology disagreed with Scripture) not to be ignored. Therefore Syncellus, the great summer-up of medieval Christian chronography, presented Manetho's epitome not in one version only but—recognizing that discrepancies existed—from both Africanus's and Eusebius's editions, and, not content with that, he offered yet a third digest of Manetho by outlining the hoax known as the *Book of Sothis*.

In modern times, Manetho has retained his authority. In 1824 Champollion made it one of his first projects to apply his decipherment of ancient Egyptian

---

59. Hekataios of Abdera (or of Teos; *FGrHist* #264), a Greek who lived a bit before Manetho, had written a philosophical and ethnographic treatise called *On the Egyptians*, which received some currency, being cited by writers down to the second century A.D. and heavily drawn on by Diodorus Siculus.

60. Did Manetho's work find true successors? Writers like Ptolemaios of Mendes (ca. first century B.C. to first century A.D., *FGrHist* #611) and Khairemon of Alexandria (first century A.D., *FGrHist* #618) may have been such, but what remains of their writings is too little to be sure.

to the trail of cartouches in the king-lists and the separate documents—keeping the list of Manetho's ruler-names at hand to help suggest or confirm. He was also eager to validate Manetho in general. Today nearly every book on Egyptology, popular and scholarly alike, presents the rulers' names in versions derived from a modern transcription but also mentions the Manethonian name as well. In many cases the name given by Manetho has become the conventional one, preferred even to more authentic versions. Manetho's method of arrangement by dynasties is still used by all.[61] Manetho has not been superseded or swept aside, and every Egyptologist regards it as a first-priority task to compare modern findings with the indications of Manetho. To be sure, the greatest weight in determining the names, order, and reign-lengths of the rulers is given to documents and monuments predating Manetho or—best of all—contemporary with the rulers themselves. And Manetho unsupported is not regarded as a reliable guide to the chronology. At the least, however, every presentation of Pharaonic Egypt since Syncellus has based itself on Manetho's foundations, specifically the list of dynasties.[62] That he was a native ancient Egyptian leads us, as it did readers in antiquity, to assume that he knew his land and his material and that we must take his reports—insofar as we know them—seriously. Only Manetho represents a complete and systematic version of native Egyptian tradition.

---

61. The extent to which Manetho's idea has proliferated may be seen in, for example, John E. Morby, *Dynasties of the World* (Oxford, 1989), which arranges into dynasties rulers from all over the world and from all periods of history.

62. Peter M. Fraser, *Ptolemaic Alexandria* (Oxford, 1972), 1:510.

CHAPTER 6

Manetho—Ancient Testimony

T1

Corpus Inscriptionum Latinarum (*Corpus of Latin Inscriptions*), VIII 1007:[1]
Manethon.

T2

Hibeh Papyri 1.72.4ff.:[2] Memorandum to the overseer Dorion from the high
priest Petosiris: Previously, in the month Choiach,[3] I made a report to you
about the seal of the temple, because Khesmenis and his son Semtheus[4] had
appropriated it on the ninth of Athyr. He did this in order to (put the seal on)[5]
whatever they would want to write to Manetho and anyone else.

T3a

Josephus *contra Apionem* (*Against Apion*) 1.73 (= Eusebius *Praeparatio
Evangelica* [*Preparation for the Gospel*] 10.13.1–2; Eusebius *Chronicon*
[*The Chronicle*] p. 70, lines 4–8 Karst, in an Armenian translation): First I
will begin from the records kept by the Egyptians. It is not possible to show

---

1. This is an inscription in Greek letters, of uncertain date, from Carthage, originally below a
marble bust (not preserved) in an ancient sanctuary of Sarapis.

2. This papyrus preserves part of a petition from the high priest of Herakles in Phebichis. The
first part of the cult name (Euthe[lac.]) is preserved. The papyrus has been dated to ca. 241 B.C.

3. The months of the Egyptian calendar were Thoth, Phaophi, Athyr, Choiach, Tybi, Mecheir,
Phanemoth, Pharmuthi, Pachon, Payni, Epeiph, and Mesore.

4. Khesmenis and Semtheus are otherwise unknown.

5. Text missing here; this completion is a reasonable conjecture.

the original documents, but there was Manetho, a man of Egyptian birth and Greek culture, as is plain from the fact that he wrote the history of his country in Greek. (Continued in F9 and F10.)

T3b

Josephus *contra Apionem* (*Against Apion*) 1.228: For this is the Manetho who undertook to translate Egyptian history from the priestly writings. (Continued in F12.)

T4

Plutarch *de Iside et Osiride* (*On Isis and Osiris*) 28 pp. 361F–362A: Ptolemy Soter saw in a dream the giant statue of Plouton[6] that was in Sinope, . . . commanding him to bring it as quickly as possible to Alexandria. Ptolemy did not know that it was the statue of Plouton and did not know that it was in Sinope. After he described the dream to his friends, a much-traveled man named Sosibios was discovered, who said that he had seen in Sinope just such a statue as the king believed he had seen. The king therefore sent Soteles and Dionysios; they spent a long time and nearly failed, but with the god's directions they stole the statue and brought it home. When it had arrived and was inspected, Timotheus the Exegete[7] and Manetho of Sebennytos, with their associates, agreed that it was a statue of Plouton, because of the Cerberus and the serpent that were also on it, and they persuaded Ptolemy that it was of no other god than Sarapis. It had not come from Sinope with this name, but after being brought to Alexandria it received the name "Sarapis,"[8] which is the Egyptian name for Plouton.

T5

Aelian *de Natura Animalium* (*On the Nature of Animals*) 10.16: . . . the Egyptian Manetho, a man who reached the pinnacle of erudition. . . . (Continued in F29a.)

---

6. A god of the underworld and of the fertility of the earth; a milder figure than Hades.
7. The Exegetai were a hereditary priesthood in the cult of Demeter at Eleusis.
8. For Sarapis, see "Manetho's Life and Work" in chapter 5.

T6

Tertullian *Apologeticum* (*Defense of Christianity*) 19.4–6: Even if the other prophets are not as great as Moses, even the most recent of them are not inferior to your leading philosophers, lawgivers, and historians. (5) It is not so much a difficult task as it is an enormous one, not so much a laborious task as it is a time-consuming one to prove this. . . . One must even open up the archives of the gentiles—Egyptians, Babylonians, Phoenicians. (6) One must call up those of their citizens who made records—a certain Manetho, an Egyptian; Berossos, a Babylonian; and Hieronymus (*FGrHist* #794), a Phoenician, king of Tyre—as well as their followers: Ptolemy of Mendes (*FGrHist* #611), Menander of Ephesus (*FGrHist* #783), Demetrius of Phaleron (*FGrHist* #643), King Juba (*FGrHist* #275), Apion (*FGrHist* #616), and Thallus (*FGrHist* #256),[9] and, for critical commentary on the others, Josephus of Judea, a native defender of Jewish antiquities.

T7

Eusebius *Praeparatio Evangelica* (*Preparation for the Gospel*) 2 preamble 5: Manetho the Egyptian has in general translated Egyptian history into the Greek language and handled in his own way the matters concerning their theology in his *Sacred Book* and other writings.

T8a

Eusebius *Chronicon* (*The Chronicle*) p. 63, lines 18–22 Karst, in an Armenian translation: From the Egyptian records of Manetho, who composed in three sections the histories of the gods, of the offspring of the gods, of the spirits of the dead, and of the mortal kings who ruled Egypt until Darius, king of the Persians.

T8b

Eusebius *Chronicon* (*The Chronicle*) p. 74, lines 7–17 Karst, in an Armenian translation: This (the material of F1, F9, and F10) is from the writings of the

---

9. For Hieronymus, Ptolemy, Menander, Demetrius, Juba, Apion, and Thallus, see Berossos T6 n. 8.

author just mentioned, Josephus,[10] from the beginning to the end, in order, Egyptian antiquity and chronicles up to their king Nektanebos, whom I have already listed above next to the others. And, after Nektanebos,[11] the Persian king Okhos acquired Egypt and ruled six years. After him, Arses, son of Okhos, ruled four years. After him, Darius ruled six years. After him, Alexander the Macedonian ruled; he slew the Persian Darius and ruled as king over both Asiatics and Egyptians, and he founded Alexandria in the sixth year of his reign. After him, because the empire was divided among many, the Ptolemies ruled over Egypt and Alexandria.

T8c

Eusebius *Chronicon* (*The Chronicle*) p. 125, line 11 Karst, in an Armenian translation: From Manetho's three books concerning Egyptian memorabilia.

T8d

Eusebius *Chronicon* (*The Chronicle*) entry for year of Abraham 1671 = 346/5 B.C. = Olympiad 108.3, in Jerome's Latin edition): Okhos held Egypt, with Nektanebos driven into Ethiopia; destruction of the Egyptian monarchy. Manetho reaches this point.

T9

Expositio Totius Mundi et Gentium (*Description of the Whole World and Its Peoples*) 2 (Riese *Geographi Latini Minores* p. 104): After Moses the order of regions and seasons was described by Berossos, a learned Chaldaean, whose writings were followed by the Egyptian prophet Manetho, and also by the learned Egyptian Apollonius.[12]

---

10. The "author just mentioned" was Josephus, but the intended reference is actually to Manetho, who was being excerpted by Josephus. What Eusebius means is "the writings of the author just mentioned, Josephus, *in which he quotes from Manetho, whose entire work covered*, from beginning to end," and so on.

11. Nektanebos II (360–343 B.C.) = Dynasty XXX.3.

12. This Apollonius is otherwise unknown.

T10a

Syncellus *Ecloga Chronographica* (*Chronological Excerpts*) 27: I think that for those of the faith this is sufficient proof that those who lived before the Great Flood inhabited the land between the ocean and Paradise and that Babylonia had not yet come into existence, nor was there yet kingship in Babylonia, as it seems to be for Berossos and those who follow him in direct contradiction of the Holy Scripture, nor was there yet an Egyptian dynasty, as there seems to be for Manetho, that fabricator and boaster, in his writings about Egyptian affairs.

T10b

Syncellus *Ecloga Chronographica* (*Chronological Excerpts*) 29–30: It is very clear that the Chaldean Empire began with Nebrod,[13] and it is just as clear, if not more so, that what Manetho of Sebennytos wrote to Ptolemy (II) Philadelphos about the Egyptian dynasties is full of lies, written both in imitation of Berossos and at about the same time as Berossos or a little later.[14] Moreover, what these men wrote is still useless even though many historians were to draw up chronological lists based on what Berossos and Manetho wrote. . . . (30) If one carefully examines the underlying chronological lists of events, one will have full confidence that the design of both is false, as both Berossos and Manetho, as I have said before, want to glorify each his own nation, Berossos the Chaldean, Manetho the Egyptian. One can only stand in amazement that they were not ashamed to place the beginning of their incredible story each in one and the same year.[15]

---

13. Nebrod = Nimrud, founder of the Assyrian Empire in Genesis 10.8–12.

14. Syncellus is reacting to the material in the *Book of Sothis*, which he regarded as genuinely Manetho's, but which we regard as spurious (see chap. 8.)

15. Syncellus's assertion sounds interesting, but it actually adds nothing new to our knowledge of either Manetho or Berossos. It arises from the following reasoning by later commentators on Manetho and Berossos (for documentation, see Syncellus 30–33). Christian chronography (based on the Septuagint version of the Old Testament) dated the Great Flood to the 2,242d year after Creation. Berossos's account of Mesopotamian history before the flood counted 120 *saroi* at 3,600 years each (see Berossos F3), or 432,000 years. This figure, immensely large compared to that derived from Scripture, was unacceptable. Syncellus himself was content to regard it as unredeemably benighted and false. He reports, however, that other, contemporary chronographers had attempted to manipulate it so as to agree with and support Scripture. The manipulation assumed that "primitive" gentile chronology was too shortsighted to grasp a solar year and that shorter periods were actually meant by the word *year*. The manipulators converted Berossos's figures by assuming that a solar *day* was intended; 432,000 days divided by 365 days per year yields 1,183 and 1/2 solar years. According to the manipulators, therefore, Berossos's informa-

T10c

Syncellus *Ecloga Chronographica* (*Chronological Excerpts*) 95, 97: For among the Egyptians there is an ancient and traditional chronography, from which I think Manetho has strayed.[16] . . . (97) And Manetho, the most distin-

---

tion actually says that he began his account 1,183 and 1/2 years before the Great Flood, which, to repeat, occurred in the 2,242d year of the world: 2,242 less 1,183 and 1/2 puts the beginning of Berossos's account in Year of the World 1058.

Similar sleight of hand was applied to what passed for Manetho's chronology, although the procedure was more complicated than for Berossus. Since there was no Great Flood explicit in Manetho's account, the manipulators hypothesized that Manetho's initial era with its reigns of "gods, offspring of gods, and spirits of the dead" (see F2a, Predynastic) represented the antediluvian age. The manipulators relied on the spurious *Book of Sothis* (see chap. 5) in dealing with "Manetho's account." This first era was, according to the *Book of Sothis*, subdivided into six dynasties of gods ruling for 11,985 years plus nine dynasties of demigods ruling for 858 years. Manetho's alleged figures for the number of years before the Flood were, plainly, also unacceptably large. As with Berossos, the two figures were reduced on the grounds that "year" had meant a smaller unit, but for "Manetho" two different bases of conversion were applied. The 11,985 years of gods were interpreted as months of 29 and 1/2 days each and thus reduced to 969 solar periods (this conversion was already being used in antiquity: Diodorus Siculus 1.26.3); the 858 years of demigods, however, were interpreted as quarter-years (or "seasons") and so reduced to 214 and 1/2 solar periods (also an ancient conversion: Diodorus Siculus 1.26.5). The sum of the two converted components of the supposed Manethonian antediluvian era is 969 plus 214 and 1/2 solar periods, equaling 1,183 and 1/2 solar periods. This, of course, is the same number as was produced for Berossos's years before the Flood, and hence both Berossos and Manetho could be said to have begun their native histories with Year of the World 1058.

Syncellus does not subscribe to these conversions carried out on Manetho and Berossos. He regards their gigantic time spans as simply false, motivated by a desire to exaggerate the antiquity of their peoples, and he feels that it is a waste of time to seek truth in them. Syncellus is in the unusual position of (a) rejecting Manetho and Berossos for their impossibly long antediluvian eras, (b) rejecting the efforts of those commentators who reduced Manetho's and Berossos's numbers so as to bring them into harmony with Scripture, and (c) blaming Manetho and Berossos for the synchronism that resulted from the harmonization.

16. This alleged "ancient and traditional chronography" (*FGrHist* #610 F2) runs as follows:

The time of Hephaistos	(uncountable because he shines night and day)
Helios, son of Hephaistos	30,000 years
Agathodaimon	184 years
Kronos and all the other twelve gods	3,984 years
Eight semidivine kings	217 years
Fifteen generations of the cycle of Sirius	443 years

Dynasty	Origin	Generations	Years
XVI.	Tanis	8	190
XVII.	Memphis	4	103
XVIII.	Memphis	14	348
XIX.	Diospolis	5	194
XX.	Diospolis	8	228

guished among the Egyptians, wrote about the same thirty dynasties and plainly based himself on it but greatly disagrees concerning the dates in these matters. (See F2b.)

T11

Codex Laurentianus 73.1:[17] Names of medical writers, Egyptian or Greek and Latin: Escolapius, . . . his sons, Asclepius grandson of Escolapius,[18] Hermes Trismegistus, Manetos, Necepso, Queen Cleopatra; also those who wrote in Greek: Chiron the Thessalian, Hippocrates . . .

T12

Suda (*Fortress of Knowledge*) s.v. "Manethos": From Diospolis[19] in Egypt, or from Sebennytos. *Physiologica* (*On Nature*) . . .[20]

XXI.	Tanis	6	121
XXII.	Tanis	3	48
XXIII.	Diospolis	2	19
XXIV.	Saïs	3	44
XV.	Ethiopia	3	44
XXVI.	Memphis	7	177
XXVII.	Persia	5	124
XXVIII.	Saïs	1	6
XXIX.	Tanis	4 (?)	39
XXX.	Tanis	1	18

Total of the thirty dynasties   36,525

(The actual total should be 36,531; it appears that Syncellus left out Dynasty XXVIII.)

17. This is a manuscript of the Laurentian Library in Florence. It was written in about the ninth century A.D., and it contains various materials. The citation in T11 comes on the back of leaf 142, just after Celsus's *de Medicina* (*On Medicine*).

18. This list is highly fictitious. Escolapius is a barbarized form of Aesculapius, which is merely the Latin version of Asklepios, the Greek god of healing, with important sanctuaries at Epidaurus and Athens. Hermes Trismegistus ("Thrice-greatest Hermes") is a pseudonym put on a body of mystical writings that was popular in antiquity and the Renaissance. Necepso is unknown. Chiron would be the centaur tutor of Achilles. Cleopatra and Hippocrates—the famous Hippocrates of Kos—are historical.

The text itself exhibits corruption, and the ascription to Manetho is owed to a modern editor's emendation. Assuming it is correct, it remains unclear why Manetho was included in this list; perhaps his work on *kyphi* (F20–F22) may furnish the reason.

19. Either Diospolis Magna (= Thebes) or Diospolis Parva.

20. See Pseudo-Manetho *Apotelesmatika* T1.

CHAPTER 7

Manetho—Fragments

History of Egypt, Volumes 1–3

F1

Josephus *contra Apionem* (*Against Apion*) 1.73: Manetho has written in Greek the history of his homeland, translating, as he himself says, from the priestly writings, and he refutes Herodotus, who through ignorance made many mistakes about Egypt.

F2a

Syncellus *Ecloga Chronographica* (*Chronological Excerpts*) 99–145 (= Eusebius *Chronicon* [*The Chronicle*] p. 63, line 15–p. 69, line 29 Karst, in an Armenian translation; Jerome *Eusebii Chronicon* pp. 20–121 Helm):[1]

---

1. In this fragment we attempt to present the epitome of Manetho's *History of Egypt*. On the epitome see "Manetho's *History of Egypt*—Reception and Transmission" in chap. 5. A split presentation is necessary because of significant discrepancies, not only between the versions of Africanus and of Eusebius, but also among the versions of Eusebius.

Africanus's version is preserved by Syncellus *Ecloga Chronographica* (*Chronological Excerpts*) 99–145;

Eusebius's version is preserved

—in an Armenian translation

—alternating with Africanus's in Syncellus *Ecloga Chronographica* (*Chronological Excerpts*) 99–145

—in Jerome's Latin edition

When the witnesses must be distinguished,

A = Africanus as transmitted by Syncellus

E = Eusebius

When the witnesses for Eusebius differ, they are distinguished as

A, E (sync)	E (arm)
Since the periods of years of Egyptian history from Mestraïm down to Nectanebo happen to be useful among those who are busied with researches into chronology, and since the chronologies taken from Manetho by ecclesiastical historians are set out with discrepancies concerning both the names and the amount of regnal years, and as to in whose reign Joseph was leader of Egypt and later Moses, who saw God, led the journey of Israel out of Egypt, I (Syncellus) thought it necessary to select two of the most famous editions and set them out side-by-side. I mean the one by Africanus and the one of Eusebius, called son of Pamphilos.	It is necessary and appropriate also to add Manetho's report on Egypt, which seems to give a firmer historical foundation.

(Predynastic:)

A	E (arm)
The dead, the demigods.	1. The first person among the Egyptians was Hephaistos,[2] who also discovered fire for them.
	2. From whom was Helios.[3]
	3. After whom was Kronos.[4]
	4. After whom was Osiris.
	5. And then Typhon,[5] brother of Osiris.

E (arm) = the Armenian translation
E (sync) = as transmitted by Syncellus
E (jer) = as transmitted by Jerome
2. Hephaistos is the Greek equivalent of the Egyptian god Ptah.
3. Helios is the Greek equivalent of the sun god Ra.
4. Kronos is the Greek equivalent of Shu.
5. Typhon is the Greek equivalent of Seth.

<table>
<tr><td></td><td>6. After whom was Oros,[6] son of Isis and Osiris.</td></tr>
<tr><td></td><td>These first reigned over the Egyptians.
7. After them, the monarchy continued until Bidis, for 13,900 years.</td></tr>
<tr><td></td><td>8. After the gods reigned the race of offspring of gods, 1,255 years.</td></tr>
<tr><td></td><td>9. And there also reigned other kings, 1,817 years.</td></tr>
<tr><td></td><td>10. After whom another 30 kings, from Memphis, 1,790 years.</td></tr>
<tr><td></td><td>11. After whom others, from This, 10 kings, 350 years.</td></tr>
<tr><td></td><td>12. And then the reign of the spirits of the dead and of the offspring of gods was 5,813 years.</td></tr>
<tr><td></td><td>Altogether there were 11,000 years.</td></tr>
</table>

(Dynastic:)

I. After the dead and the demigods comes the First Dynasty, with 8 kings of whom Menes was the first. He was an excellent leader. In what follows are recorded the rulers from all of the ruling houses in succession.

I.1. Menes of Thinis, whom Herodotus calls Men, and his 7 descendants.

A	E (arm)	E (sync)
He ruled 62 years.	He ruled 30 years.	He ruled 60 years.

He led the army across the frontier and won great glory. He was killed by a hippopotamus.

I.2. Athothis, his son.

A	E
He ruled 57 years.	He ruled 27 years.

He built the palace in Memphis. He was a skilled physician and wrote books on anatomy.

I.3. Kenkenes, his son.

A	E
He ruled 31 years.	He ruled 39 years.

---

6. Oros = Horus (equated by the Greeks with Apollo).

I.4.

A	E (arm)	E (sync)
Ouenephes,	Vavenephis,	Ouenephes,

his son.

A	E
He ruled 23 years.	He ruled 42 years.

In his reign a great famine gripped Egypt. Also he built the pyramids around Kokhome.[7]

I.5.

A	E
Ousaphaidos,	Ousaphais,

his son. He ruled 20 years.

I.6.

A	E
Miebidos,	Niebais,

his son. He ruled 26 years.

I.7.

A	E (arm)	E (sync)
Semempses,	Memphses,	Semempses,

his son. He ruled 18 years. In his reign there were many extraordinary events, and there was an immense disaster.

I.8.

A	E (arm)	E (sync)
Bienekhes,	Vibenthis,	Oubienthis,

his son. He ruled 26 years.

Altogether they ruled

A	E (arm)	E (sync)
253 years.	270 years.	252 years.

II. Second Dynasty: 9 kings from Thinis

II.1.

A	E (arm)	E (sync)
Boethos ruled 38 years.	Bokchos.	Bokhos.

In his reign a great chasm opened up at Boubastos, and many people died.

---

7. Or Ko Hill. Neither name corresponds to a known place.

II.2.

A	E (arm)	E (sync)
Kaiekhos ruled 39 years.	Kechoos.	Khoös.

In his reign the bulls Apis in Memphis and Mnevis in Heliopolis and the Mendesian goat were recognized as gods.

II.3.

A	E
Binothris ruled 47 years.	Biophis.

In his reign it was judged that women are entitled to kingship.

A	E
II.4. Tlas ruled 17 years. II.5. Sethenes ruled 41 years. II.6. Khaires ruled 17 years.	4–6. Next came 3 more kings, in whose reigns nothing extraordinary happened.

II.7.

A	E
Nepherkheres ruled 25 years.	A seventh king.

There is a myth that in his reign the Nile ran mixed with honey for eleven days.

II.8. Sesokhris ruled 48 years. It is said that he was five cubits and three palms (= ca. eight and one-half feet) tall.[8]

II.9.

A	E
Kheneres ruled 30 years.	Under the ninth king nothing worth mention happened.

A	E (arm)	E (sync)
The first and second dynasties together lasted for 555 years.	They ruled 297 years.	The first and second dynasties together lasted for 549 years.

III. Third Dynasty:

A	E
9 kings from Memphis.	8 kings from Memphis.

8. Or "five cubits (ca. seven and one-half feet) tall and three palms (ca. twelve inches) thick back to front."

III.1.

A	E
Nekherophes ruled 28 years.	Necherochis.

In his reign the Libyans revolted from the Egyptians and surrendered because the moon grew unusually large.

III.2.

A	E
Tosorthros ruled 29 years.	Sesorthos.

For his medical skill he was esteemed as Asklepios by the Egyptians, and he invented the art of building with cut stones, and he studied writing.

A	E
III.3. Tyreis ruled 7 years. III.4. Mesokhris ruled 17 years. III.5. Soüphis ruled 16 years. III.6. Tosertasis ruled 19 years. III.7. Akhes ruled 42 years. III.8. Sephouris ruled 30 years. III.9. Kerpheres ruled 26 years.	3–8. The other 6 did nothing worth mention.

Altogether they ruled

A	E (arm)	E (sync)
214 years.	197 years.	198 years.

The three dynasties together lasted for

A	E (arm)	E (sync)
769 years.		747 years.

IV. Fourth Dynasty:

A	E (arm)	E (sync)
8	17	17

kings from Memphis, of a different family.

A	E
IV.1. Soris ruled 29 years. IV.2. Souphis ruled 63 years. He built the Great Pyramid, which Herodotus says was built by Kheops. He was arrogant toward the gods. He wrote the *Sacred Book*, highly regarded by the Egyptians.	

IV.3.

A	E
Souphis ruled 66 years.	Souphis built the Great Pyramid, which Herodotus says was built by Kheops. He was arrogant toward the gods until he repented and wrote the *Sacred Book*, highly regarded by the Egyptians.

A	E
IV.4. Menkheres ruled 63 years. IV.5. Rhatoises ruled 25 years. IV.6. Bikheris ruled 22 years. IV.7. Seberkheres ruled 7 years. IV.8. Thamphthis ruled 9 years.	Nothing worth mention is recorded about the rest.

Together they ruled

A	E
277 years.[9]	448 years.

The four dynasties together lasted

A	E (arm)	E (sync)
1,046 years.		1,195 years.

V. Fifth Dynasty:

A	E
8 kings	31 kings

from Elephantine.

A	E (arm)	E (sync)
V.1. Ouserkheres ruled 28 years.	V.1.	
	Othios.	Othoes
	He was killed by his bodyguards.	
V.2. Sephres ruled 13 years.		
V.3. Nepherkheres ruled 20 years.		

---

9. A second manuscript of Syncellus gives 274. The sum of the separate figures is 284.

V.4. Sisires ruled 7 years.	V.4. Phiops. He began his reign at six years of age and ruled until he was one hundred.
V.5. Kheres ruled 20 years.	
V.6. Rhathoures ruled 44 years.	
V.7. Menkheres ruled 9 years.	
V.8. Tankheres ruled 44 years.	
V.9. Onnos ruled 33 years.	

Added to the

A	E (arm)	E (sync)
1,046		1,195

years of the preceding four dynasties, the total of years is

A	E (arm)	E (sync)
1,294.		1,295.

VI. Sixth Dynasty:

A	E
6 kings from Memphis.	

A	E
VI.1. Othoes ruled 30 years. He was killed by his bodyguards.	(See Dynasty V.1.)
VI.2. Phios ruled 53 years.	
VI.3. Methousouphis ruled 7 years.	
VI.4. Phiops. He began his reign at six years of age and ruled until he was one hundred.	(See Dynasty V.4.)
VI.5. Mentesouphis ruled 1 year.	

VI.6. Nitokris, the bravest and most beautiful of her time, blonde in complexion, who built the third pyramid. She ruled 12 years.
Altogether they ruled 203 years.

With these added to the

A	E (arm)	E (sync)
1,294 years		1,295 years

of the preceding five dynasties, the total of years is

A	E (arm)	E (sync)
1,497.		1,498.

VII. Seventh Dynasty:

A	E
70	5

kings from Memphis, who ruled

A	E (arm)	E (sync)
70 days.	75 years.	75 days.

VIII. Eighth Dynasty:

A	E
27 kings	5 kings

from Memphis, who ruled

A	E
146 years.	100 years.

Total for the first eight dynasties:

A	E (arm)	E (sync)
1,639 years.		1,598 years.

IX. Ninth Dynasty:

A	E
19 kings	4 kings

from Herakleopolis, who ruled

A	E
409 years.	100 years.

IX.1. The first was

A	E (arm)	E (sync)
Akhthoes.	Ochthois.	Akhthoes.

He was the cruelest of all so far. He hurt people all over Egypt, but later he went mad and was killed by a crocodile.

X. Tenth Dynasty: 19 kings from Herakleopolis, who ruled for 185 years.

XI. Eleventh Dynasty: 16 kings from Diospolis, who ruled 43 years.

After them Ammenemes ruled 16 years.

Volume 1 of Manetho reaches this point. It covers 192 kings and

A	E (arm)	E (sync)
2,300 years, 70 days.	2,300 years.	2,300 years, 79 days.

From volume 2 of Manetho.

XII. Twelfth Dynasty: 7 kings from Diospolis.

XII.1. Sesonkhosis, son of Ammenemes, ruled 46 years.

XII.2. Ammenemes ruled 38 years. He was killed by his own eunuchs.

XII.3. Sesostris ruled 48 years.

A	E
	They say that he was four cubits, three palms, and two fingers (ca. seven feet and two inches) tall.

He conquered all Asia in 9 years, and Europe as far as Thrace. He erected monuments everywhere to announce his power over the nations, inscribing on the monuments male genitals for a brave people and female genitals for the cowardly. Because of his deeds he was ranked next to Osiris by the Egyptians.

XII.4.

A	E (arm)	E (sync)
Lamares.	Lampares.	Lamares.

He built the Labyrinth in Arsinoe to be his tomb.

A	E
XII.5. Ameres ruled 8 years.	His successors ruled 42 years.
XII.6. Ammenemes ruled 8 years.	
XII.7. Skemiophris, his sister, ruled 4 years.	

Altogether they ruled

A	E
160 years.	245 years.

XIII. Thirteenth Dynasty: 60 kings from Diospolis, who ruled 453 years.

XIV. Fourteenth Dynasty: 76 kings from Xoïs, who ruled

A	E (arm)	E (sync)
184 years.	484 years.	184 years.[10]

---

10. Syncellus reports that he found the figure 284 in another copy of Eusebius.

XV. Fifteenth Dynasty:

A	E
6 kings of the Shepherds. They captured Memphis and founded a city in the Sethroite Nome. From there they set out to conquer the Egyptians.	kings from Diospolis, who ruled 250 years.
XV.1. Saites ruled 19 years. The Saite Nome is named for him.	
XV.2. Bnon ruled 44 years.	
XV.3. Pakhnan ruled 61 years.	
XV.4. Staan ruled 50 years.	
XV.5. Arkhles ruled 49 years.	
XV.6. Aphobis ruled 61 years.	
Total, 284 years.	

XVI. Sixteenth Dynasty:

A	E (arm, sync)	E (jer)
other Shepherds, 32 kings, who ruled 518 years.	5 kings from Thebes, who ruled 190 years.	Thebans ruled 190 years.

XVII. Seventeenth Dynasty:

A	E (arm, sync)	E (jer)
other Shepherds, 43 kings, and 43 Thebans from Diospolis. Altogether the Shepherds and Thebans ruled 151 years.	Shepherds, Phoenician brothers, foreign kings, who even captured Memphis.	
(See Dynasty XV.)	1. Saites, their first king, ruled 19 years. The Saite Nome is named for him. They also built a city in the Sethroite Nome. From there they set out to conquer the Egyptians.	

| | | 2. Bnon, the second, ruled 40 years. | |

A	E (arm)	E (sync)	E (jer)
	3. After him Archles ruled 30 years.	3. Apophis ruled 14 years.	
	4. Apophis ruled 14 years.	4. After him Arkhles ruled 30 years.	

A	E (arm, sync)	E (jer)
	Altogether they ruled 103 years.	Shepherds ruled 103 years.

XVIII. Eighteenth Dynasty:

A	E (arm, sync)	E (jer)
16 kings from Diospolis.	14 kings from Diospolis.	kings from Diospolis.

XVIII. 1.

A	E (arm)	E (sync, jer)
Amos.	Amoses.	Amosis.
	He ruled 25 years.	

XVIII.2.

A	E
Khebros.	Khebron.

He ruled 13 years.

XVIII.3.

A	E (arm)	E (sync, jer)
Amenophthis ruled 24 years.	Amophis ruled 21 years.	Ammenophis ruled 21 years.

A	E (arm)	E (sync)	E (jer)
XVIII.4. Amensis ruled 22 years.	XVIII.4. Memphres. He ruled 12 years.	XVIII.4. Miphres. He ruled 12 years.	XVIII.3. Memphres. He ruled 12 years.

A	E
XVIII.5. Misaphris ruled 13 years.	

A	E (arm)	E (sync)	E (jer)
XVIII.6. Misphrag-mouthosis.	XVIII.5. Myspharmou-thosis.	XVIII.5. Misphragmou-thosis.	Mispharmou-thosis.

He ruled 26 years.

A	E (arm, sync)	E (jer)
XVIII.7.	XVIII.6.	

Touthmosis ruled 9 years.

A	E (arm)	E (sync)	E (jer)
XVIII.8. Amenophis.	XVIII.7. Amnophis.	XVIII.7. Amenophis.	Ammenophis.

He ruled 31 years. He is believed to be the Memnon of the talking statue.[11]

A	E (arm)	E (sync)	E (jer)
XVIII.9.	XVIII.8.	XVIII.8.	

Oros ruled

A	E (arm)	E (sync)	E (jer)
37 years.	28 years.	36 years.[12]	38 years.
XVIII.10. Akherres	XVIII.9. Akhenhkheres	XVIII.9. Akhenkherses	Achencheres
ruled 32 years.	ruled 16 years.		ruled 12 years.
XVIII.11. Rhathos ruled 6 years.		XVIII.10. Athoris ruled 39 years.	Athoris ruled 8 years.
		XVIII.11. Khenkheres ruled 16 years.	Chencheres ruled 16 years.

---

11. The mortuary temple of Amenophis III lay across from Luxor. The approach to it featured a pair of giant statues of the king. For some reason—perhaps because the names seemed similar—Greeks identified the king portrayed here as Memnon, the Ethiopian hero who fought in the Trojan War. The northern statue became a great tourist attraction because of its habit of making a twanging sound: see Pausanias *Graeciae Descriptio* (*Description of Greece*) 1.42.5.

12. Syncellus notes that another copy of Eusebius reads 38 years.

XVIII.12. Khebres ruled 12 years.			
	XVIII.10. Akherres ruled 8 years.	XVIII.12. Akherres ruled 12 years.	Acheres ruled 8 years.
XVIII.13. Akherres ruled 12 years.	XVIII.11. Kherres ruled 15 years.	XVIII.13. Kherres ruled 15 years.	Cherres ruled 15 years.
XVIII.14. Armesis ruled 5 years.	XVIII.12. Armais, also called Danaos, ruled 5 years. Then he was exiled from Egypt and fled for refuge to his brother Aigyptos. He emigrated and reached the land of the Greeks. He gained power in Argos and ruled over the Argives.	XVIII.14. Armais, also called Danaos, ruled 5 years. Then he was exiled from Egypt. Fleeing from his brother Aigyptos, he reached Greece, where he gained power in Argos and ruled over the Argives.	Armais, also called Danaus, ruled 5 years.
XVIII.15. Rhamesses ruled 1 year.	XVIII.13. Ramesses,	XVIII.15. Rhamesses,	Remesses,
	also called Aigyptos, ruled 68 years.		
XVIII.16. Amenophath ruled 19 years.	XVIII.14. Amenophis ruled 40 years.	XVIII.16. Amenophis ruled 40 years.	Menofis ruled 40 years.
Altogether they ruled			
263 years.	348 years.		

XIX. Nineteenth Dynasty:

A	E (arm, sync)	E (jer)
6 kings from Diospolis.	5 kings from Diospolis.	

XIX.1. Sethos.

A	E
He ruled 51 years.	He ruled 55 years.

XIX.2.

A	E
Rhapsakes ruled 61 years.	Rhampses ruled 66 years.

XIX.3.

A	E (arm)	E (sync)	E (jer)
Amenephthes ruled 20 years.	Amenephthis ruled 8 years.	Ammenephthis ruled 40 years.	Amenophis ruled 40 years.

A	E
4. Rhammeses ruled 60 years.	
5. Ammenemnes ruled 5 years.	4. Ammenemes ruled 26 years.
6.	5.

Thouoris ruled 7 years. In Homer he is called Polybos, husband of Alkandra.[13] He was king when Troy was captured.

A	E (arm, sync)	E (jer)
Total, 209 years.	Total, 194 years.	

A	E (arm)	E (sync)	E (jer)
Total for Manetho's second volume: 96 kings, 2,121 years.	Total for Manetho's second volume: 92 kings, 2,121 years.	Total for Manetho's second volume: 92 kings, 1,121 years.	

---

13. Eusebius (Armenian version) has "a muscular man," probably as a mistranslation of Manetho's Greek phrase that actually means "husband of Alkandra." (This ruler is probably to be identified with Queen Twosret.)

From volume 3 of Manetho.

XX. Twentieth Dynasty:

A, E (arm, sync)	E (jer)
12 kings from Diospolis.	

A	E (arm)	E (sync, jer)
They ruled 135 years.	They ruled 172 years.	They ruled 178 years.

XXI. Twenty-first Dynasty:

A, E (arm, sync)	E (jer)
7 kings from Tanis.	

XXI.1. Smendes ruled 26 years.

XXI.2.

A, E (sync, jer)	E (arm)
Psousennes.	Psusennos.
He ruled 46 years.	He ruled 41 years.

XXI.3.

A	E
Nephelkheres.	Nepherkheres.

A , E (arm, sync)	E (jer)
He ruled 4 years.	He ruled 3 years.

XXI.4.

A, E (arm)	E (sync, jer)
Amenophthis.	Ammenophthis.

He ruled 9 years.

XXI.5. Osokhor ruled 6 years.

XXI.6.

A, E (sync, jer)	E (arm)
Psinakhes.	Psinnakhes.

He ruled 9 years.

XXI.7. Psousennes ruled

A	E
14 years.	35 years.

A, E (arm, sync)	E (jer)
Altogether they ruled 130 years.	

XXII. Twenty-second Dynasty:

A	E (arm, sync)	E (jer)
9	3	

kings from Bubastis.

XXII.1.

A	E (arm)	E (sync, jer)
Sesonkhis.	Sesonkhusis.	Sesonkhosis.

He ruled 21 years.

XXII.2.

A, E (sync, jer)	E (arm)
Osorthon.	Osorthos.

He ruled 15 years.

A	E
XXII.3–5. 3 more kings, who ruled 25 years.	
6. Takelothis ruled 13 years.	3. Takelothis ruled 13 years.
7–9. 3 more kings, who ruled 42 years.	

A	E (arm, sync)	E (jer)
Altogether they ruled 120 years.	Altogether they ruled 49 years.	

XXIII. Twenty-third Dynasty:

A	E (arm, sync)	E (jer)
4 kings	3 kings	

from Tanis.

XXIII. 1

A	E
Petoubates ruled 40 years. The first Olympiad was held during his reign.[14]	Petoubastis ruled 25 years.

XXIII.2

A	E
Osorkho ruled 8 years.	Osorthon ruled 9 years.

The Egyptians called him Herakles.

---

14. The first Olympiad covers the years from 776 to 772 B.C.

XXIII.3

A, E (sync, jer)	E (arm)
Psammous.	Phramus.

He ruled 10 years.

A	E
XXIII.4. Zet ruled 31 years.	

A	E (arm, sync)	E (jer)
Altogether they ruled 89 years.	Altogether they ruled 44 years.	

XXIV. Twenty-fourth Dynasty:

A, E (arm, sync)	E (jer)
Bokhkhoris from Saïs.	Bocchoris.

He ruled

A	E
6 years.	44 years.

In his reign a lamb spoke.[15]

A, E (arm, sync)	E (jer)
	He made laws for the Egyptians.

A[16]	E (arm)	E (sync)	E (jer)
		Total for this dynasty, 44 years.	

XXV. Twenty-fifth Dynasty:

A, E (arm, sync)	E (jer)
3 kings from Ethiopia.	

XXV.1.

A, E (sync, jer)	E (arm)
Sabakon.	Sapakon.

---

15. This probably alludes to the "Prophecy of the Lamb," known from other sources. It fore-told a nine-hundred-year period of disasters; Egypt would be conquered by Assyria, and the gods would be removed to Nineveh. Egypt was indeed soon conquered by Assyria, in 671 B.C. during Dynasty XXV. Egypt was then liberated by Psammetikhos of Dynasty XXVI.

16. Africanus also has here the phrase "990 years," unclear and perhaps a corrupt reflex of the nine-hundred-year period in the "Prophecy of the Lamb."

A, E (arm, sync)	E (jer)
He captured Bokhkhoris and burned him alive.	

He ruled

A	E
8 years.	12 years.

XXV.2. Sebikhos,

A, E (arm, sync)	E (jer)
his son.	

He ruled

A	E
14 years.	12 years.

XXV.3.

A	E
Tarkos ruled 18 years.	Tarakos ruled 20 years.

XXVI. Twenty-sixth Dynasty:

A, E (arm, sync)	E (jer)
9 kings from Saïs.	

A	E (arm)	E (sync)	E (jer)
	XXVI.1. Ameres the Ethiopian ruled 18 years.	XXVI.1. Ammeris the Ethiopian ruled 12 years.	XXVI.1. Amerres the Ethiopian ruled 12 years.
XXVI.1. Stephinates.	XXVI.2. Stephinathes.	XXVI.2. Stephinathis.	Next, Stephinathis.

He ruled 7 years.

A	E (arm, sync)	E (jer)
XXVI.2.	XXVI.3.	

Nekhepsos.
He ruled 6 years.

A	E (arm, sync)	E (jer)
XXVI.3.	XXVI.4.	

Nekhao.
He ruled 8 years.

A	E (arm)	E (sync)	E (jer)
XXVI.4. Psammetikhos ruled 54 years.	XXVI.5. Psametikhos ruled 44 years.	XXVI.5. Psammetikhos ruled 45 years.	Psammeticus ruled 44 years.

A	E (arm, sync)	E (jer)
XXVI.5.	XXVI.6.	

A second Nekhao.

A, E (arm. sync)	E (jer)
	He was also called Nekhepsos.

He ruled 6 years.

A	E (arm)	E (sync)	E (jer)
XXVI.6	XXVI.7		
Another Psammouthis ruled 6 years.	The other Psamuthes, also called Psametichos, ruled 17 years.	Another Psammouthis, also called Psammetikhos, ruled 17 years.	Another Psammuthes, also called Psammeticus, ruled 12 years.

A	E (arm)	E (sync)	E (jer)
XXVI.7	XXVI.8		
Ouaphris ruled 19 years.	Vaphres ruled 25 years.	Ouaphris ruled 25 years.	Uafres ruled 30 years.

A	E (arm, sync)	E (jer)
XXVI.8	XXVI.9	
Amosis ruled 44 years.	Amosis ruled 42 years.	Amasis ruled 42 years.

A	E
XXVI.9. Psammekherites ruled 6 months.	

A	E (arm)	E (sync)	E (jer)
Altogether they ruled 150 years, 6 months.	Altogether they ruled 167 years.	Altogether they ruled 163 years.	

XXVII. Twenty-seventh Dynasty:

A, E (arm, sync)	E (jer)
8	

kings from Persia.

A	E (arm)	E (sync)	E (jer)
XXVII.1. Kambyses became king of Egypt in his fifth			Cambyses conquered Egypt in his sixth

year as king of Persia

A	E (arm)	E (sync)	E (jer)
He ruled 6 years.	He ruled 3 years.		

A	E (arm, sync)	E (jer)
	XXVII. 2. The Magoi ruled 7 months.	
XXVII.2. Dareios, son of Hystaspes, ruled 36 years.	XXVII.3. Dareios ruled 36 years.	
XXVII.3. Xerxes the Great ruled 21 years.	XXVII.4. Xerxes, son of Darcios, ruled 21 years.	

A	E
XXVII.4. Artabanos ruled 7 months.	

A	E (arm)	E (sync)	E (jer)
XXVII.5. Artaxerxes ruled 41 years.	XXVII.5. Artashes	XXVII.5. Artaxerxes Longhand	
	ruled 40 years.		

A	E (arm, sync)	E (jer)
	XXVII.6. Xerxes	
	the Second	

ruled 2 months.	

A, E (arm, sync)	E (jer)
XXVII.7. Sogdianos ruled 7 months.	
XXVII.8. Dareios, son of Xerxes, ruled 19 years.	The last was Darius, son of Xerxes.

Altogether they ruled

A	E (arm, sync)	E (jer)
124 years, 4 months.	120 years, 4 months.	111 years.

A	E (arm)	E (sync)	E (jer)
XXVIII. Twenty-eighth Dynasty:			Egypt rebelled against the Persians.
Amyrteos	Amyrte	Amyrtaios	Amyrtaeus

of Saïs ruled 6 years.

XXIX. Twenty-ninth Dynasty:

A, E (arm, sync)	E (jer)
4 kings from Mendes.	kings from Mendes.
XXIX.1. Nepherites ruled 6 years.	Neferites ruled 6 years.
XXIX.2 Akhoris ruled 13 years.	Next, Akhoris ruled 12 years.

A	E (arm)	E (sync)	E (jer)
XXIX.3. Psamouthis	XXIX.3. Psamuthes	XXIX.3. Psammouthis	Psammuthes

ruled 1 year.

A, E (sync, jer)	E (arm)
	XXIX.4. Muthes ruled 1 year.

A	E (arm)	E (sync)	E (jer)
XXIX.4. Nephorites ruled 4 months.	XXIX.5 Nepherites ruled 4 months.	XXIX.4. Nepherites ruled 4 months.	Next, Nepherites ruled 4 months.

A, E (arm, jer)	E (sync)
	XXIX.5. Mouthis ruled 1 year.

A, E (arm, sync)	E (jer)
	Next, Nectanebis ruled 18 years.
	Teo ruled 2 years.

A	E (arm, sync)	E (jer)
Altogether they ruled		
20 years, 4 months.	21 years, 4 months.	

XXX. Thirtieth Dynasty:

A, E (arm, sync)	E (jer)
3 kings from Sebennytos.	

A	E (arm)	E (sync)	E (jer)
XXX.1.	XXX.1.	XXX.1.	
Nektanebes.	Nektanebis.	Nektanebes.	
He ruled 18 years.	He ruled 10 years.		

A, E (arm, sync)	E (jer)
XXX.2. Teos ruled 2 years.	(See Dynasty XXIX.)

A	E (arm, sync)	E (jer)
XXX.3. Nektanebos ruled		Nectanebus ruled
18 years.	8 years.	18 years.
Total, 38 years.	Total, 20 years.	

A, E (arm, sync)	E (jer)
	Destruction of the Egyptian monarchy.

A	E (arm)	E (sync)	E (jer)
XXXI. Thirty-first Dynasty: 3 kings from Persia.	XXXI. Thirty-first Dynasty: Persians.	XXXI. Thirty-first Dynasty: 3 kings from Persia.	

A	E (arm, sync)	E (jer)
XXXI.1. In his twentieth year as king of Persia, Okhos acquired Egypt and ruled		Ochus took Egypt after driving Nectanebus into Ethiopia. This was the destruction of the Egyptian monarchy. Manetho reached this point.
2 years.	6 years.	
XXXI.2. Arses ruled 3 years.	XXXI.2. Next, Arses, son of Okhos, ruled 4 years.	
XXXI.3. Dareios ruled 4 years.	XXXI.3. Next Dareios, whom Alexander of Macedon killed, ruled 6 years.	
Total of years in volume 3 of Manetho, 1,550. Manetho reached this point.	This is from volume 3 of Manetho.	
The sequel comes from Greek writers.		

F2b

Syncellus *Ecloga Chronographica* (*Chronological Excerpts*) 97: With the 113 generations in the three volumes recorded in thirty dynasties, their time reaches a total of 3,555 years, beginning with the 1,586th year of the world and ending at the 5,147th year of the world, or about 15 years before Alexander the Macedonian's conquest of the world.

F2c

Syncellus *Ecloga Chronographica* (*Chronological Excerpts*) 486: As far as Okhos and Nektanebos, Manetho recorded the thirty-one dynasties of Egypt,

1,050 years of his third volume. Later matters are from writers of Greek history; fifteen Macedonian kings.

History of Egypt, Volume 1 (Predynastic and Dynasties I–XI)

F3a

Malalas, *Chronographia* (*Chronicle*) p. 21 Bonn: When therefore Hermes himself arrived in Egypt (from Italy), Mestraim from the family of Kham reigned over the Egyptians; on his death the Egyptians made Hermes king, and he reigned arrogantly over the Egyptians for thirty-nine years.

And after him Hephaistos reigned over the Egyptians for 1,680 days, which makes 4 years, 7 months, 3 days; for the Egyptians then did not know how to measure years, but they called the period of the day "years." They called the same Hephaistos a god, for he was a warrior and mystic. He became lame when his horse fell during a war. The same Hephaistos established it as law for women to have one husband and remain faithful, and for those found in adultery to be punished. . . . The same Hephaistos, in consequence of a mystical prayer, received out of the air the brilliant idea of making weapons from iron . . . for before him they made war with clubs and stones. After the death of Hephaistos, his son Helios was king of the Egyptians for 4,477 days, which would be 12 years and 97 days; for neither the Egyptians at that time nor anyone else knew how to calculate a number, but instead some counted the periods of the moon as years while others counted the periods of days as years. Reckoning by twelve-month periods was developed later, after the names for taxation intervals were introduced.

After the death of the king Helios, . . . Sosis was king of the Egyptians. After his reign Osiris was king, and after Osiris, Horus was king. After Horus, the king was Thoulis, who, with a great army, captured all the land as far as the ocean. And during the conquest he arrogantly approached the oracle in the African land, and after sacrificing he made inquiry, saying, "Tell me, O mighty in fire, undeceiving, blessed one who runs a course through the blazing upper heaven: Who before my reign was able to conquer all, or who will conquer all after me?" And he received this response: "First was god, then reason, and spirit with them; all were born together and converge in one, which has eternal power. Walk with swift feet, mortal, as you fulfill your uncertain destiny." And immediately on leaving the oracular shrine, he was seized by his own people and slain in Africa.

Manetho recorded these old and ancient reigns of the Egyptians. In his writings he mentions that the names of the five planets are different, because they used to call the star of Kronos "the shining one"; Zeus's star was "the glowing one," Ares's "the fiery," Aphrodite's "the most beautiful," and Hermes's "the glistening."

F3b

Lydus *de Mensibus* (*On the Months*) 4.86: In volume 3[17] of his *History of Egypt*, Manetho says that the first man to be king among the Egyptians was Hephaistos, who also discovered fire and gave it to them. After him came his son Helios, and then Helios's son Kronos. Next was Osiris, and then Osiris's brother Typhon.

F4

Malalas *Chronographia* (*Chronicle*) p. 59 Bonn: The Egyptian kingships before him (Pharao/Narakho; cf. F7a–b) were recorded by the very learned Manetho.

F5

Excerpta Latina Barbari (*Excerpts in Bad Latin*) fol. 38a: We have found the Egyptian monarchy to be the oldest of all monarchies. We write the record of its beginning, as it is told by Manetho.

First I shall do the reigns of the gods, written by themselves, as follows:

1. Some say the god Hephaistos[18] ruled in Egypt	680 years.
2. After him Sol, son of Hephaistos,	77 years.
3. After him Sosinosiris	320 years.
4. After him Prince Oros	28 years.
5. After him Typhon	45 years.
The total regnal years of the gods:	1,550.

Next the reigns of the demigods are as follows:

---

17. Lydus's error; he should have written volume 1.

18. This writer of bad Latin wrote *Ifestus*; we have regularized it and other such idiosyncrasies.

1. First Anubes (corrupt)		83 years.
2. After him (corrupt)		67 years.
I.	After these he puts in kings of the dead, calling them also demigods and heroes	2,100 years.
II.	Mineus and his seven descendants ruled	253 years.
III.	Bochus and eight others	302 years.
IV.	Necherocheus and seven others	214 years.
V.	Likewise seventeen others	277 years.
VI.	Likewise twenty-one others	258 years.
VII.	Othoi and seven others	203 years.
VIII.	Likewise also fourteen others	140 years.
IX.	Likewise also twenty others	409 years.
X.	Likewise also seven others	204 years.

This is the end of Manetho's first volume, containing 2,100 years.[19]

History of Egypt, Volume 2 (Dynasties XII–XIX)

F6

Excerpta Latina Barbari (*Excerpts in Bad Latin*) fol. 38a:

XI.	Dynasty of Diospolis	160 years.
XII.	Dynasty of Bubastis	153 years.
XIII.	Dynasty of Tanis	184 years.
XIV.	Dynasty of Sebennytos	224 years.
XV.	Dynasty of Memphis	318 years.
XVI.	Dynasty of Heliopolis	221 years.
XVII.	Dynasty of Hermoupolis	260 years.

---

19. This is incorrect. Our better witnesses (F2a) give 2,300 years.

The second volume reaches the Seventeenth Dynasty, covering, as it explains, 1,520 years.[20] These are the dynasties of the Egyptians.

F7a

Malalas *Chronographia* (*Chronicle*) p. 21 Bonn: Afterward the king of the Egyptians was Sostris, the first from the tribe of Ham, who took arms and warred against the Assyrians, and he subjugated them and the Chaldeans and the Persians as far as Babylon. Likewise he subjugated Asia and all Europe and Scythia and Mysia. . . .

And the king Sostris, taking possession of Egypt, died after his victory, and after him the king of the land of the Egyptians was Pharao, also called Narakho. And from his line came the rest of the kings of the Egyptians.

F7b

Malalas *Chronographia* (*Chronicle*) p. 59 Bonn: Of the Egyptians (until the time of Abraham) the first king from the tribe of Ham, son of Noah, was Pharao, also called Narakho.

F8

Scholiast on Plato *Timaeus* 21E (p. 282 Greene): *Saïs:* From Manetho's *History of Egypt*: The Seventeenth Dynasty were Shepherds, Phoenician brothers, foreign kings, who also took Memphis; their first king, Saites, ruled 19 years, and the Saite Nome is named for him; they also founded a city in the Sethroite Nome, and setting out from there they conquered the Egyptians. Their second king, Bnon, ruled 40 years; the third, Arkhaës, ruled 30 years; the fourth, Aphophis, 14 years. Total: 103 years.

Saïs added twelve hours to the month, so that it was of 30 days, and 5 days to the year, and it became one of 365 days.

F9

Josephus *contra Apionem* (*Against Apion*) 1.74–92 (= Eusebius *Chronicon* [*Chronicle*] p. 70, line 3–p. 72, line 24 Karst; in an Armenian translation;

---

20. This is incorrect. F2a gives 2,121 years.

Eusebius *Praeparatio Evangelica* [*Preparation for the Gospel*] 10.13): This Manetho, in the second volume of his *History of Egypt,* writes about us as follows—I will quote his exact words, just as if I were producing a witness in court: (75) "Toutimaios.[21] In his reign God, I know not why, breathed against us, and suddenly from the east people of unknown race boldly invaded our land, and they easily seized it without a battle, (76) and capturing the governors of the land they then cruelly burned the cities and destroyed the temples of the gods, and they treated all the inhabitants with utmost hostility, slaughtering some and enslaving the wives and children of others. (77) Furthermore they enthroned one of their own, whose name was Salitis; and he established himself in Memphis, exacting tribute from both Upper and Lower Egypt and posting garrisons in strategic locations; he especially fortified the eastern district, foreseeing that the Assyrians would some day grow stronger and desire to attack his kingdom. (78) In the Sethroite Nome he found a very well-situated city, lying on the east side of the Bubastite River and called Avaris for ancient religious reasons: he rebuilt this place and gave it impregnable walls and installed in it a guard of 240,000 soldiers. (79) He would come here in the summer to distribute food and pay and also to carry out maneuvers carefully intended to frighten those across the frontier. He died after 19 years of rule.

(80) After him another named Beon[22] ruled 44 years.

After whom another, Apakhnas, ruled 36 years and 7 months.

And then Apophis for 61 years, and Iannas for 50 years and 1 month.

(81) And lastly Assis, 49 years and 2 months.

And these were the first six rulers among them, always making war and always more and more destructive in their desire to destroy the Egyptians root and branch."

(82) The entire tribe was named *Hyksos,* that is, "king-shepherds": for ʿ*uk* in the language of priestly writings means "a king," while in the vernacular *sos* means "shepherd" and "shepherds," and *Hyksos* is the resultant compound.

Some say that they were Arabs.

(83) In another copy it says that the expression *hyk* does not mean kings but the opposite and that the compound word would mean "captive-shep-

---

21. The text here seems corrupt. Most editors divine that a pharaoh's name, perhaps a version of, for example, Thutmose, underlies this word.

22. This name appears as Bnon in F2a. The text of Josephus is perhaps corrupt.

herds"; for in Egyptian *hyk* and *hak*—note the *h*—clearly mean "captives"; and this seems to me more persuasive and closer to ancient history.[23]

(84) Manetho says that these previously mentioned kings—both the "Shepherds" and those descended from them—controlled Egypt for 511 years. (85) He says that after this there arose a revolt against the Shepherds from the people in the Thebaid and the rest of Egypt, and a great and long war broke out between them. (86) He says that in the reign of a king named Misphragmouthosis the Shepherds were defeated, driven out of the rest of Egypt, and blockaded in a place containing 5,000 acres; the place was named Avaris. (87) The Shepherds, he says, surrounded this place with a strong and high wall to protect their possessions and booty. (88) Thoummosis, the son of Misphragmouthosis, besieged them and tried to capture them by force, with an army of 480,000 around the walls. But when he had given up the siege, he made a treaty whereby the Shepherds might all leave Egypt and go unharmed wherever they wished. (89) Under this agreement, the Shepherds with all their households and possessions, being no fewer than 240,000, left Egypt and journeyed through the desert into Syria, and in the land now called Judea, (90) fearing the Assyrians who were in control of Asia, they built a city large enough for all their myriads of people, and they named it Jerusalem.

(91) In another book of his *History of Egypt,* Manetho says that, in the sacred books of the Egyptians, the tribe known as Shepherds are called captives, and rightly so, because tending sheep was an ancient custom of our earliest ancestors, and from their nomadic way of life they were called Shepherds. (92) It is also reasonable that they were called captives in the Egyptian records, because our ancestor Joseph told the king of Egypt that he was a captive, and with the king's permission he later sent for his brothers to come to Egypt . . .

F10

Josephus *contra Apionem* (*Against Apion*) 1.93–105 (= Eusebius *Chronicon* [*Chronicle*] p. 72, line 25–p. 74, line 6 Karst, in an Armenian translation; Theophilus *ad Autolycum* [*Against Autolycus*] 3.20): I will therefore return to my citations on chronology from Manetho's writings. (94) He says as follows: "After the people of the Shepherds made their exodus out of Egypt to

---

23. Modern Egyptologists view the Hyksos as Asiatic invaders who dominated Egypt in Dynasties XV and XVI, ca. 1650–1550 B.C., and they interpret the name *Hyksos* as meaning "Lords of the Foreign Lands," thus disagreeing with Josephus's version(s) of Manetho's explanation(s). The epitome, however, does gloss Hyksos as "Foreign Kings" (see F2a, D. XVII.)

Jerusalem, Tethmosis, the king who expelled them, reigned 25 more years and 4 months and then died.

(95) And his son Khebron inherited the throne from him and reigned 13 years.

After him Amenophis reigned 20 years and 7 months.

His sister Amesses, 21 years and 9 months.

Her son Mephres, 12 years and 9 months.

His son Mephramouthosis, 25 years and 10 months.

(96) His son Thmosis,[24] 9 years and 8 months.

His son Amenophis, 30 years and 10 months.

His son Oros, 36 years and 5 months.

His daughter Akenkheres, 12 years and 1 month.

Her brother Rhathotis, 9 years.

(97) His son Akenkheres, 12 years and 5 months.

His son Akenkheres the Second, 12 years and 3 months.

His son Harmais, 4 years and 1 month.

His son Rhamesses, 1 year and 4 months.

His son Rhamesses Miamoun, 66 years and 2 months.

His son Amenophis, 19 years and 6 months.

(98) And his son Sethos, who is also called Rhamesses, having a cavalry force and a navy, appointed his brother Harmais as viceroy of Egypt and gave him all royal power, but commanded him not to wear a crown or touch the queen, who was mother of his children, and to keep away from the other royal concubines. (99) He himself went on an expedition against Cyprus and Phoenicia, and also against the Assyrians and the Medes. He conquered some in battle, and he captured others without a battle because they feared his large army. Elated by his successes, he extended his campaigns and conquered the cities and lands to the east. (100) After waiting until it seemed safe, Harmais, the brother left behind in Egypt, began fearlessly to disobey all of his brother's instructions. He raped the queen and used the concubines mercilessly. At the urging of his friends, he wore a crown and supplanted his brother. (101) The man in charge of the temples of Egypt wrote a letter and sent it to Sethos, telling him the full story of how his brother Harmais had supplanted him. Sethos therefore returned instantly to Pelusium and recaptured his throne." (102) The country is called "Egypt" from this same name, because it is said that Sethos was called Aigyptos, and his brother Harmais was called Danaos.

---

24. The text is perhaps corrupt, covering a version of Touthmosis.

(103) That is the account of Manetho. If the time of the years mentioned is added up, it is clear that those called "Shepherds," our ancestors, left Egypt and settled this land 393 years before Danaos arrived at Argos. The Argives, however, view Danaos as extremely ancient. (104) From the written records of the Egyptians, therefore, Manetho has furnished two extremely important pieces of testimony about us. The first is that we were immigrants into Egypt. The second is that our departure from there was so ancient as to antedate the Trojan War by nearly a thousand years. (105) As for the things that Manetho has added that come not from the written records of the Egyptians but, as he himself admits, from nameless oral tradition, I shall refute these things later (see F12) and show in detail that his false tales deserve no belief.

F11

Josephus *contra Apionem* (*Against Apion*) 2.16: Manetho says that the Exodus of the Jews from Egypt took place 393 years before the flight of Danaos to Argos. Lysimakhos (*FGrHist* #621) puts it in the reign of Bokkhoris, that is, 1,700 years earlier. Molon (*FGrHist* #728) and others have other views. (17) Most believable of all is of course[25] Apion (*FGrHist* #616), who put the Exodus precisely in the seventh Olympiad (752–748 B.C.).

F12

Josephus *contra Apionem* (*Against Apion*) 1.223, 226–53, 287: It was the Egyptians who began the slanders against us. Others, wishing to ingratiate themselves with the Egyptians, have also tried to pervert the truth. They have falsely denied our ancestors' arrival in Egypt as well as the Exodus. . . . (226) Some of them have become so insanely narrow-minded as to dare to contradict their own earlier writings, and they blindly failed to see that they were contradicting themselves. (227) I shall first discuss the account of one whose testimony for our antiquity I recently used.

(228) This is the Manetho who promised to translate Egyptian history from the priestly writings. He declared that our ancestors, tens of thousands of them, had come into Egypt and conquered the inhabitants. He then agreed that they had later gone into exile, occupied the land now called Judea, founded Jerusalem, and built the temple. Up to this point he followed the

---

25. Josephus is being sarcastic toward Apion.

written records. (229) Then, however, he promised to record the myths and legends about the Jews. With this license he inserted unbelievable stories, wanting to confuse us with a mass of Egyptians who were, he says, deported from Egypt for leprosy and other diseases.

(230) He mentioned King Amenophis. Because this name was a fiction, he did not dare to specify the regnal years, although he gave the exact number of years for the other kings. To this king he attached certain mythical tales, forgetting that his account had put the Exodus of the Shepherds to Jerusalem 518 years earlier. (231) For Tethmosis was king at the time of the Exodus, and according to Manetho there were 393 years for the kings from Tethmosis down to the two brothers Sethos and Hermaios. Manetho says that Sethos was named Aigyptos and Hermaios was named Danaos. After expelling Hermaios, Sethos ruled fifty-nine years, and after him his son Rhampses ruled sixty-six years. (232) Manetho therefore admitted that this many years had passed since our ancestors left Egypt, but he then interpolated King Amenophis. He says that this king felt a desire to see the gods, just as Or, one of the preceding kings, had done. He told his desire to his namesake Amenophis son of Paapis, who was reputed to be partly divine because of his wisdom and his knowledge of the future. (233) This namesake then told the king that he would be able to see gods if he cleansed the whole country of lepers and other "unclean" people. (234) The king gladly rounded up all those in Egypt with deformed bodies, eighty thousand of them. (235) He put them to work in the stone-quarries in the part of the country east of the Nile, so that they might be productive as well as segregated from the other Egyptians. Manetho says that among them were some learned priests afflicted with leprosy. (236) But Amenophis, the wise prophet, became afraid that he and the king would suffer the wrath of the gods if the mistreatment of the priests became known. He also said that the unclean people would find allies and sieze control of Egypt for thirteen years. Afraid to tell this to the king, he put his whole prophecy in writing and committed suicide. The king became despondent.

(237) Manetho's exact words are now as follows: "After those in the quarries had suffered for a long time, they asked the king to give them a separate dwelling place and refuge, the city Avaris that had been deserted by the Shepherds. He granted their request. According to religious belief, the city was from the beginning sacred to Typhon. (238) When they had occupied this city and had this place as a base for revolt, they appointed Osarsephos, said to be a priest of Heliopolis, as their leader, and they took an oath of total obedi-

ence to him. (239) His first act was to legislate that they should not worship
the gods or show reverence for any of the animals regarded as sacred by the
Egyptians, not even the holiest. They should sacrifice and use all of them, and
they should have nothing to do with any person except those who shared in
the oath. (240) After imposing these laws and many others completely
counter to Egyptian culture, he ordered them to put all hands to work fortify-
ing the walls of the city and preparing for the war against King Amenophis.
(241) Osarsephos himself formed a council with the other "unclean" priests
and sent ambassadors to the Shepherds, those who had been expelled. . . . He
explained to them what had happened to him and the other dishonored ones,
and he asked them to join wholeheartedly in an expedition against Egypt.
(242) He offered first to lead them to their ancestral homeland Avaris and to
supply their people generously with everything they needed, to fight for them
whenever necessary, and to give them easy conquest of the land. (243) They
were overjoyed, and all twenty thousand set out eagerly together. They soon
arrived at Avaris. Amenophis, the king of the Egyptians, was deeply disturbed
when he learned about their invasion, because he remembered the prediction
of Amenophis son of Paapis. (244) He first gathered a great number of Egyptians and conferred with their leaders. He then sent for all the most sacred
animals in the temples to be brought to him, and he sent orders to the priests
in each district to hide the wooden images of the gods as well as possible.
(245) He sent his five-year-old son Sethos, also called Rhamesses, named
after Amenophis's father Rhapses, away to a friend. Amenophis himself set
out across the country with three hundred thousand of the best Egyptian
soldiers. Although they encountered the enemy, he did not join battle, (246)
because he thought he should not fight against the gods. He turned back and
arrived at Memphis, where he collected Apis and the other sacred animals
that had been sent to him there, and he immediately set out for Ethiopia with
his whole large army of Egyptians. The king of Ethiopia was in his debt.
(247) Amenophis and all his people were welcomed there, and the Ethiopian
king gave them all the produce they needed. He gave them enough cities and
villages to live in for the predicted thirteen years of exile. He also posted an
Ethiopian army on the Egyptian frontier to guard Amenophis and his people.
(248) Such was the situation in Ethiopia. Meanwhile, the army that had come
back to Egypt . . . and joined with the "unclean" Egyptians treated the people
so impiously that their previous occupation as "Shepherds" seemed like a
golden age to those who saw their current sacrileges. (249) They not only
burned cities and villages, plundered the sanctuaries, and befouled the images

of the gods, but they also kept the kitchens going to cook the sacred animals that the people revered. They forced priests and prophets to slay and butcher the animals, and they threw the men out naked." (250) It is said that the man who gave them their constitution and laws was a priest of the people of Heliopolis, named Osarseph from Osiris the god of Heliopolis. When he changed his allegiance, he changed his name and was called Moses.

(251) These, then, are the Egyptian legends about the Jews. There are more, which I pass over for the sake of brevity. I shall, however, give some more of Manetho's tale. After all this Amenophis invaded from Ethiopia with a large force, and his son Rhampses also had an army. These two met up with the Shepherds and the "unclean" ones, and they defeated them. They killed many and pursued the rest as far as the borders of Syria. This, and similar material, is what Manetho wrote.

(252) I shall prove that he is obviously a ridiculous liar, after I emphasize one point that will be useful in arguing against others. Manetho has admitted that we were not originally Egyptians, that we entered from elsewhere, conquered Egypt, and then left. (253) But I shall refute him from his own statements and prove that we were not mixed in with the later class of diseased Egyptians, and that the one who led them was not Moses, who had lived many generations earlier. . . . (287) I therefore think it has become plain enough that, when Manetho followed the ancient written records, he came close to the truth. But when he turned to the anonymous myths, he either combined them implausibly or relied on anti-Jewish accounts.

F13

Cosmas *Topographia Christiana* (*Christian Topography*) 12 (p. 327 line 11 Winstedt): Those who have written histories of Egypt, that is, Manetho, Khairemon (*FGrHist* #618), Apollonios Molon (*FGrHist* #728), Lysimakhos (*FGrHist* #621), and the grammarian Apion (*FGrHist* #616), have mentioned Moses and the Exodus of the children of Israel from Egypt.[26] As Egyptians writing about Egyptian matters, they are in good agreement about topography. Some of them also attack Moses as a troublemaker, who stirred up a host

26. All of these writers of Egyptian history are regarded as having featured popular fables of an anti-Jewish character. Their dates follow: Khairemon of Alexandria, first century A.D.; Apollonios Molon of Rhodes, second to first centuries B.C.; Lysimakhos, perhaps first century B.C. to first century A.D.; Apion of Alexandria, the foe of Josephus, first century A.D.

of derelicts and invalids and led them out of Egypt. And they escaped to Mount Sinai and Jerusalem and were called Jews.

F14

Ecloga Historiarum (Historical Selections)—(full title: *Historical Selections from the Book of Moses and from the Distingushed Foreign Historians and from Holy Scripture, Narrating in Sections up to the Reign of Anastasios*)—in J. A. Cramer, ed., *Anecdota Graeca e Codicibus Manuscriptis Bibliothecae Regiae Parisiensis* (Oxford, 1839) 2:189: The year 4068, in which is acknowledged the discovery of the grapevine by Dionysos, not the son of Semele, but the one born from Ammon and Amaltheia,[27] as the Egyptians say. . . . Then also is acknowledged the first Herakles in Phoenicia. . . . Then also Danaos is king of Egypt according to Manetho. . . . Then also Egypt, previously called Aëreia, received its current name.

History of Egypt, Volume 3 (Dynasties XX–XXX / XXXI)

F15

Baden Papyrus (F. Bilabel, ed., *Baden Papyri*, Publications from the Baden Papyrus-Collections 4 [1924] = *Die kleine Historikerfragmente auf Papyrus* [1922], 34), no. 59 (fifth century A.D.):[28]

In the fourth year of his reign over the Persians, (Kambyses) became king (of Egypt) and reigned six years.

The Magoi reigned seven months.

Dareios son of Hystaspes reigned thirty-six years.

Xerxes the Great reigned (lac.) years.

Artabanos reigned (lac.) months.

---

27. In mainstream pan-Hellenic myth, Dionysos is the son of Zeus and the Theban princess Semele, who was burned to death when she insisted that Zeus reveal himself in his full divine glory. The embryo was rescued and implanted in Zeus's thigh, where it grew to birth (see Euripides's play *Bacchae*). Ammon was a Libyan version of Zeus, worshiped at the oasis of Siwah. Amaltheia was a she-goat.

28. Although this text does not mention Manetho, it is included because its phrasing strongly resembles the epitome's presentation of Manetho's D. XXVII (see F2a.)

Artaxerxes Longhand, son, reigned (lac.) years.
Xerxes II reigned (lac.) months.
Sogdianos reigned (lac.) months.
Dareios Nothos reigned (lac.) years.
(lac.) ph (lac.) son (lac.)

F16

Moses of Chorene *Historia Armeniae* (*History of Armenia*) 2.12: This Nektanebos was the last king of the Egyptians. His story is told by Manetho, and
some have said that he was the father of Alexander.

Against Herodotus

F17

Eustathius *Commentarii ad Homeri Iliadem* (*Commentary on Homer's Iliad*)
11.480: **Lîs**, "lion," just as **leôn**, "lion," comes from **laô**, "I see," according to
the grammarian Orus, because the lion is so sharp-sighted. Also, as Manetho
says in *Against Herodotus*, the lion does not sleep—which is incredible, for it
would not stay always awake, but rather, the ancients say, it sleeps with its
eyes open, on the watch for a gazelle—**dorkas**, corrupted from **derkô**, "I
see"—or a rabbit—**lagôs**, from **laô**, "I see."

Sacred Book

(This title is given by T7. No fragments survive.)

On Antiquity and Religion

F18

Porphyrius *de Abstinentia* (*On Abstinence*) 2.55: Amosis put an end to the
custom of human sacrifice in Egyptian Heliopolis, as Manetho testifies in *On
Antiquity and Religion*. Human beings used to be sacrificed to Hera, and they
were inspected, just as the pure calves that are sought for and marked with a
seal. Three were sacrificed each day. Amosis ordered life-size waxen images
to take their place.

On Festivals

F19

Lydus *de Mensibus* (*On the Months*) 4.87: One ought to know that, as Manetho says in *On Festivals*, an eclipse of the sun brings a harmful flux around the human head and stomach.

On the Preparation of Kyphi

F20

Plutarch *de Iside et Osiride* (*On Isis and Osiris*) 52 p. 372C: And it is said that Horus, son of Isis, was the first of all to sacrifice to Helios on the fourth day of the first part of the month, as it is written in *The Birthday of Horus*. Indeed, there is each day a three-part use of incense to Helios: first, resin at the Sun's rising, then myrrh when he is in the middle of the sky, and finally the substance called *kyphi*[29] at Sun's setting. Later I will give an explanation of each of these.

F21

Plutarch *de Iside et Osiride* (*On Isis and Osiris*) 80 pp. 383E–384C: *kyphi* is a mixture of sixteen ingredients compounded: honey, wine, raisin, galingale, resin, myrrh, thorny trefoil, hartwort, mastic, asphalt, thorn apple, dock, both kinds of juniper—they call one "the greater" and the other "the lesser"—cardamom, and reed. These are mixed in an orderly way, and the ointment recipes of sacred writings are read when they are being mixed. . . . They use *kyphi* both as a beverage and as an unguent; for it is believed to be a purgative when drunk and an emollient in cream form. As separate substances, resin is a product of the sun, and myrrh is a product of the plants that weep from the sun's heat, but the ingredients of *kyphi* are rather the ones to give cheer at nightfall for such beings as are nourished by cool breezes and shade and dew and moisture. . . . It therefore makes good sense that the former in-

---

29. *Kyphi* was generally well known among the Greeks and Egyptians in both cult and medicine, where it was valued for its narcotic, euphoric properties. See Galen 13.199.

censes, used as simple substances that are generated by the sun, are used during the day, while the latter, a compound with all sorts of qualities, is the incense for nightfall.

F22

Suda (*Fortress of Knowledge*) s.v. *kyphi*: Manetho the Egyptian prepared this, but there is controversy over the method of preparation.

Digest of Physics

F23

Diogenes Laertius *Vitae Philosophorum* (*Lives of the Philosophers*) 1.10: The philosophy of the Egyptians, about the gods and justice, is of this sort: they say the beginning to be substance, and that then the four elements were separated out of it, and certain animals were formed, and the gods were Sun and Moon, the one called Osiris and the other Isis; they allude enigmatically to them through the scarab, serpent, hawk, and other animals, as Manetho says in the *Digest of Physics* and Hekataios[30] (*FGrHist* #264) in the first book about the philosophy of the Egyptians. They build statues and sanctuaries so that the form of the god may not be known. (11) The universe is subject to birth and death and is spherical; the stars are fire, and by mixing with them things come into existence on the earth; the moon is eclipsed by falling into the earth's shadow; the soul both abides and transmigrates; rains come in accordance with the turning of the atmosphere.

Miscellaneous

F24

Eusebius *Praeparatio Evangelica* (*Preparation for the Gospel*) 3.2.6: These are the stories of the Greeks. Let us now hear the oldest stories of the barbarians, namely, those of the Egyptians. They say that Isis and Osiris are the sun and the moon; Zeus is the spirit that moves through all things, Hephaistos is

---

30. Hekataios of Abdera (late fourth to early third centuries B.C.) wrote a *History of Egypt,* philosophical and ethnographic in tone (*FGrHist* #264).

fire, and the earth is named Demeter; moisture is regarded as Ocean among the Egyptians, as also their river Nile, to which they attribute the origins of the gods; and they say that they call the air Athena. These five gods—I mean the air and the water and the fire and the earth and the spirit—travel on the entire world, taking on the forms and appearances of men and of all sorts of animals, different ones at different times; and mortals bearing the same names came into being, named Sun and Kronos and Rhea, also Zeus and Hera and Hephaistos and Hestia. Manetho writes rather extensively about these things.

F25

Plutarch *de Iside et Osiride* (*On Isis and Osiris*) 9 p. 354C: Furthermore, although most believe that "Amoun" (which we corrupt into "Ammon") is a proper name given to Zeus by the Egyptians, Manetho of Sebennytos thinks that "that which has been concealed" and "concealment" are manifested by this word, while Hekataios of Abdera (*FGrHist* #264) says that the Egyptians use this word among themselves whenever they address someone, because the word is a form of address. Therefore they call the first god, whom they believe to be identical with The All, "Amoun," as though summoning someone invisible and hidden and urging him to become visible and manifest to them.

F26

Plutarch *de Iside et Osiride* (*On Isis and Osiris*) 49 p. 371(B)C: But Typhon is the part of the soul that is like the Titans: passionate, impulsive, irrational, and unstable. He is the part of the body that is morbid and diseased and causes disturbances, such as storms, extremes of temperature, and eclipes of the sun and moon. These are like attacks and outbursts of Typhon. And the name "Seth," by which they call Typhon, means this: it means "that which overpowers and subdues by violence," and it often means "reversal" and also "outbreak." Some say that Bebon was one of the companions of Typhon, but Manetho says that Typhon himself was called Bebon; the name means "constraint" or "hindrance," meaning that the power of Typhon obstructs actions that are proceeding on their way and traveling toward the proper goal. (50) Therefore, they assign to him the most stupid of domesticated animals,

the ass, and the most savage of wild animals, the crocodile and the hippopotamus.

F27

Plutarch *de Iside et Osiride* (*On Isis and Osiris*) 62 p. 376(A)B: Egyptian lore
is also like these (i.e., divine names admitting of etymological explanation).
For they often call Isis by the name of Athena, expressing this sort of idea: "I
came from myself," which manifests self-initiated motion; but Typhon, as it
is said, is named Seth and Bebon and Smy, names signifying a violent and
obstructive restraint or an opposition or reversal. Furthermore they call the
lodestone the "bone of Horus" and iron the "bone of Typhon," as Manetho
records; for just as iron is often like a thing pulled and drawn to the stone but
often also turns away and is driven in the opposite direction, so also with the
cosmic motion that preserves and is good and is rational. At one time it at-
tracts and draws and softens, persuading that harsh Typhonian motion, but at
other times it has reversed its power and turned the other around and plunged
it into confusion.

F28

Plutarch *de Iside et Osiride* (*On Isis and Osiris*) 73 p. 380(C)D: Many say
that the soul of Typhon is dispersed among these animals, and this myth
seems to encode the idea that every irrational and bestial soul is a portion of
the evil spirit and that men appease and conciliate that spirit by tending and
worshiping these animals. If a long and severe drought occurs, bringing many
fatal diseases or other strange and unexplainable disasters, then the priests
lead away some of the honored animals, calmly and by night, and they begin
the ritual by threatening and frightening them. If the drought persists, they go
on to consecrate and slaughter them. This is a sort of punishment of the spirit
and also a purification for the greatest pollutions. And indeed in the city of
Eilethyia they burned living human beings, as Manetho has recorded, calling
them "Typhonians," and they winnowed their ashes and made them vanish by
scattering them. But this was done publicly, at a certain time in the dog days,
whereas the consecrations of honored animals take place in secret at irregular
times as the need arises, and most people are unaware of them—except when
they hold the funeral of Apis. Then they pick out some of all the animals

present and lay them to rest together with Apis, in the belief that this gives pain back to Typhon and diminishes his pleasure, because Apis, with a few other animals, is deemed worthy to be sacred to Osiris, and they accord the greatest honors to him.

F29a

Aelian *de Natura Animalium* (*On the Nature of Animals*) 10.16: Because of her gluttony, the sow is merciless even toward her own offspring, and even when she chances on a human body does not restrain herself but eats it; the Egyptians therefore hated her as a loathsome animal. . . . but I hear that the Egyptian Manetho, a man who had reached the pinnacle of erudition, said that a person who has tasted of sow's milk becomes full of white and scaly leprosy. All Asians indeed hate these diseases. The Egyptians believe that the sow is abominated by both the Sun and the Moon; when they hold a festival to the Moon, they sacrifice sows to her this once a year, but at other times they are unwilling to sacrifice this animal to her or to any other god, since she is an abomination. . . . However, Eudoxos[31] says that the Egyptians refrain from sacrificing swine out of respect for them, because when the grain has been sown, they drive the herds of swine onto the fields, and the swine trample the wheat and drive it into the moister ground so that it remains alive and is not destroyed by the birds.

F29b

Plutarch *de Iside et Osiride* (*On Isis and Osiris*) 8 pp. 353F–354A:[32] Likewise they also think that the sow is an unholy animal, because she is most likely to breed in the waning of the moon, and those who drink her milk have their bodies break out in leprosy and scabrous callouses. (354A) There is a story added by some who were once sacrificing and eating a pig at the full moon, that Typhon chasing a pig toward the full moon found the wooden coffin in which the body of Osiris lay and ripped it to pieces. Not everyone

---

31. Eudoxos of Knidos (fourth century B.C.), the famous astronomer and geometrician, visited Egypt and is credited with introducing Egyptian astronomy into Greece.

32. Although this passage does not mention Manetho, it seems to reflect the same text as F29a, which is attributed to Manetho. Also, Plutarch has cited Manetho elsewhere in *de Iside et Osiride* (F20, F21, F25–F28).

accepts this tale, believing it to be, like many other things, a recent misunderstanding.

F30

Josephus *Antiquitates Judaicae* (*Jewish Antiquities*) 1.107: All the historians, Greeks and non-Greek, who wrote foundation stories support me in this. Manetho, who wrote Egyptian history, and Berossos, the compiler of Babylonian history, and Mokhos (*FGrHist* #784 F3), and Hestiaios (*FGrHist* #786 F2), and besides them the Egyptian Hieronymos (*FGrHist* #787 F1), writers of Phoenician history—they agree with what I am saying, and also Hesiod, Hekataios (*FGrHist* #1 F35), Hellanikos (*FGrHist* #4 F202), Akousilaos (*FGrHist* #2 F46), Ephoros (*FGrHist* #70 F238), and Nikolaos (*FGrHist* #90 F141)—their judgment is that the ancients lived a thousand years.[33]

---

33. For further information on the writers named here, see Berossos F15c n. 57.

CHAPTER 8

Pseudo-Manetho—
Ancient Testimony and Fragments

Apotelesmatika (Astrological Influences)

T1

Suda (Fortress of Knowledge) s.v. "Manethos": From Diospolis in Egypt, or from Sebennytos . . . *Apotelesmatika (Astrological Influences)*[1] in verse; and some other astronomical writings.

F1

Pseudo-Manetho *Apotelesmatika (Astrological Influences)* 1(5).1–15: May you rejoice, O Ptolemy, having received the kingly honor of our land, world-begetting Egypt; I bring you these gifts, worthy of royal power, the manifestations of the heavenly stars, of those that do not wander and of those that do, . . . being sleepless at nights and toiling much in the days, . . . so that I may tell quite unerringly all the very things that Petosiris[2] himself has fluently spoken, . . . so that you may learn that we, whose lot it is to dwell in holy Egypt, are in all ways learned men.

---

1. On this work and on the *Book of Sothis*, see "Manetho's Life and Work" in chap. 5.
2. Petosiris was the name of a well-known priest of Thoth (= Hermes) at Hermoupolis, who died around 300 B.C., named here as a (fictitious) mentor of "Manetho."

F2

Pseudo-Manetho *Apotelesmatika* (*Astrological Influences*) 2(6).1–11: From
the unenterable sacred books, King Ptolemy, and from the secret
monuments that all-wise Hermes[3] erected, finding Asklepios[4] a counselor
of wise understanding, . . . for none has gained the glory of such wisdom but
Petosiris alone, by far the dearest man to me.

Book of Sothis

T1a

Syncellus *Ecloga Chronographica* (*Chronological Excerpts*) 32: Manetho
of Sebennytos, chief priest of the polluted temples in Egypt, born—later
than Berossos—in the time of Ptolemy Philadelphos, writes to the same
Ptolemy, telling lies like Berossos. (See *Book of Sothis* F2a–b.)

T1b

Syncellus *Ecloga Chronographica* (*Chronological Excerpts*) 72: Also concerning the dynasty of the Egyptians, it remains to excerpt briefly out of
Manetho of Sebennytos, who bore the title of chief priest of the idols in
Egypt in the time of Ptolemy Philadelphos, and who—from, he says, the
monuments lying in the Seriadic land in the sacred language and inscribed
in hieroglyphic characters by Thoth the first Hermes and translated after the
deluge from the sacred language into the Greek language in hieroglyphics
and disposed into books by Agathodaimon, son of the second Hermes,
father of Tat, in the inner sancta of the temples of Egypt—in the *Book of
Sothis* made dedication to the same king, Ptolemy II Philadelphos, in the
following words.[5] (See *Book of Sothis* F1.)

---

3. Hermes (= Thoth) was made the inspiring god of a large body of forged mystical writing
in late antiquity.

4. Asklepios was a Greek god of healing, with cults at various places. His most famous
sanctuary was at Epidauros in Greece.

5. This passage furnishes the title *Book of Sothis* for this forgery. "Sothis" is a Greek
version of "Shopdu," the Egyptian name for Sirius (the Dog Star). It is in the title because the
ancient Egyptians began each calendar year (365 days) with the annual reappearance of Sothis
in the morning sky—an event that also fell close in time to the annual Nile flood in early
summer. Since the *Book of Sothis* gives great prominence to time-reckoning—it gives the
rulers in chronological order and gives the length of each reign in years—Sothis, the bringer of

F1

Syncellus *Ecloga Chronographica* (*Chronological Excerpts*) 73.14: Letter of Manetho of Sebennytos to Ptolemy Philadelphos: "To the Great King Ptolemy Philadelphos Augustus, Manetho the high priest and scribe of the sacred temples in Egypt, born in Sebennytos and resident in Heliopolis, greets my lord Ptolemy.

We must, O Greatest King, think about all matters that you wish us to examine. Since you are seeking to know the future of the world, you will see, in accordance with your command to me, the sacred books that I have studied, written by your forefather Hermes Trismegistus. Strength to you, my lord King!"

That is what he tells about his translation of the books by the second Hermes. Then he gives his account of five Egyptian tribes in thirty dynasties,[6] of those called gods and demigods and the dead and mortals.

F2a

Syncellus *Ecloga Chronographica* (*Chronological Excerpts*) 32.13: Concerning, therefore, the six dynasties of six gods—none of which really existed—Manetho says that they covered 11,985 years, and he says that the first of them, the god Hephaistos, reigned 9,000 years. . . .

First Dynasty
  1. Hephaistos was ruler of the   9,000 years.[7] [Panodoros: 727 3/4]
     Egyptians

---

each year, is a suitable emblem. The book is also referred to by Syncellus as the "Cycle of the Dog Star" (*Book of Sothis* F3, Syncellus 193). In fact, the morning rising of Sirius coincided exactly with the beginning of the 365-day civil year only once every 1,461 years, a period known as the Sothic cycle or the "Cycle of the Dog Star" (see *Book of Sothis* F4 n. 15.)

6. In the sequel (*Book of Sothis* F2a–b and F3) Syncellus's presentation does not, apart from occasional hints, show the expected division into dynasties.

7. According to Syncellus, the numbers that the *Book of Sothis* had given for these reigns were converted to smaller numbers by Christian chronograpers, including, by name, Panodoros (an Egyptian monk of the late fourth to early fifth century A.D.). For a discussion of the reasons for this conversion, see Manetho T10b n. 15. What Panodoros did was to regard *Sothis*'s "years" for the six reigns of the gods as actually being lunar months (at a rate of ca. 29 and 1/2 days per month) and to thus reduce the figures down to solar years. Syncellus's text presents the Panodoran figures, but it is possible, on Syncellus's information, to reconstruct the original figures, and that is what we have done here. The numbers shown are the presumed originals, while Panodoros's alterations—as actually given in Syncellus—are shown in brackets. Syncellus explicitly reports the first figure, 9,000 years for Hephaistos. For the next five reigns

2. Helios, son of Hephaistos, was ruler of the Egyptians	992 years. [Panodoros: 80 1/6]
3. Agathodaimon was ruler of the Egyptians	700 years. [Panodoros: 56 7/12]
4. Kronos was ruler of the Egyptians	501 years. [Panodoros: 40 1/2]
5. Osiris and Isis were rulers of the Egyptians	433 years. [Panodoros: 35]
6. Typhon was ruler of the Egyptians[8]	359 years. [Panodoros: 29]

(Second and Third Dynasties)[9]

7. Horos the demigod was ruler of the Egyptians	100 years. [Panodoros: 25][10]
8. Ares the demigod was ruler of the Egyptians	92 years. [Panodoros: 23]
9. Anubis the demigod was ruler of the Egyptians	68 years. [Panodoros: 17]
10. Herakles the demigod was ruler of the Egyptians	60 years. [Panodoros: 15]
11. Apollo the demigod was ruler of the Egyptians	100 years. [Panodoros: 25]

---

we have arithmetically undone Panodoros's work. Our formula is {(Panodoran figure) x 365} ÷ 29.5 = original *Sothis* figure; fractional years have been rounded up, since *Sothis* probably did not employ fractions, not having Panodoros's need to harmonize with an external figure (one based on Scripture). Lastly, Syncellus states the original total of these six reigns as 11,985 years, and this is in fact the total of our conjectural restoration (9,000 + 992 + 700 + 501 + 433 + 359 = 11,985.)

8. At this point the text of Syncellus gives the sixth item as "(lac.) was ruler of the Egyptians (lac.)." This would result in sixteen rulers here, but Syncellus's own statements call for six gods + nine demigods = fifteen. It seems best to regard the sixth item as a copyist's error, and we have deleted it (as Jacoby in *FGrHist* #609 F27 also recommended), so that the series from Typhon through Zeus appears as items six through fifteen.

9. We have added this heading on the basis of Syncellus's information (*Book of Sothis* F2b) that the nine demigods made up two dynasties.

10. Panodoros's basis for reducing the figures for the nine reigns of demigods was different from the one he used on the preceding six reigns of gods. Instead of assuming that the *Book of Sothis*'s "years" were actually lunar months, he assumed this time that they were in fact quarter-years (*horai*, "seasons"). To regain the original figures, we have multiplied by four the Panodoran figures given in Syncellus. According to Syncellus, Panodoros reduced the total 858 *horai* of *Sothis* to 214 and 1/2 years, but the separate Panodoran figures cited by Syncellus (25 + 23 + 17 +15 + 25 + 30 + 27 + 32 + 20) add up to only 214, and so our restored *Sothis* figures total 856 rather than 858. We suppose that an additional 1/2 belonging with one of the Panodoran figures was omitted by a copyist.

12. Ammon the demigod was ruler
    of the Egyptians   120 years. [Panodoros: 30]
13. Tithoes the demigod was ruler
    of the Egyptians   108 years. [Panodoros: 27]
14. Sosos the demigod was ruler of
    the Egyptians   128 years. [Panodoros: 32]
15. Zeus the demigod was ruler of
    the Egyptians   80 years. [Panodoros: 20]

F2b

Syncellus *Ecloga Chronographica* (*Chronological Excerpts*) 75.15: For the two dynasties of nine demigods, . . . Panodoros strives to calculate 214 and 1/2 years from 858 *horai*, or quarters of a year.

F3

Syncellus *Ecloga Chronographica* (*Chronological Excerpts*) 170.4ff.:

Years of kings of Egypt[11]
1. Menes was the first ruler of Egypt,   35 years.
2. Kourodes was ruler of Egypt   63 years.
3. Aristarkhos was ruler of the Egyptians   34 years.

---

11. Syncellus's comment on no. 25 (Konkharis) shows that this series is part of the excerpts from the *Book of Sothis,* which began in *Book of Sothis* F2 with the reigns of gods and demigods. This catalog of eighty-six human rulers is broken up by Syncellus into fifteen portions.

At this point, we wish to declare how we have edited the rest of the material that Syncellus presented as the *Book of Sothis.* We believe, in view of the false cover letter from "Manetho" to Ptolemy (*Book of Sothis* F1), that the work was posing as an Egyptian, and therefore pagan, document. But Syncellus's presentation contains many features that can derive only from Judeo-Christian historiography. We assume that these features were added to the original *Book of Sothis* by Judeo-Christian editors, and we have, as far as possible, removed all such matter. The suppressed material includes the Year of the World dates furnished for the first year of each reign and items in the comments on some of the rulers (e.g, no. 22, Rhamessameno: "This is the first Pharaoh mentioned in Holy Scripture. The patriarch Abraham entered Egypt in this reign.") Also removed are the Hebrew names "Mestraia" for Egypt and "Mestraim" for Menes.

At the same time, the comments also contain material of Hellenic or more general interest, and some of these items are the same as appear in the epitome of genuine Manetho. We infer that the preparer of the *Book of Sothis* made use of the epitome, and that such items were transferred into the original *Sothis.* We have preserved this non-Judeo-Christian commentary, although not all of it is parallel to our other information (Manetho F2a–b) about the contents of the epitome, and some may have been added by editors.

4. Spanios was ruler of the Egyptians	36 years.
5 and 6. Two unnamed kings of the Egyptians,	72 years.
7. Osiropis was ruler of the Egyptians	23 years.
8. Sesonkhosis was ruler of the Egyptians	49 years.
9. Amenemes was ruler of the Egyptians	29 years.
(179)	
10. Amasis was ruler of the Egyptians	2 years.
11. Akesephthres was ruler of the Egyptians	13 years.
12. Ankhoreus was ruler of the Egyptians	9 years.
13. Armiyses was ruler of the Egyptians	4 years.
14. Khamois was ruler of the Egyptians	12 years.
15. Miamous was ruler of the Egyptians	14 years.
16. Amesesis was ruler of the Egyptians	65 years.
17. Ouses was ruler of the Egyptians	50 years.
18. Rhameses was ruler of the Egyptians	29 years.
(189)	
19. Rhamesomenes was ruler of Egypt	15 years.
20. Ousimares was ruler of Egypt	31 years.
21. Rhamesseseos was ruler of Egypt	23 years.
22. Rhamessameno was ruler of Egypt	19 years.
23. Rhamasse Ioubasse was ruler of Egypt	39 years.
(193)	
24. Rhamesse son of Ouaphres was ruler of Egypt	29 years.
25. Konkharis was ruler of Egypt	5 years.

By this year, the fifth year of Konkharis the twenty-fifth ruler of Egypt, during the sixteenth dynasty of what is called in Manetho the "Cycle of the Dog Star," there have been seven hundred years. and twenty-five kings since the first king and founder of Egypt. . . . The throne passed to four Tanite kings, who ruled Egypt for 254 years in the Seventeenth Dynasty, as is tabulated below.[12]

---

12. At this point, Syncellus injects a discussion comparing Josephus's presentation of Dynasties XVII–XIX (Manetho F9–F12) with that of "Manetho" (by which Syncellus means the *Book of Sothis*). Syncellus states that he prefers Josephus to Manetho, which really means preferring Josephus's version of Manetho to *Sothis* (Pseudo-Manetho). Syncellus seems to imply that he will correct *Sothis*'s figures on the basis of Josephus, but it does not appear that this editing has been applied to the actual presentation here of *Sothis*. Only in regard to no. 31, Kertos, does Syncellus note a discrepancy with Josephus, and this in such a way that we

26. Silites was ruler of the Egyptians   19 years.

First of the six kings of Manetho's Seventeenth Dynasty

(204)
27. Baion was ruler of the Egyptians   44 years.
28. Apakhnas was ruler of the Egyptians   36 years.
29. Aphophis was ruler of the Egyptians   61 years.
(232)
30. Sethos was ruler of the Egyptians   50 years.
31. Kertos was ruler of the Egyptians   44 years.[13]
32. Asseth was ruler of the Egyptians   20 years.

This king added the 5 extra days to the year, and in his reign, they say, the Egyptian year officially became one of 365 days, instead of 360 as before. In his reign the calf was deified and called Apis.

33. Amosis, also called Tethmosis, was ruler of
     the Egyptians   28 years.
(278)
34. Khebron was ruler of the Egyptians   13 years.
35. Amemphis was ruler of the Egyptians   15 years.
36. Amenses was ruler of the Egyptians   11 years.
37. Misphragmouthosis was ruler of the Egyp-
     tians   16 years.
38. Misphres was ruler of the Egyptians   23 years.
39. Touthmosis was ruler of the Egyptians   39 years.
(286)
40. Amenophthis was ruler of the Egyptians   34 years.

This Amenophthis is believed to be Memnon and a speaking stone. The Persian king Kambyses later cut the stone apart, thinking that there was witchcraft in it, as Polyainos of Athens (*FGrHist* #639) records.

The Ethiopians, having left the River Indus, settled near Egypt.

---

assume that the other figures, which receive no such note, are the untampered-with figures of "Manetho"-*Sothis.*

13. It is here that Syncellus noted "29 according to Josephus, but 44 according to Manetho" (see the preceding footnote). We have put in the 44 as representing *Sothis* and left the other figures as given by Syncellus.

41. Oros was ruler of the Egyptians	48 years.
42. Akhenkheres was ruler of the Egyptians	25 years.
43. Athoris was ruler of the Egyptians	29 years.
44. Khenkheres was ruler of the Egyptians	26 years.
(293)	
45. Akherres was ruler of the Egyptians	8 or 30 years.
46. Armaios, also called Danaos, was ruler of the Egyptians	9 years.

Armaios, also called Danaos, fleeing his brother Rhamesses, also called Aigyptos, abdicated his throne in Egypt and arrived in Greece. His brother Rhamesses, also called Aigyptos, ruled Egypt for sixty-eight years, and he changed the name of the land to Egypt, after his own name. . . . Danaos, also called Armaios, got control of Argos, expelled Sthenelos son of Krotopos, and became king of the Argives. His descendants were called Danaids down to the time of Eurystheus son of Sthenelos son of Perseus. After them the Pelopids, beginning with Atreus, inherited the throne.

(302)	
47. Rhamesses, also called Aigyptos, was ruler of the Egyptians	68 years.
48. Amenophis was ruler of the Egyptians	8 years.
49. Thouoris was ruler of the Egyptians	17 years.
50. Nekhepsos was ruler of the Egyptians	19 years.
51. Psammouthis was ruler of the Egyptians	13 years.
52. (lac.) was ruler of the Egyptians	4 years.
53. Kertos was ruler of the Egyptians	20 years.
54. Rhampsis was ruler of the Egyptians	45 years.
55. Amenses, also called Ammenemes, was ruler of the Egyptians	26 years.
(319)	
56. Okhyras was ruler of the Egyptians	14 years.
57. Amendes was ruler of the Egyptians	27 years.
58. Thouoris was ruler of the Egyptians	50 years.

This is the one called Polybos in Homer, presented as the husband of Alkandra (*Odyssey* 4.126), with whom they say Menelaos and Helen stayed as they wandered after the fall of Troy.

59. Athothis, also called Physanos, was ruler of
    the Egyptians   28 years.

In his reign earthquakes occurred in Egypt. They had never happened
there before.

60. Kenkenes was ruler of the Egyptians   39 years.
61. Ouennephis was ruler of the Egyptians   42 years.
(332)
62. Sousakeim was ruler of the Egyptians   34 years.
63. Psouenos was ruler of the Egyptians   25 years.
64. Ammenophis was ruler of the Egyptians   9 years.
65. Nephekheres was ruler of the Egyptians   6 years.
66. Saites was ruler of the Egyptians   15 years.
67. Psinakhes was ruler of the Egyptians   9 years.
68. Petoubastes was ruler of the Egyptians   44 years.
69. Osorthon was ruler of the Egyptians   9 years.
70. Psammos was ruler of the Egyptians   10 years.
71. Konkharis was ruler of the Egyptians   21 years.
(347)
72. Osorthon was ruler of the Egyptians   15 years.
73. Takalophis was ruler of the Egyptians   13 years.
74. Bokkhoris was ruler of the Egyptians   44 years.

Bokkhoris made laws for the Egyptians. Story has it that a lamb spoke in
his reign.

75. Sabakon the Ethiopian was ruler of the
    Egyptians   12 years.

This man captured Bokkhoris in war and burned him alive.

76. Sebekhon was ruler of the Egyptians   12 years.
(360)
77. Tarakes was ruler of the Egyptians   20 years.
78. Amaës was ruler of the Egyptians   38 years.
79. Stephinathes was ruler of the Egyptians   27 years.
80. Nekhepsos was ruler of the Egyptians   13 years.
(396)
81. Nekhao was ruler of the Egyptians   8 years.

82. Psammetikhos was ruler of the Egyptians   14 years.
83. Nekhao II was ruler of the Egyptians   9 years.
84. A second Psamouthis, also called Psam-
    metikhos, was ruler of the Egyptians   17 years.
85. Ouaphris was ruler of the Egyptians   34 years.
86. Amosis was ruler of the Egyptians   50 years.

The kingship of the Egyptians, ten dynasties[14] and eighty-six kings, lasted . . . 2,211 years. It was destroyed by Kambyses in the reign of Amosis, the eighty-sixth king of Egypt, counting from the first king, Menes. In Amosis's reign Egypt resisted Kambyses, and he conquered it by force of arms and hard battles. He found Pythagoras here as a traveler seeking learning, and he included him with the other prisoners of war taken by the Persians. At this time, they say, Pythagoras came to Mesopotamia and partook of its learning. Later he left this place also and went to Italy. He was in exile from his native Samos because of the tyrant Polykrates. He lived the rest of his life in Italy and established a school. Egypt remained under the Persians until Dareios the son of Xerxes. It was in the Twenty-seventh Dynasty that the Persians conquered Egypt, in the fifth year of Kambyses.

F4

Iamblichus *de Mysteriis Aegyptiorum* (*On the Mysteries of the Egyptians*) 8.1: Because there are many completely different essences, tradition gives them many causes and different rankings, and different ancient priests hold different views. Hermes has therefore given a complete list in the 20,000 books that Seleukos (Seleukos of Alexandria, *FGrHist* #634) copied, or in the 36,525 books, as Manetho records. Individual essences are explained in many places by various writers who borrow ancient explanations.[15]

---

14. This number is probably an error made by Syncellus or those who made copies of his text. We believe our main witnesses (in Manetho F2a), that Manetho presented thirty-one or thirty dynasties.

15. The status of this passage is uncertain. It seems to have a Sothic reference, because the number 36,525 represents 25 Sothic cycles (the heliacal rising of Sirius actually coincided with the beginning of the calendar year each 1,461 years), and it may perhaps belong with the other citations from the *Book of Sothis*. Other scholars have put it with Manetho's *Digest of Physics* (Manetho F23) or with yet another pseudo-Manethonian work that was separate from the *Book of Sothis*.

CHAPTER 9

Manetho—Tables

Table A. Time Outline—Egypt

Major Divisions of Ancient Egyptian History[1]

Chalcolithic, ca. 4300–3000 B.C.
Archaic (Early Dynastic), ca. 3050–2575 B.C.
    Unification of the Two Lands
    Dynasties I–II
Old Kingdom, ca. 2575–2134 B.C.
    Dynasties III–VI
    Age of the Pyramids
First Intermediate Period, ca. 2134–2040 B.C.
    Dynasties VII–XI
Middle Kingdom, ca. 2040–1640 B.C.
    Dynasties XI–XIII
Second Intermediate Period, ca. 1640–1532 B.C.
    Dynasties XIV–XVII
    Hyksos Domination
New Kingdom, ca. 1550–1070 B.C.
    Dynasties XVIII–XX
Third Intermediate Period, ca. 1070–712 B.C.
    Dynasties XXI–XXIV

---

1. These divisions are based on John Baines and Jaromir Málek, *Atlas of Ancient Egypt* (New York, 1982), 8–9.

Late Period, ca. 712–332 B.C.
   Dynasties XXV–XXXI
   Ethiopian Domination (Dynasty XXV)
   Saite Renaissance (Dynasty XXVI)
   Persian Domination (Dynasty XXVII, Dynasty XXXI)
Greco-Macedonian Period, 332–30 B.C.
   Alexander the Great (332–323 B.C.)
   Regency of Ptolemy (323–305 B.C.
   Ptolemaic Dynasty (305–30 B.C.)
Roman Empire, 30 B.C.–A.D. 330
Byzantine Empire, A.D. 330–642
Arab Conquest, A.D. 642

Table B. Ancient Egyptian Ruler-Lists, Manetho's List, and a Modern List Compared

Sign	Name	Date	Contents	Remains
OKA	Old Kingdom Annals	D. V–D. VI	Predynastic king-list (perhaps 140 kings): dynastic annals from Menes (D. I.1) to Niuserre (D. V.6), year by year, with important events and heights of Nile inundations	Six fragments (see next three items), preserving perhaps 10 percent of the orginal
P	Palermo Stone (chief fragment of **OKA**)			
C	Four Cairo fragments			
L	London fragment			
K	Karnak list	Early D. XV (Thutmose III)	Names of 61 kings, selectively, not in order, from DD. III, IV, V, VI, XI, XII, XIII, XIV, XVII	48 names read
A	Abydos list	Seti I (D. XIX.2)	76 kings D.I–D. XIX; 2d Intermediate Period, Hyksos, and Atenists are ignored	Quite complete
T	Turin papyrus	ca. Ramesses II (D. XIX.3)	300+ kings, from gods to late D. XVII; names, lengths of rule and life (yrs., mos., days) with some totalling	Ca. fifty fragments yielding 80–90 names and other information
S	Saqqara list	Ramesses II (D. XIX.3)	58 kings: names from D. I.6 ("Miebidos") to D. XIX.1–3; omissions as in **A**	47 names
R	Ramesses's list at Abydos	Ramesses II	An updated duplicate of **A**	Less complete than **A**

K and **R**, listed above for the sake of completeness, are not used in the comparative charts that follow.

Predynastic:[2]

Manetho	OKA	T	Modern[3]
Gods	"Kings of Lower Egypt"		
Hephaistos	(lac.)pu	Ptah (lac.)	(lac.)pu
Helios	Seka	Ra (lac.)	Seka
Sosis/Agathodaimon	Khayu	Shu (lac.)	Khayu
Kronos	Tiu	Geb (lac.)	Tiu
Osiris/Osiris-Isis	Tjesh	Osiris (lac.)	Tjesh
Typhon	Neheb (?)	Seth: 200 years	Neheb (?)
(?)Bidis	Wadjnadj		Wadjnadj
(?)Thoulis	Mekha		Mekha
	(lac.)a		(lac.)a
Total:13,900 years			

9 (or 8) Offspring of Gods ("Demigods," "Heroes")	"Kings of Upper Egypt"		.
Horos		Horus: 300 years	
Ares		Djehuti (= Thoth): 3,126 (?) years	
Anubis		Ma'at (lac.)	
Herakles		Her (lac.)	
Apollo		Total (lac.)	
Ammon		9 gods	
Tithoes			
Sosos			
Zeus			
Total: 1,255 years			

---

2. This presentation of Manetho's predynastic list is based on the Armenian translation of Eusebius (see F2a), with supplements based on Malalas (F3a), Lydus (F3b), the *Excerpta Latina Barbari* (F5), and Pseudo-Manetho (*Book of Sothis* F2). Like T, Manetho gave reign-lengths for the gods, demigods, and so on. We give the numbers from Eusebius only. It is unfortunate that no details are available from Africanus.

3. The basis for our modern list is *CAH*[3], supplemented by Jürgen von Beckerath, *Abriss der Geschichte des alten Ägypten* (Vienna, 1971).

Manetho	OKA	T	Modern
Other kings: 1,817 years		20 *akhu* "blessed spirits" (from Hierakonpolis?)	
		10 *akhu* (from Buto?)	
		(lac.) *akhu* (from Heliopolis?)	
		20 (lac.)	
30 kings from Memphis: 1,790 years		19 Powers (?) from Memphis: 11 years, 4 months, 22 days	
10 kings from Thinis: 350 years		19 *akhu* of Lower Egypt	
Spirits of the Dead ("Demigods"): 5,813 years		7 Speakers (?) for the Father, women, *akhu* Followers of Horus	

Dynastic:

DD. I–II: Archaic and Early Dynastic Period (ca. 3100–2686 B.C.)

Manetho	OKA	A	T	S	Modern
D. I, 8 kings from Thinis					8 kings, ca. 3100–2890 B.C.: 210 years
Menes: 62 (60)[4] years		Meni	Meni		Narmer/Men
Athothis: 57 (27) years	Atet: 55(?) years	Teti	Iti		Aha/Iti
Kenkenes: 31 (39) years		Itet	(lac.)		Djer/Iti: 47 years

---

4. If Africanus and Eusebius disagree on years of reign, Eusebius is in rounded brackets.

Manetho	OKA	A	T	S	Modern
Ouenephes: 23 (42) years		Ita	(lac.)ai		
Ousaphaidos: 20 years		(Hesepti?)	Zemti (Khaseti?)		Den/Khaseti: 55–60 years
Miebidos: 26 years		Merbiape	Merbiapen	Merbiapen	Merbiape: 7 years
Semempses: 18 years		(?)	Semsem		Semerkhet: 8 years
Bienekhes/ Oubienthis: 26 years		Khebeh	(lac.)beh	Khebwe	Qaa, Sen: 25 years
Total: 253 (252) years					

D. II, 9 kings from Thinis					10 kings, ca. 2890–2686 B.C.
Boethos/ Bokhos: 38 years		Bedjau	(lac.)bau	Baunetjer	Hetepsekhemy Hetep
Kaiekhos/ Khoös: 39 years		Kakau	Kakau	Kakau	Reneb Nubnefer
Binothris/ Biophis: 47 years	Netjeren: >35 years	Banetjeren	(lac.)netjeren	Baunetjerwe	Nynetjer Nynetjer: 45–47 years
Tlas: 17 years		Wadjnas	(lac.)	Wadjnas	Weneg (Wadjnes): 19 years
Sethenes: 41 years		Sendi	Sendi	Sendj	Sened
Khaires: 17 years					Peribsen
			Aka		Aka

Manetho	OKA	A	T	S	Modern
Nepher-kheres: 25 years				Neferkare	
Sesokhris: 48 years			Neferka-sekre: 8 years	Neferka-sekre	Neferkasokar
Kheneres: 30 years					
			Hudjefa: 11 years	Hudjefa	Khasekhem: 21 (?) years
		Djadjaï			
			Bebti: 27 years	Bebi	Khasekhemwy: 17 years
Total: 302 (297) years					Total: 205 years

D. III–D. VI: Old Kingdom (ca. 2575–2134 B.C.)

D. III, 9 kings from Memphis					5 rulers, ca. 2686–2613 B.C.
Nekheroph-es/Nekher-okhis: 28 years		Nebka	Nebka: 19 years		Nebka: 19 years
Tosorthros/ Sesorthos: 29 years		(lac.) Djesersa	Djes-er(it?): 19 years	Djeser	Djoser: 19 years
Tyreis: 7 years		Teti	Djeserti: 6 years	Djeserteti	Djoser Teti: 6 years
Mesokhris: 17 years		Sedjes	(lac.)dje-fa: 6 years	Nebkare	Khaba: 6 years
Soüphis: 16 years		Neferkare			

Manetho	OKA	A	T	S	Modern
Tosertasis: 19 years					
Akhes: 42 years			Huni: 24 years	Huni	Huni: 24 years
Sephouris: 30 years					
Kerpheres: 26 years					
Total: 214 years					Total: 74 years

Manetho	OKA	A	T	S	Modern
D. IV, 8 kings from Memphis					ca. 2613–2494 B.C., 8 rulers
Soris: 29 years	Sne-feru: <16 years	Sneferu	Sneferu: 24 years	Sneferu	Sneferu: 24 years
Souphis: 63 years	(lac.)-fu	Khufu	(lac.): 23 years	Khufuf	Khufu (Cheops): 23 years
Souphis: 66 years		Redjedef	(lac.): 8 years	Redjedef	Redjedef: 8 years
		Khafre	Khauf-(lac.)	Khaufre	Khephren: 25 (?) years
			(lac.)		Baufre (?)
Menkheres: 63 years		Men-kaure	(lac.): 18 years	Menkaure	Menkaure: 28 (?) years
Rhatoises: 25 years			(lac.): 4 years	(lac.)	
Bikheris: 22 years			(lac.): 2 years	(lac.)	
Seberkher-es: 7 years	Shep-seskaf	Shepses-kaf		(lac.)	Shepseskaf: 4 years

Manetho	OKA	A	T	S	Modern
Thamph-this: 9 years				(lac.)[5]	Djedefptah (?) (Thamphthis): 2 years
Total: 277 years					Total: 120 years

Manetho	OKA	A	T	S	Modern
D. V, 8 kings from Elephantine					9 rulers, ca. 2494–2345 B.C.
Ouserkhe-res: 28 years	User-kaf	Userkaf	(lac.)kaf: 7 years	Userkaf	Userkaf: 7 years
Sephres: 13 years	Sahu-re: 12/13 (?) years	Sahure	(lac.): 12 years	Sahure	Sahure: 14 years
Nepherkhe-res: 20 years	Nefer-irkare	Kakau	(lac.)	Neferirkare	Neferirkare Kakai: 10 years
Sisires: 7 years			(lac.): 7 years	Shepseska-re	Shepseskare Isi: 7 years
Kheres: 20 years	Nefer-efre	Neferefre	(lac.): x +1 years	Khaneferre	Neferefre: 7 years
Rhathoures: 44 years	Nius-erre[6]	Neuserre	(lac.): 11 years		Niuserre: 31 years
Menkheres: 9 years		Menkau-hor	Menka-hor: 8 years	Menkahor	Menkauhor: 8 years
Tankheres: 44 years		Djedkare	Djed: 28 years	Shukare	Djedkare Asosi: 39 (?) years

---

5. There is another small list, inscribed during ca. D. XII, which lists Khufu, Redjedef, Khafre, Hardjedef, and Rebaef.

6. This is as far as OKA takes us.

Manetho	A	T	S	Modern
Onnos: 33 years	Unis	Unis: 30 years	Unas	Unas: 30 years
Total of D.I–D.V: 1,294 (1,295) years		Total kings from Meniti (?) to (lac.)		Total: 150 years

D. VI, 6 kings from Memphis				ca. 2345–2181 B.C., 7 rulers
Othoes: 30 years	Teti	(lac.)	Teti	Teti: 12 years
	Userkare	(lac.)		Userkare: 1 (?) year
Phios: 53 years	Merire	(lac.): 20 years	Pepi	Meryre Phio(p)s I: 49 years
Methousouphis: 7 years	Merenre	(lac.): 44 (?) years	Mer-enre	Merenre Antyemsaf I: 14 years
Phiops: 99 years	Neferkare	(lac.): 90+ years	Nefer-kare	Neferkare Phiops II: 94 (?) years
Menthesouphis: 1 year	Merenre Usefem-saf (?)	(lac.): 1 year		Merenre Antyemsaf II: 1 year
Nitokris: 12 years	Neterkare	Nitokerti: (lac.)		Netjerikare Menkare (?) (Nitocris): 2 years
		Neferka, child (lac.)		
		Neferes: 2 years, 1 month, 1day		
		Ibi: 4 years, 2 months		
		(lac.)		
		(lac.)		
		(lac.)		
		(lac.)		

Manetho	A	T	S	Modern
		(Total) kings (from Teti to [lac.]): 181		
Total: 203 years		Total since Meni: 955 years, 10+ days		Total: 165 years

DD.VII–XI, for which no details from Manetho survive, make up the First Intermediate Period, a time of confusion in all records. The modern list indicates ca. 33 rulers over ca. 2181–1991 B.C.: 191 years

Manetho	A	T	S	Modern
D. VII, 5 kings from Memphis: 70 (75) days (no details)	(See foot-note)[7]			9 rulers, ca. 2181–2173 B.C.
	Menkare			
	Neferkare			Neferkare "the Younger"
	Neferkare Neby			Neferkare Neby
	Djedkare Shema			Djedkare Shema
	Neferkare Khendu			Neferkare Khendu
	Merenhor			Merenhor
	Sneferka			Neferkamin
	Nekare			Nykare
	Neferkare Tereru			Neferkare Tereru
	Neferka-hor			Neferkahor

7. Although Alan H. Gardiner, *Egypt of the Pharaohs* (Oxford, 1961), regards D. VII as "spurious"—not detectable in any list or any other monument or document, we follow for convenience *CAH³*, which does divide the successors of Nitokris between D. VII and D. VIII.

Manetho	A	T	S	Modern
D. VIII, 27 (5) kings from Memphis: 146 (100) years (no details)		(Apparently ignored by T)	(Ignored by S)	6 rulers, ca. 2173–2160 B.C.: 13+ years
	Neferkare Pepysonb			Wadjkare Pepysonb: 4+ years
	Sneferka Anu			Neferkamin Anu: 2 years, 1 month
	(Ka?)-kaure			Kakare Ibi: 4 years, 2 months
	Nefer-kaure			Neferkare: 2 years, 1 month
	Nefer-kauhor			Neferhauhor Kapuibi: 1 year, 15 days
	Neferir-kare			Neferirkare

Manetho	A	T	S	Modern
D. IX, 19 (4) kings from Herakleopolis: 409 (100) years	(Ignored by A)		(Ignored by S)	(Unsettled; reflects T and a few monuments)
		(lac.)		
		(lac.)		
(The only detail is:)		Neferkare		
Akhthoes		Akhthoy		
		(lac.)[8]		

Manetho	A	T	S	Modern
D. X, 19 kings from Herakleopolis: 185 years (no details)	(Ignored by A)		(Ignored by S)	(Unsettled; reflects T and a few monuments)

D. XI–D. XVII: Middle Kingdom and Second Intermediate Period, including the Hyksos (ca. 2040–1532 B.C.)

---

8. From this point through D. X, fourteen reigns are lost from T.

Manetho	A	T	S	Modern
D. XI, 16 kings from Diospolis: 43 years. (no details)				7 rulers, 2133–1991 B.C.: 142 years
		(lac.) [9]		Mentuhotpe I and Inyotef I (2133–2118)
		(lac.)		Inyotef II (2117–2069)
		(lac.)		Inytotef III (2068–2061)
		(lac.)		
	Nebkhru-re	Menthot-pe: 57 years	Nebkhrure	Mentuhotpe II (2060–2010)
	Sankhka-re	Menthot-pe: 12 years	Sankhkare	Sankhkare Mentuhotpe III (2009–1998)
		Total: 143 years		Mentuhotpe IV (1997–1991)
		(Kings of the) residence Ittowe		
After them Ammenemes: 16 years	Sehetep-ibre	Sehetep-ibre: 29 (?) years	Sehetep-ibre	(assigned to next dynasty)

Manetho	A	T	S	Modern
D. XII, 7 kings from Diospolis				1991–1786 B.C., 8 rulers
				Sehetepibre Ammenemes I (1991–1962)

---

9. See preceding footnote.

Manetho	A	T	S	Modern
Sesonkhosis: 46 years	Kheper-kare	Kheperkare: 45 years	Kheper-kare	Kheperkare Sesostris I (1971–1928)
Ammenemes: 38 years	Nebka-re	(lac.): 10+ (or 30+) years	Nubkare	Nubkare Ammenemes II (1929–1895)
	Kha-kheper-re	(lac.): 10 years	Kha-kheperre	Khakheperre Sesostris II (1897–1878)
Sesostris: 48 years	Kha-kaure	(lac.): 30+ years	Khakare	Khakare Sesostris III (1878–1843)
Lamares: 8 years	Nema-re	(lac.): 40+ years	Nemare	Nymare Ammenemes III (1842–1797)
Ameres: 8 years				
Ammenemes: 8 years	Makh-rure	Makhrure: 9 years, 3 months, 27 days	Makheru-re	Makerure Ammenemes IV (1798–1790)
Skemiophris: 4 years		Sebeknofrure: 3 years, 10 months, 24 days	Sebekka-re	Sobkkare Sobkneferu (1789–1786)
Total: 160 years		Total, kings of the residence Ittowe, 8 kings:[10] 213 years, 1 month, 16 days		Total: 205 years

10. T is including the preceding Sehetepibre (= Ammenemes I) in this count. Ittowe is believed to have been near el-Lisht, on the west bank of the Nile, close to the Faiyum.

Manetho	A	T	S	Modern
D. XIII, 60 kings from Diospolis: 453 years	(Ignored by A)	(See footnote)[11]	(Ignored by S)	D. XIII–D. XVII overlap. Many kings, brief reigns. Total span, 1786–ca. 1567 B.C.: 219 years
D. XIV, 76 kings from Xoïs: 184 years	(Ignored by A)		(Ignored by S)	See preceding.
D. XV, 6 kings of the "Shepherds," based in the Sethroite Nome[12]	(Ignored by A)	(Chieftain of a foreign country) Khamudy (Total, chieftains) of a foreign country, 6: 108 years[13]	(Ignored by S)	(Agrees that this dynasty and the next two are Hyksos-dominated.)
Saites: 19 years				
Bnon: 44 years				
Pakhnan: 61 years				
Staan: 50 years				
Arkhles: 49 years				
Aphobis: 61 years				
Total: 284 years				

---

11. Except for the Shepherds named in D. XV, we have no details from Manetho from here (D. XIII) through D. XVII. Only in D. XVIII can we resume comparing Manetho with other lists—but only with A and S, for T has run out by then. In this interval Manetho counted 258 kings, 1,590 years; T had places for at least 160 reigns. Of them around one hundred names are at least partly readable; they are not shown in our table, except for two lines that we have put next to the Shepherds of Manetho's D. XV.

12. For simplicity this dynasty, as well as the next, is presented just as in Africanus (F2a); the other witnesses—Eusebius (F2a), Josephus (F9), Pseudo-Manetho (*Book of Sothis* F3)—differ greatly. "Shepherds" is given as Manetho's name for the intruders, now generally called Hyksos, by Africanus. Eusebius's version of Manetho, however, also calls them "foreign kings," which resembles both the description in T ("chieftains of a foreign country") and modern scholars' interpretation of "Hyksos" as "Lords of the Foreign Lands" (see chap. 5, n. 18.)

13. See above note 11 on D. XIII. (Khamudy's name is not in a cartouche.)

Manetho	A	T	S	Modern
D. XVI, 32 more "Shepherds": 518 years[14] (no details)	(Ignored by A)		(Ignored by S)	

Manetho	A	T	S	Modern
D. XVII, more "Shepherds," 43 kings; also 43 Theban kings from Diospolis: 151 years (no details)	(Ignored by A)	(T is lost from here on.)	(Ignored by S)	

D. XVIII–D.XX: New Kingdom (ca. 1550–1070 B.C.)

Manetho	A	S	Modern
D. XVIII, 16 (14) kings from Diospolis[15]			14 rulers, 1567–1320 B.C. 247 years
Amosis: 25 years, 4 months	Nebpehtire	Nebpehtire	Nebpehtire Amosis (1570–1546)
Amenophis: 20 years, 7 months	Djeserkare	Djeserkare	Djeserkare Amenophis I (1546–1526)
Mephres: 12 years, 9 months	Akheperkare	Akheperkare	Akheperkare Thutmose I (1525–ca. 1512)
Khebron: 13 years	Akheperenre	Akheperenre	Akheperenre Thutmose II (1512–1504)
Amensis: 21years, 9 months			Makare Hatshepsut (1503–1482)
Misphragmouthosis: 25 years, 10 months	Menkheperre	Menkheperre	Menkheperre Thutmose III (1504–1450)

14. This, given by Africanus, is surely not the number Manetho had. Nor is it historically credible.

15. All the witnesses for Manetho's sequence in D. XVIII–D. XIX—Josephus in F10, Africanus and Eusebius in F2a—appear confused. We give the reconstruction of H. W. Helck, *Untersuchungen zu Manetho und den ägyptischen Königslisten, Untersuchungen zur Geschiche und Altertumskunde Aegyptens* 18 (Berlin, 1956), 41–45, 64–71.

Manetho	A	S	Modern
Amenophis: 30 years, 10 months (?)	Akheperure	Akheperure	Akheprure Amenophis II (1450–1425)
Touthmosis: 9 years, 8 months	Men-kheperure	Men-kheperure	Menkheprure Thutmose IV (1425–1417)
Oros: 38 years, 7 months	Nebmaatre	Nebmaatre	Nebmare Amenophis III (1417–1379)
Akherres: 16 years (?)			Neferkheprure Amen-ophis IV (Akhenaten) (1379–1362)
Rhathos: 5 years, 5 months (?)			Ankhkheprure Smenkh-kare (1364–1361)
Khebres: 8 years, x months (?)			Nebkheprure Tutankhamun (1361–1352)
Akherres: 4 years, 1 month			Kheperkheprure Ay (1352–1348)
Harmais: 12 years, 3 months	Djeser-kheperure Setepenre	Djeser-kheperure Setepenre	Djeserkheprure Horemhab (1348–1320)

Manetho	A	S	Modern
D. XIX, 6 (5) kings from Diospolis			8 rulers, 1320–1200 B.C.: 121 years
Ramesses I: 1 year, 4 months	Menpehtire	Menpehtire	Menpehtire Ramesses I (1320–1318)
Sethos I: 19 years	Menmare	Menmare	Menmare Sethos I (1318–1304)
Ramesses II : 66 years, 2 months		Usermare Setepenre	Usermare Ramesses II (1304–1237)
Merneptah: 19 years, 6 months			Merneptah (1236–1223)
Sethos II "Ramses"			Amenmesses (1222–1217 [?])
Amenmose: 5 years, x months			Sethos II (1216–1210 [?])
Thouoris: 7 years, x months			Siptah and Twosre (1209–1200 [?])

(From this point on there are no earlier lists to compare.)

Manetho	Modern
D. XX, 12 kings from Diospolis: 135 (178 or 172) years[16]	10 rulers, 1200–1085 /80 B.C.: 115/120 years
	Sethnakhte (1200–1198)
	Ramesses III (1198–1166)
	Ramesses IV (1166–1160)
	Ramesses V (1160–1156)
	Ramesses VI (1156–1148)
	Ramesses VII (1148–1147)
	Ramesses VIII (1147–1140)
	Ramesses IX (1140–1121)
	Ramesses X (1121–1113)
	Ramesses XI (1113–1085/80)

D. XXI–D. XXIV: Third Intermediate Period (ca. 1070–712 B.C.)

D. XXI, 7 kings from Tanis	7 rulers, 1080–945 B.C.
Smendes: 26 years	Smendes (1080–1054)
Psousennes: 41 years	Psusennes and Neferkare (1054–1004)
Nepherkheres: 4 years	
Amenophthis: 9 years	Amenophthis (1004–985)
Osokhor: 6 years	Osokhor (985–979)
Psinakhes: 9 years	Netrikheperre-setepenamun Siamun (979–960)
Psousennes: 14 (35) years	Psusennes II (960–945)
Total: 130 years	Total: 140 years

D. XXII, 9 kings from Bubastis	9 rulers, ca. 945–715 B.C. (overlaps with next dynasties)
Sesonkhosis: 21 years	Shoshenk I (ca. 945–924)
Osorthon: 15 years	Osorkon I (ca. 924–889)
3 others: 25 years	Takeloth I and Shoshenk II (ca. 880–874)

---

16. No names are transmitted by Africanus or Eusebius. Pseudo-Manetho (= *Book of Sothis* F3) has some.

Manetho	Modern
Takelothis: 13 years	Osorkon II (ca. 874–850)
3 others: 42 years	Takeloth II (ca. 850–825)
	Shoshenk III (ca. 825–773)
	Pimay (ca. 773–767)
	Shoshenk V (ca. 767–730)
	Osorkon IV (ca. 730–715)
Total: 120 years	Total: 230 years

D. XXIII, 4 (3) kings from Tanis	7 rulers, 817–715 B.C. (overlaps)
Petoubates: 40 (25) years	Usermare-setepenamun Petubastis (ca. 792–767)
Osorkho: 8 (9) years	Shoshenk IV (ca. 793–787)
Psammous: 10 years	Osorkon III (ca. 787–759)
Zet (?):[17] 31 years	Takeloth III (ca. 764–757 [?])
	Rudamun (ca. 757 [?]–754)
	Iuput II (ca. 754–720 [or 715])
	Shoshenk VI (?) (ca. 720–715 [?])
Total: 89 (44) years	Total: 102 years

D. XXIV	2 rulers, 727–715 B.C.: 12 years (overlaps)
	Shepsesre Tefnakht (ca. 727–718)
Bokhkhoris from Saïs: 6 (44) years	Wahkare Bokkhoris (718–712)

D. XXV–D. XXXI: Late Period (ca. 712–332 B.C.)

D. XXV, 3 kings from Ethiopia	6 rulers, Kushites/Nubians 745–655 B.C. (overlaps)
	Ma(?)-re Kashta (ca. 745–740)
	Usermare Piye (740–713)
Sabakon: 8 (12) years	Neferkare Shabako (713/12–698)
Sebikhos: 14 (12) years	Djedkare Shebitko (698–690)
Tarkos: 18 (20) years	Khunefertemre Taharko (690–664)
	Bikare Tanwatamun (664–655)
Total: 40 (44) years	Total: 90 years

---

17. Omitted by Eusebius; questionable name in Africanus.

Manetho	Modern
D. XXVI, 9 kings from Saïs	6 rulers from Saïs, 664–525 B.C. (overlaps)[18]
Stephinates: 7[19] years	
Nekhepsos: 6 years	
Nekhao: 8 years	
Psammouthis/Psammetikhos: 54 (44 or 45) years	Wahibre Psametik I (664–610)
Nekhao II: 6 years	Uhemibre Nekhow (610–595)
Psammouthis/Psammetikhos II: 6 (17) years	Neferibre Psametik II (595–589)
Ouaphris: 19 (25) years	Haïbre Apriës (589–570/68)
Amosis: 44 (42) years	Khnemibre Amosis (570–526)
Psammikherites: 6 months	Ankhkaenre Psametik III (526–525)
Total: 150 years, 6 months (163 years)	Total: 139 years

D. XXVII, 8 kings from Persia	8 Persian rulers, 525–404 B.C.
Kambyses: 6 (3) years	Kambyses (525–522)[20]
Magoi: 7 months	Magoi (March–Sept. 522)
Dareios son of Hystaspes: 36 years	Dareios I (521–486)
Xerxes the Great (son of Darius): 21 years	Xerxes I (485–465)
Artabanos: 7 months[21]	Artabanos (ursurper/regent) (465–464)
Artaxerxes: 41 (40) years	Atraxerxes (464–424)
Xerxes II: 2 months	Xerxes II (424)
Sogdianos: 7 months	Sogdianos (424)
Dareios son of Xerxes: 19 years	Dareios II (423–405)
Total: 124 (120) years, 4 months	Total: 121 years

---

18. All dates from here on are absolute.

19. Eusebius begins with "Amerres, an Ethiopian: 12 years" and omits Psammekherites, the last in Africanus.

20. Begins with his fifth year as king of Persia.

21. Not in Eusebius.

Manetho	Modern
D. XXVIII	1 ruler: 5 (?) years
Amyrteos (-aios) from Saïs: 6 years	Amyrtaios (404 [?]–399)

Manetho	Modern
D. XXIX, 4 kings from Mendes	5 rulers, 399–380 B.C.
Nepherites: 6 years	Bienre-merenter Nepherites I (399–393)
Akhoris: 13 years	Muthes and Psammuthes (393)
Psammouthis: 1 years	Akhoris (393–380)
Nepherites: 4 months	Nepherites II (380)
Total: 20 (21) years, 4 months.	Total: 20 years

Manetho	Modern
D. XXX, 3 kings from Sebennytos	3 rulers, 380–342 B.C.
Nektanebes: 18 (10) years	Kheperkare Nektanebis (380–362)
Teos: 2 years	Irmaenre Teos (362–360)
Nektanebos: 18 (8) years	Sedenemibre Nektanebos (362–340)
Total: 38 (20) years	Total: 38 years

Manetho	Modern
D. XXXI, 3 kings from Persia[22]	3 rulers, 342–332 B.C.: 11 years
Okhos: 2 (6) years	Artaxerxes III Okhos (342–338)
Arses (son of Okhos): 3 (4) years	Arses (337–336)
	Counter-king: Senenre-setepenptah Khabash (336–335)
Dareios: 4 (6) years	Dareios III (335–332)

---

22. There is controversy as to whether Manetho actually included D. XXXI or a later editor added it.

Table C. Jacoby's Numbering for Manetho's Testimony and
Fragments Compared with Our Corresponding Numbering

Jacoby[23]		Verbrugghe and Wickersham
T1	*Suda* s.v. *kyphi*	F22
T2	*Suda* s.v. *Manethos*	T12, Pseudo-Manetho *Apotelesmatika* T1
T3	Plutarch *de Iside et Osiride* 28 pp. 361F–362A	T4
T4	*P. Hibeh* 1.72.4ff.	T2
T5	*CIL* VIII 1007	T1
T6a	Josephus *Antiquitates Judaicae* 1.107 = Eusebius *Praeparatio Evangelica* 9.13.5 = Syncellus *Ecloga Chronographica* 78	F30
T6b	Tertullian *Apologeticum* 19.4	T6
T6c	*Expositio Totius Mundi et Gentium* 2	T9
T7a	Josephus *contra Apionem* 1.73 = Eusebius *Praeparatio Evangelica* 10.13.1–2 = Eusebius *Chronicon* p. 70, line 4 Karst	T3a
T7b	Josephus *contra Apionem* 1.228	T3b
T7c	Josephus *contra Apionem* 1.104	F10
T8a	Eusebius *Chronicon* p. 63, line 18 Karst	T8a
T8b	Eusebius *Chronicon* p. 125, line 11 Karst	T8c
T8c	Eusebius *Chronicon* (Jerome) year of Abraham 1671 = 346/5 B.C. = Olympiad 108. 3	T8d
T8d	Eusebius *Chronicon* p. 74, line 7 Karst	T8b
T8e	Syncellus *Ecloga Chronographica* 486	F2c
T9	Eusebius *Praeparatio Evangelica* 2 preamble 5	T7
T10	Syncellus *Ecloga Chronographica* 95; 97	T10c, F2b
T11a	Syncellus *Ecloga Chronographica* 72	Pseudo-Manetho *Book of Sothis* T1b
T11b	Syncellus *Ecloga Chronographica* 32	Pseudo-Manetho *Book of Sothis* T1a

---

23. The most recent critical edition of the remains of Manetho's writings is that of Jacoby, in his *FGrHist*, vol. III C 1 (1958), pp. 5–112. In Jacoby's continuous numbering of writers, Manetho is *FGrHist* #609.

Jacoby		Verbrugghe and Wickersham
T11c	Syncellus *Ecloga Chronographica* 29	T10b
T11d	Syncellus *Ecloga Chronographica* 27	T10a
T11e	Syncellus *Ecloga Chronographica* 95, 97	T10c, F2b
T12a	Pseudo-Manetho *Apotelesmatika* 1.1–15	Pseudo-Manetho *Apotelesmatika* F1
T12b	Pseudo-Manetho *Apotelesmatika* 2.1–11	Pseudo-Manetho *Apotelesmatika* F2
T13	*Codex Laurentianus* 73.1	T11
T14a	Josephus *contra Apionem* 1.73	T3a
T14b	Aelian *de Natura Animalium* 10.16	T5
F1	Josephus *contra Apionem* 1.73	F1
F2	Syncellus *Ecloga Chronographica* 99–144	F2a
F3a	Eusebius *Chronicon* p. 63, line 15–p. 69, line 29 Karst	F2a
F3b	Eusebius *Chronicon* (Syncellus 102–45)	F2a
F3c	Eusebius *Chronicon* (Jerome) pp. 20–121 Helm	F2a
F4	*Excerpta Latina Barbari* fol. 38a	F5, F6
F5a	Malalas *Chronographia* p. 21.4 Bonn	F3a, F7a
F5b	Malalas *Chronographia* p. 59.12 Bonn	F4, F7b
F6	*Ecloga Historiarum*, in Cramer *Anecdota Graeca* vol. 2, p. 189	F14
F7	Scholiast on Plato *Timaeus* 21E	F8
F8	Josephus *contra Apionem* 1.74–92 =Eusebius *Chronicon* p. 70, line 3–p. 72, line 24 Karst = Eusebius *Praeparatio Evangelica* 10.13	F9
F9	Josephus *contra Apionem* 1.93–105 = Eusebius *Chronicon* p. 72, line 25–p. 74, line 6 Karst = [Theophilus] *ad Autolycum* 3.20	F10
F10a	Josephus *contra Apionem* 1.223–53	F12
F10b	Cosmas *Topographia Christiana* 12	F13
F11	*Baden Papyri* 4	F15
F12	Moses of Chorene *Historia Armeniae* 2.12	F16
F13	Eustathius *Commentarii ad Homeri Iliadem* 11.480 = *Etymologicon Magnum* p. 560.20	F17
F14	Porphyrius *de Abstinentia* 2.55 = Eusebius *Praeparatio Evangelica* 4.16.4 = Theodoretus *de Curandis Graecorum Affectionibus* 7.42	F18

Jacoby		Verbrugghe and Wickersham
F15	Lydus *de Mensibus* 4.87	F19
F16a	*Suda* s.v. *kyphi*	F22
F16b	Plutarch *de Iside et Osiride* 52 p. 372C	F20
F16c	Plutarch *de Iside et Osiride* 80 pp. 383E–84C	F21
F17	Diogenes Laertius *Vitae Philosophorum* 1.10	F23
F18	Eusebius *Praeparatio Evangelica* 3.2.6	F24
F19	Plutarch *de Iside et Osiride* 9 p. 354C	F25
F20	Plutarch *de Iside et Osiride* 49 p. 371(B)C	F26
F21	Plutarch *de Iside et Osiride* 62 p. 376(A)B	F27
F22	Plutarch *de Iside et Osiride* 73 p. 380(C)D	F28
F23a	Aelian *de Natura Animalium* 10.16	F29a
F23b	Plutarch *de Iside et Osiride* 8 p. 353F	F29b
F24	Josephus *Antiquitates Judaicae* 1.107	F30
F25	Syncellus *Ecloga Chronographica* 73–76	Pseudo-Manetho *Book of Sothis* F1, F2b
F26	Iamblichus *de Mysteriis Aegyptiorum* 8.1	Pseudo-Manetho *Book of Sothis* F4
F27	Syncellus *Ecloga Chronographica* 32–34	Pseudo-Manetho *Book of Sothis* F2a
F28	Syncellus *Ecloga Chronographica* 170–396	Pseudo-Manetho *Book of Sothis* F3

Table D. Our Numbering Corresponding to Jacoby's and Waddell's Numbering for Manetho's Testimony and Fragments

Verbrugghe/ Wickersham	Jacoby	Waddell[24]
T1	T5	(p. xiii)
T2	T4	(p. xix)
T3a	T7a, T14a	Fr. 42
T3b	T7b	Fr. 54
T4	T3	Fr. 80
T5	T14b	Fr. 81
T6	T6b	—
T7	T9	Fr. 76
T8a	T8a	Fr. 1
T8b	T8d	—
T8c	T8b	—
T8d	T8c	(pp. 182–83, n. 1)
T9	T6c	—
T10a	T11d	—
T10b	T11c	—
T10c	T10, T11e	App. III
T11	T13	—
T12	T2	(p. x)
F1	F1	Fr. 42
F2a	F2	Frs. 6, 8, 11, 14, 18, 20, 23, 25, 27, 29, 31, 34, 38, 41(a), 43, 45, 47, 52, 55, 57(a), 58, 60, 62, 64, 66, 68, 70, 72(a), 73(a), 74(a), 75(a)

---

24. W. G. Waddell's *Manetho* is the only other English translation of Manetho. It was originally published in the Loeb Classical Library in 1940, together with the *Tetrabiblos* (*Treatise in Four Books*) of the astronomer Ptolemy. It has been reprinted a few times. In the latest reprint (1980), Manetho is bound alone, without Ptolemy. Waddell presents Müller's text of 1878 (*Fragmenta Historicorum Graecorum*) together with a facing English translation. Inasmuch as Müller's edition has been superseded by Jacoby's, we felt that there was scope for a new English translation, one based on Jacoby. A dash (—) means that the text is not noticed in Waddell.

Verbrugghe/ Wickersham	Jacoby	Waddell
	F3a	Frs. 1, 7(b), 10, 12(b), 16, 19(b), 21(b), 26(b), 28(b), 29(b), 32(b), 36, 41(c), 44(b), 45(b), 48(b), 53(b), 56(b), 57(c), 59(b), 61(b), 65(b), 67(b), 69(b), 71(b), 73(c), 74(c), 75(c)
	F3b	Frs. 7(a), 9, 12(a), 15, 19(a), 21(a), 24(a), 26(a), 28(a), 30(a), 32(a), 35, 39(a), 41(b), 44(a), 46(a), 48(a), 53(a), 56(a), 57(b), 59(a), 61(a), 63(a), 65(a), 67(a), 69(a), 71(a), 72(b), 73(b), 74(b), 75(b)
	F3c	—
F2b	T10, T11e	App. III
F2c	T8e	(pp. 184–85 n. 1)
F3a	F5a	Fr. 5
F3b	(p.12 n)	(p. 2 n. 1)
F4	F5b	Fr. 5
F5	F4	Fr. 4
F6	F4	Fr. 4
F7a	F5a	Fr. 5
F7b	F5b	Fr. 5
F8	F7	Fr. 49
F9	F8	Fr. 42
F10	T7c, F9a	Frs. 50, 51
F11	F9b	—
F12	F10a	Fr. 54
F13	F10b	—
F14	F6	—
F15	F11	(p. vii n. 1)
F16	F12	—
F17	F13	Fr. 88
F18	F14	Fr. 85
F19	F15	Fr. 84
F20	F16b	—
F21	F16c	Fr. 87
F22	T1, F16a	(p. x)
F23	F17	Fr. 82

Verbrugghe/ Wickersham	Jacoby	Waddell
F24	F18	Fr. 83
F25	F19	Fr. 77
F26	F20	Fr. 78
F27	F21	Fr. 79
F28	F22	Fr. 86
F29a	F23a	Fr. 81
F29b	F23b	—
F30	T6a, F24	—

Verbrugghe/Wickersham	Jacoby	Waddell
Pseudo-Manetho *Apotelesmatika* T1	T2	(p. x)
Pseudo-Manetho *Apotelesmatika* F1	T12a	(p. xiv)
Pseudo-Manetho *Apotelesmatika* F2	T12b	(p. xiv)
Pseudo-Manetho *Book of Sothis* T1a	T11b	Fr. 3
Pseudo-Manetho *Book of Sothis* T1b	T11a	App. I
Pseudo-Manetho *Book of Sothis* F1	F25	Fr. 2; App. I
Pseudo-Manetho *Book of Sothis* F2a	F27	Fr. 3
Pseudo-Manetho *Book of Sothis* F2b	F25	Fr. 2, App. I
Pseudo-Manetho *Book of Sothis* F3	F28	App. IV
Pseudo-Manetho *Book of Sothis* F4	F26	—

Table E. Ancient and Medieval Authors Who Preserve or
Mention Manetho

Africanus
    Chronographiae = Syncellus *Ecloga Chronographica* 99–144   F2a
Aelian
    de Natura Animalium 10.16   T5, F29a
Codex Laurentianus 73.1   T11
Cosmas
    Topographia Christiana 12   F13
Diogenes Laertius
    Vitae Philosophorum 1.10   F23
Ecloga Historiarum   F14
Eusebius
    Chronicon p. 63, line 15–p. 69, line 29 Karst   F2a
    Chronicon p. 63, lines 18–22 Karst   T8a
    Chronicon p. 70, line 3–p. 72, line 24 Karst   F9
    Chronicon p. 70, lines 4–8 Karst   T3a
    Chronicon p. 72, line 25–p. 74, line 6 Karst = Josephus *contra*   F10
        Apionem 1.93–105
    Chronicon p. 74, lines 7–17 Karst   T8b
    Chronicon p. 125, line 11 Karst   T8c
    Chronicon = Syncellus *Ecloga Chronographica* 99–145   F2a
    Chronicon (Jerome) year of Abraham 1671   T8d
    Chronicon (Jerome) pp. 20–121 Helm   F2a
    Praeparatio Evangelica 2 preamble 5   T7
    Praeparatio Evangelica 3.2.6   F24
    Praeparatio Evangelica 4.16.4 = Porphyrius *de Abstinentia*   F18
        2.55 = Theodoretus *de Curandis Graecorum Affectionibus*
        7.42
    Praeparatio Evangelica 9.13.5 = Josephus *Antiquitates*   F30
        Judaicae 1.107 = Syncellus *Ecloga Chronographica* 78
    Praeparatio Evangelica 10.13.1–2 = Josephus *contra Apionem*   T3a, F9
        1.73 = Eusebius *Chronicon* p. 70, lines 4–8 Karst
Eustathius
    Commentarii ad Homeri Iliadem 11.480 = *Etymologicon*   F17
        Magnum p. 560.20
Excerpta Latina Barbari fol. 38a   F5, F6

Expositio Totius Mundi et Gentium 2	T9
Iamblichus	
de Mysteriis Aegyptiorum 8.1	Pseudo-Manetho
	Book of Sothis F4
Inscriptions	
Corpus Inscriptionum Latinarum VIII 1007	T1
Jerome	
Eusebii *Chronicon* year of Abraham 1671	T8d
Eusebii *Chronicon* pp. 20–121 Helm	F2a
Josephus	
Antiquitates Judaicae 1.107 = Eusebius *Praeparatio Evangelica* 9.13.5 = Syncellus *Ecloga Chronographica* 78	F30
contra Apionem 1.73 = Eusebius *Praeparatio Evangelica* 10.13.1–2 = Eusebius *Chronicon* p. 70, lines 4–8 Karst	T3a, F1
contra Apionem 1.74–92 = Eusebius *Chronicon* p. 70, line 3– p. 72, line 24 Karst = Eusebius *Praeparatio Evangelica* 10.13	F9
contra Apionem 1.93–105 = Eusebius *Chronicon* p. 72, line 25–p. 74, line 24 Karst = Theophilus, *ad Autolycum* 3.20	F10
contra Apionem 1.223–53	F12
contra Apionem 1.228	T3b
contra Apionem 2.16	F11
Lydus	
de Mensibus 4.86	F3b
de Mensibus 4.87	F19
Malalas	
Chronographia p. 21 Bonn	F3a, F7a
Chronographia p. 59 Bonn	F4, F7b
Moses of Chorene	
Historia Armeniae 2.12	F16
Papyri	
Baden Papyri 4	F15
Hibeh Papyri 1.72.4ff.	T2
Plutarch	
de Iside et Osiride 8 p. 353F	F29b
de Iside et Osiride 9 p. 354C	F25
de Iside et Osiride 49 p. 371(B)C	F26
de Iside et Osiride 52 p. 372C	F20
de Iside et Osiride 62 p. 376(A)B	F27

Bibliography

ANET³ = Pritchard, James B. *Ancient New Eastern Texts Relating to the Old Testament*. 3d ed. Princeton, 1969.

Baines, John, and Jaromir Málek. *Atlas of Ancient Egypt*. New York, 1982.

Beaulieu, Paul-Alain. *The Reign of Nabonidus, King of Babylon 556–539 B.C.* 3d ed. New Haven, 1989.

Beckerath, Jürgen von. *Abriss der Geschichte des alten Ägypten*. Vienna, 1971.

———. *Handbuch der ägyptischen Königsnamen*. Munich and Berlin, 1984.

Bickerman, E. J. *Chronology of the Ancient World*. Ithaca, 1968.

Brinkman, J. A. *A Political History of Post-Kassite Babylonia 1158–722 B.C.* Vol. 43 of *Analecta Orientalia*. Rome, 1968.

———. "Appendix: Mesopotamian Chronology of the Historical Period." In *Ancient Mesopotamia: Portrait of a Dead Civilization*, ed. A. Leo Oppenheim, rev. Erica Reeves, 335–40. Chicago, 1977.

Burstein, Stanley. *The Babyloniaca of Berossus*. Sources and Monographs: Sources from the Ancient Near East, vol. 1, no. 5. Malibu, 1978.

CAH² = *Cambridge Ancient History*. Vols. 3–5. 2d ed. Cambridge, 1982–92.

CAH³ = *Cambridge Ancient History*. Vols. 1–2. 3d ed. Cambridge, 1970–75

Dijk, Jan van. "Die Inschriftenfunde: II. Die Tontafeln aus dem res-Heiligtum." In *XVIII. vorläufiger Bericht über die von dem Deutschen Archäologischen Institut und der Deutschen Orient-Gesellschaft aus Mitteln der Deutschen Forschungsgemeinschaft unternommenen Ausgrabungen in Uruk-Warka (1959/1960)*, ed. Heinrich J. Lenzen, 43–61. Berlin, 1962.

Donbaz, Veysel. "Two Neo-Assyrian Stelae in the Antakya and Kahramanmaraš Museums." *Annual Review of the Royal Inscriptions of Mesopotamia Project* 8 (1990): 5–24.

Drews, Robert. "Assyria in Classical Universal Histories." *Historia* 14 (1963): 129–42.

———. "The Babylonian Chronicles and Berossus." *Iraq* 37 (1975): 39–55.

FGrHist = Jacoby, Felix. *Die Fragmente der griechischen Historiker*. Leiden and Berlin, 3 vols. in 15, 1923–58. Testimonia and fragments of Berossos in *FGrHist* vol. III C 1 (1958), 364–97. Berossos = *FGrHist* #680; Manetho in *FGrHist* vol. III C 1 (1958), 5–112. Manetho = *FGrHist* #609.

FHG = Müller, Carolus. *Fragmenta Historicorum Graecorum* (Paris, 5 vols., 1841–70). Testimonia and fragments of Manetho in *FHG* vol. II (1848), 511–616.

Foster, Benjamin R. *Before the Muses: An Anthology of Akkadian Literature.* 2 vols. Bethesda, 1993.

Fraser, Peter M. *Ptolemaic Alexandria.* 3 vols. Oxford, 1972.

Gardiner, Alan H. *Egypt of the Pharaohs.* Oxford, 1961.

—. *Egyptian Grammar.* 3d ed. Oxford, 1982.

Glassner, Jean-Jacques. *La Chute d'Akkadé: L'évenement et sa mémoire.* Berlin, 1986.

Grayson, A. K. "Assyria and Babylonia." *Orientalia* 49 (1980): 140–94.

—. *Assyrian and Babylonian Chronicles.* Locust Valley, N. Y., 1975.

Gruen, Erich S. "Cultural Fictions and Cultural Identity." *Transactions of the American Philological Association* 123 (1993): 1–14.

Hallo, William, and William Simpson. *The Ancient Near East: A History.* New York, 1971.

Helck, H. W. "Manethon (1)." In *Der kleine Pauly,* ed. K. Ziegler and W. Sontheimer, 3:952–53. Munich, 1975.

—. *Untersuchungen zu Manetho und den ägyptischen Königslisten.* Untersuchungen zur Geschichte und Altertumskunde Aegyptens 18. Berlin, 1956.

Helck, H. W., and Eberhard Otto. *Kleines Wörterbuch der Aegyptologie.* Wiesbaden, 1987

Jacobsen, Thorkild. *The Sumerian King List.* Chicago, 1939.

Jacoby, Felix. *Die Fragmente der griechischen Historiker.* Vols. 1–3. Leiden and Berlin, 1923–58. (Abbr. *FGrHist.*) Testimonia and fragments of Berossos in *FGrHist* vol. III C 1 (1958), 364–97. Berossos = *FGrHist* #680; testimonia and fragments of Manetho in *FGrHist* vol. III C 1 (1958), 5–112. Manetho = *FGrHist* #609.

Karst, Josef. *Die Chronik aus dem Armenischen übersetzt.* Vol. 5 of *Eusebius, Werke.* Leipzig, 1911.

Komoroczy, G. "Berosos and the Mesopotamian Literature." *Acta Antiqua Academica Scientiarum Hungarica* 21 (1973): 125–52.

Kuhrt, Amélie. "Berossus' *Babyloniaka* and Seleucid Rule in Babylonia." In *Hellenism and the East.,* ed. Amélie Kuhrt and Susan Sherwin-White, 53–56. London, 1987.

Lambert, W. G. "Berossus and Babylonian Eschatology." *Iraq* 38 (1976): 170–73.

Lichtheim, Miriam. *Ancient Egyptian Literature, Volume III: The Late Period.* Berkeley, 1980.

Lieu, Samuel N. C. *Manichaeism in the Later Roman Empire and Medieval China.* 2d ed. Tübingen, 1992.

Luckenbill, Daniel. *Ancient Records of Assyria and Babylonia.* 2 vols. Chicago, 1927.

Málek, Jaromir. "The Original Version of the Royal Canon of Turin." *Journal of Egyptian Archaelogy* 68 (1982): 93–106.

McCullough, W. Stewart. *A Short History of Syriac Christianity to the Rise of Islam.* Chico, California, 1982.

Mendels, D. "The Five Empires: A Note on a Propagandistic *Topos*." *American Journal of Philology* 102 (1981): 330–37, with addendum by H. Tadmor, 338–39.

Morby, John E. *Dynasties of the World.* Oxford, 1989.

Müller, Carolus. *Fragmenta Historicorum Graecorum.* 5 vols. Paris, 1841–70. (Abbr. *FHG.*) Testimonia and fragments of Manetho in *FHG* vol. II (1848), 511–616.

Neugebauer, O., and H. B. van Hoesen. *Greek Horoscopes.* Philadelphia, 1959.

Parpola, Simo. "The Murderer of Sennacherib." In *Death in Mesopotamia,* ed. Bendt Alster, 171–82. Copenhagen, 1980.

Pritchard, James B. *Ancient New Eastern Texts Relating to the Old Testament.* 3d ed. Princeton, 1969. (Abbr. *ANET³.*)

Redford, D. B. *Pharaonic King-Lists, Annals, and Day-Books: A Contribution to the Study of the Egyptian Sense of History.* SSEA Publication 4. Mississauga, Ontario, 1986.

Schnabel, Paul. *Berossos und die Babylonisch-Hellenistische Literatur.* Leipzig, 1923.

Seters, John van. *The Hyksos, a New Investigation.* New Haven, 1966.

Sherwin-White, Susan, and Amélie Kuhrt. *From Samarkhand to Sardis.* Berkeley, 1993.

Soden, Wolfram von. "Zweisprachigkeit in der geistigen Kultur Babyloniens." *Österreichische Akademie der Wissenschaften, Philosophisch-Historische Klasse* 235 (1960): 1–33.

Spek, R. J. van der. "The Babylonian City." In *Hellenism and the East,* ed. Amélie Kuhrt and Susan Sherwin-White, 57–74. London, 1987.

Thompson, Dorothy J. *Memphis under the Ptolemies.* Princeton, 1989.

Veyne, Paul. *Did the Greeks Believe in Their Myths?* Trans. P. Wissing. Chicago, 1987.

Wachsmuth, Kurt. *Einleitung in das Studium der alten Geschichte.* Leipzig, 1895.

Waddell, W. G. *Manetho.* Cambridge, Mass., and London, 1940. Reprint, 1980.

Wiseman, D. J. *Nebuchadressar and Babylon.* Oxford, 1983.

Wright, William. A *Short History of Syriac Literature.* In *Encyclopaedia Britannica,* 9th ed., vol. 22 (1887). Reprinted and enlarged, Philo Press, 1894, 1966.

Index